FACILITATING SEVEN WAYS OF LEARNING

FACILITATING SEVEN WAYS OF LEARNING

A Resource for More Purposeful, Effective, and Enjoyable College Teaching

James R. Davis and
Bridget D. Arend

Foreword by L. Dee Fink

STERLING, VIRGINIA

Sty/us

COPYRIGHT © 2013 BY
STYLUS PUBLISHING, LLC.

Published by Stylus Publishing, LLC
22883 Quicksilver Drive
Sterling, Virginia 20166-2102

Library of Congress Cataloging-in-Publication Data
Davis, James R., 1936–
Facilitating seven ways of learning : a resource for more
purposeful, effective, and enjoyable college teaching / by
James R. Davis and Bridget Arend ; foreword by Dee Fink.
 p. cm.
Includes bibliographical references and index.
ISBN 978-1-57922-840-8 (cloth : alk. paper)
ISBN 978-1-57922-841-5 (pbk. : alk. paper)
ISBN 978-1-57922-842-2 (lib ebook)
ISBN 978-1-57922-843-9 (ebook)
1. College teaching. I. Arend, Bridget, 1970– II. Title.
LB2331.D377 2013
378.1'25—dc23   2012024271

13-digit ISBN: 978-1-57922-840-8 (cloth)
13-digit ISBN: 978-1-57922-841-5 (paper)
13-digit ISBN: 978-1-57922-842-4 (library networkable
 e-edition)
13-digit ISBN: 978-1-57922-843-9 (consumer e-edition)

Bulk Purchases

Quantity discounts are available for use in workshops
and for staff development.
Call 1-800-232-0223

First Edition, 2013

10 9 8 7 6

To Adelaide and Marcela
To Chris, Zach, and Chloe

CONTENTS

FOREWORD

Davis and Arend start this book with a discussion of the need for a paradigm shift about the way we teach in higher education. They are absolutely right. In my view, though, there is a need for two paradigm shifts: one on *how* we teach, and another on how we *prepare* to teach.

The integrated nature of today's world and the revolution in information technology that provides wide and rapid access to information are two of the major factors creating the need for the first paradigm shift. What are the reasons for claiming that we also need the second paradigm shift?

Potential Value of Higher Education

Given what we know today about the nature of learning and multiple ways of improving teaching, it is both vital and absolutely feasible for all colleges and universities to provide students with significant learning experiences in each of the following four domains of life:

1. *Preparation for the workforce:* Develop the wider range of competencies that have become important in the world of work today. These competencies include being innovative; looking at issues from multiple perspectives; and working effectively in teams, especially with people different from oneself.
2. *Citizenship:* Become more informed and thoughtful citizens in the multiple political bodies in which they will participate.
3. *Social relations:* Learn how to engage others in more positive ways, in both formal and informal relationships.
4. *Personal life:* Find ways to make one's own life more fulfilling and meaningful.

What is needed for all of these possibilities to become a reality? That everyone who teaches in higher education fully understands and knows how to apply the powerful ideas about teaching and learning that have been created in the scholarship of teaching and learning over the last 25 years, a body of literature to which this book makes a valuable addition. This includes, among other capabilities, knowing how to formulate good learning goals for multiple kinds of learning; use small groups effectively; assess complex kinds of learning; engage students in active learning; develop rubrics; accommodate students with diverse characteristics; teach large classes; teach creativity; teach critical thinking; help students become self-directing learners; and use technology in ways that actually promote better learning.[1]

The Problem

The problem is that only a few professors are using these ideas. For example, as indicated in the research cited by the authors, the vast majority of faculty are still using passive learning in their teaching, even though books fully describing the benefits and procedures for active learning were published over 20 years ago. The fact that these new and powerful ideas about teaching and learning are largely ignored is the dilemma and shame of higher education today.

Why aren't more of us using these ideas? Because the second paradigm shift has not occurred. Decision makers at our institutions of higher education have not yet seen fit to provide opportunities for teachers to learn about teaching and learning, either *before* they become professors or *after* they start teaching. When I do workshops each year on dozens of campuses around the country and around the world, I ask professors whether they had any formal instruction on college teaching while in graduate school. Only 10–15 percent answer in the affirmative—even though 50–70 percent of all graduate students in the major research universities go on to become college teachers.[2] And two-thirds of all institutions of higher education in the United States still do not have substantial, meaningful faculty development programs that can provide in-service programs on teaching for professors.[3]

We can all hope that someday soon university leaders will decide it is no longer an acceptable practice to charge students an ever-increasing amount for tuition and then put them in classes taught by professors who know their subject matter well but are blissfully ignorant of the powerful ideas about teaching and learning that are essential for personal and societal success in the twenty-first century.

Contribution of This Book

When this second paradigm shift does occur, and when institutions begin expecting all professors—junior and senior—to be knowledgeable *about* and know how to *use* these new ideas about teaching and learning (and a few institutions around the world have initiated policies and procedures that support exactly this expectation), *Facilitating Seven Ways of Learning* will undoubtedly take its place as a major resource. Why?

Two of the major ideas that have emerged in the last decade or so are the beliefs that (a) teaching should be learning-centered, and (b) teachers need to learn how to design their courses in a learning-centered way. Course design refers to the decision-making aspect of teaching. Before a course or program of instruction begins, teachers have to make decisions about how they want their courses to unfold and what kinds of learning experiences they want their students to have.

Three books on learning-centered course design were published around the year 2000 with very similar ideas. In 1998, Grant Wiggins and Jay McTighe published *Understanding by Design*. This book popularized the phrase "backward design." By this, they meant that when we design a course, we should start by identifying the kind of learning we hope students will achieve by the end of the course and then "work backward" by asking what kinds of learning activities and assessment activities will lead to that kind of learning. Most of the examples in this book came from pre-collegiate levels of instruction but the principles apply to any level of instruction. John Biggs published a book in 1999 entitled *Teaching for Quality Learning at University: What the Student Does* in which he called for "constructive alignment." This concept means that the learning activities and the assessment activities in a course should be aligned with the desired learning outcomes. Given that Biggs was from Tasmania, this book is relatively well known in universities in British Commonwealth countries.

Then in 2003, my book, *Creating Significant Learning Experiences,* was published. At the time I was not aware of either of the two preceding books, but my concept of Integrated Course Design (see the following figure) is essentially the same as their versions of learning-centered course design. After collecting relevant information about the teaching and learning situation, one should identify the important learning goals for the course and then decide what learning and assessment activities are necessary for students to achieve those learning goals.

As advocated in all three of these books, once a good set of learning goals have been created or selected, the teacher is ready to identify the learning activities that are necessary and appropriate for those particular learning goals—and that is where this book comes in. The seven ways of learning identified by Davis and Arend will add a great deal of precision to the task

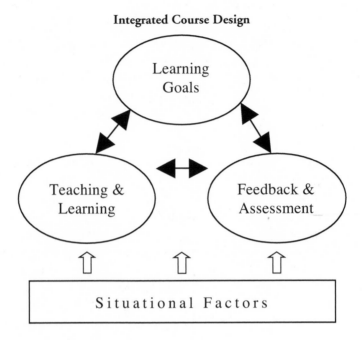

of selecting the right set of learning activities for a rich or, in my language, significant set of learning goals.

Another feature of this book that adds major value is the fact that the authors clearly understand the important relationships in learning-centered, integrated course design. Therefore, for each of the seven ways of learning (i.e., the seven sets of learning activities) they comment on the learning goals and the assessment activities that are appropriate for that way of learning.

For those of us who care about our students' learning—and I believe that is the attitude of the majority of teachers—this book offers valuable strategies for improving learning, and will be worth reading for years to come!

L. Dee Fink
Norman, Oklahoma
August 2012

Notes

1. An annotated bibliography of numerous books that have had a major influence on my own teaching is available in a document called "Major New Ideas That

Can Empower College Teaching." It is available at: www.finkconsulting/major-pub lications under the category of "College Teaching."

2. This figure is based on research I conducted on PhD graduates at the University of Oklahoma; when I compared this percentage to that for other major research universities, most were very similar.

3. This figure is based on nationwide research conducted by Sally Kuhlenschmidt at Western Kentucky University: "Distribution and Penetration of Teaching-Learning Development Units in Higher Education: Implications for Strategic Planning and Research," *To Improve the Academy* 29 (2011): 274–287.

College teaching is changing. It has always been challenging, but now it is becoming downright difficult. Heightened expectations about using technology are pushing professors to teach in completely new ways. Pressures to assess learning outcomes are being thrust upon faculty by accrediting agencies. With the academic disciplines no longer able to contain the explosion of knowledge, new subjects are emerging and old ones are being reconceptualized. What had been the professor's privileged "store of knowledge" is now available in libraries and on the Internet through instantaneous searches. New types of students—some very well prepared, others poorly—are coming to college as residents, commuters, or working adults. The dominant paradigm of lecture followed by discussion is being challenged by a bewildering array of new teaching methods. Commercial cure-alls are being peddled for a price. Online learning has emerged as a viable alternative to the classroom, and heated debates are being held about the best use of the physical classroom. The college teaching scene is confusing, to say the least. Conscientious professors can hardly keep up anymore with what they are supposed to do to be successful teachers.

Not all of this is bad. The century-old lecture paradigm deserves to be challenged. Opportunities to enhance learning through new technologies merit exploration. Calls to enable greater numbers of students to earn a college degree justify a reexamination of the basic purposes of higher education. Results from a century of research on learning warrant application to college teaching. The increased availability of information in the new era surely requires some rethinking of the outcomes and methods of college teaching. Some are even saying that the key driver of reform in higher education should be the transformation of teaching. In any case, the stable environment college teaching once took place in no longer exists. The name of the game hasn't changed, but in the past twenty years, someone changed the rules, the playbook, the equipment, and the venue.

The confusion about teaching is serious in itself, but the shocking consequence is that students don't appear to be learning what they need to know for life in the twenty-first century. Derek Bok, former president of Harvard University, puts it this way in his book *Our Underachieving Colleges*:

Many seniors graduate without being able to write well enough to satisfy their employers. Many cannot reason clearly or perform competently in analyzing complex, non-technical problems, even though faculties rank critical thinking as the primary goal of a college education. Few undergraduates receiving a degree are able to speak or read a foreign language. Most have never taken a course in quantitative reasoning or acquired the knowledge needed to be a reasonably informed citizen in a democracy. And these are only some of the problems.[1]

The dilemma is this: we college professors are trained to be researchers, not teachers, and the amount of time and energy we have for faculty development (on-the-job training for teaching) is limited by the opposing pressure for publishable scholarship. It is natural to fall back on the traditional paradigm of lecture and discussion. Yet college teachers today are expected by students, parents, administrators, and accrediting bodies to get results, that is, to facilitate real learning—deep, serious, lasting, and transformative learning for their students. Society needs it; the students deserve it. Many college teachers, however, find it very challenging to function effectively in this new environment of high expectations and confusing alternatives.

The Proposal

One response to these challenges is to hold firm to the belief that what worked in the past is still effective, and to question, therefore, whether the reform of teaching is actually necessary. Another response is to experiment, trying this and that, without much of a sense of how to select among the options or evaluate their effectiveness. A third approach, the one we propose, is to think carefully about desired learning outcomes—what we hope students will know or be able to do—and facilitate the way of learning that will most likely produce the desired results.

One thing a century of research on learning has demonstrated clearly is that learning is not one thing but many. The learning associated with developing a skill is different from the learning associated with understanding and remembering information, which in turn is different from thinking critically and creatively, solving problems, making decisions, or reworking attitudes—to name a few of the things that college teachers hope their students will be able to do. Differing outcomes involve different ways of learning. Learning a skill through a carefully arranged sequence of steps with appropriate feedback is one way of learning. Learning information through a carefully designed presentation is another. Learning to think critically by asking questions is still another. A *way of learning* is a cluster of coherent arrangements and activities designed to produce specific learning outcomes. What makes the seven ways of learning presented in this book distinctive is that they are well researched, based on established theories of learning, and verified through practice and observation over many years. Effective college teaching needs to be rooted in established ways of learning.

The Promises

The promises to the readers of this book are the following:

- At the most basic level, this book provides an overview of seven distinct ways of learning that are clearly explained and well illustrated. Reading about one way of learning per night for a week will give you the detailed background you need. Along the way you will be introduced, as historical grounding, to what was learned about learning in the twentieth century.
- By reading this book you will learn how to select the most appropriate way of learning for your particular content and outcomes. This will help you organize your teaching conceptually and allow you to select subject matter and activities from a sometimes bewildering array of options, thus helping you feel more in control of your teaching.
- When it comes time to implement a particular way of learning with students, you will have at your fingertips a useful and very extensive set of practical guidelines. Exploring new ways of learning will take some experimentation and practice, and you will need to be creative in applying what you know about learning to the way you teach. The examples interspersed in the text will assist you in this process and enable you to become more purposeful in the conscious choices you make about your teaching.
- By grounding your teaching in these seven ways of learning, you will enable your students to learn more and perform better, and you will probably enjoy your teaching more. With new successes you will feel more comfortable in engaging students in a greater number of ways of learning. Your teaching will be less frustrating, more effective, and more satisfying, as it is meant to be.

Facilitating Seven Ways of Learning is not an overview of teaching for beginning teachers. It is not filled with tips on how to prepare a syllabus or get through the first day of class. Other books already do a good job of this. Many of the most popular books about college teaching are designed as how-to guidebooks that provide advice for nearly every issue related to teaching and learning from course design to grading.[2] Some books in this area have a slightly targeted focus, such as teaching methods for first-generation students or teaching methods for new faculty or graduate students.[3] Other excellent college teaching books focus on a particular philosophy, a format for course design, learning principles, or attributes of successful college teachers.[4]

Many books provide useful lenses to view college teaching, and they combine theory with advice and examples for practical application. In addition, numerous other resources—journals, newsletters, products, and websites—are designed to support the college teacher. However, none of these books or resources addresses the issue of teaching and learning from the perspective of matching goals to distinct ways of learning based on well-established theories of learning. We believe this is what makes our book unique.

In truth, this book may be a little advanced. It is designed for those of you who want to get beyond methods, tactics, fads, and commercial products to do some serious independent thinking about learning. It can be used by professors who work with future faculty in programs designed to prepare graduate students for teaching, and it can be used in centers for teaching and learning to work with beginning teachers over time, or to help continuing faculty reexamine a particular aspect of their teaching. The book will be most useful for those of you who are ready to move your teaching to the upper-division level by examining and applying what is known about learning. This is a book for those who are willing to take the time to learn about learning and who want to join or lead the movement to transform college teaching.

Content and Organization

Facilitating Seven Ways of Learning: A Resource for More Purposeful, Effective, and Enjoyable College Teaching is divided into three sections. Part One, "Understanding Teaching and Learning," opens with chapter 1, "The Lecture Paradigm and the New Context of Teaching and Learning." The concept of *paradigm* is introduced to describe the most dominant and familiar method of college teaching: lecture and discussion. Traditional lecture and discussion has come under criticism from a number of directions as the dominant and exclusive paradigm for college teaching. A century of learning about learning has given visibility to other important and useful ways of learning. The new era has given greater urgency and importance to more complex forms of knowledge in the workplace and in personal life. Furthermore, the workplace itself demands a broader range of skills and abilities. As the dominant paradigm has begun to crumble, other ways of learning have emerged.

Although we have delineated a particular approach to teaching—using distinct ways of learning to attain specific objectives—we recognize that other ideas about college teaching do exist. These are explored in chapter 2, "Alternative Approaches to Teaching and Learning." It is important for you to recognize these many different approaches to teaching, to be able to identify and evaluate them, and to know where ours fits among them. In this way you will have a broad scan of the scope of activity of college teaching, be able to recognize other approaches when you encounter them, and know what it means to teach by using established ways of learning.

In chapter 3, "Using the Seven Ways of Learning for Teaching," we address such questions as, Why is there often a disconnection between teaching and learning? What is a way of learning? What is a well-established theory of learning? This chapter provides detailed guidance on how to establish learning outcomes that project what your students will know and be able to do. Suggestions are also made for selecting the appropriate way of learning to match intended outcomes. This clears the way for you to delve into our more detailed elaboration of the seven ways of learning.

Part Two, "Organizing Teaching and Learning," contains individual chapters on each of the seven ways of learning. These are listed in the table of contents and include a range of ideas about learning, not always compatible with each other, and growing out of the research and theory building of the twentieth century. Each way of learning is described fully and illustrated with examples from different academic fields and types of institutions. The teacher's role in facilitating each way of learning is clearly delineated. Discussion of the uses of appropriate technologies and methods of assessment are embedded in the presentation of each way of learning, confirming our belief that these matters tend to be specific to particular ways of learning.

Part Three, "Transforming College Teaching," consists of the concluding chapter, "More Purposeful, Effective, and Enjoyable College Teaching." As you begin to use more differentiated and varied patterns of teaching and learning, you will become more purposeful in the specification of outcomes and the selection of appropriate ways of learning to achieve intended results.

As you do so, skillfully implementing each selected way of learning, you will become more effective, and as you become more effective, you will probably find teaching to be more enjoyable. Individual teachers get better one lesson at a time, but the overall postsecondary environment individual teachers work in still contains many challenges. Besides the traditional teaching paradigm, there is a student paradigm, a promotion and tenure paradigm, and a graduate education paradigm. This is where you can become involved with the broader and more significant changes that need to occur in colleges and universities so that college teaching can prosper and thrive.

Visit http://sevenwaysoflearning.com for more resources and examples or to share your own methods for successfully implementing these ways of learning.

Acknowledgments

We are indebted to the scholars and researchers who have explored, theorized, studied, crafted, and elaborated the ways of learning presented in this book. Living as we do in an age where the contributions of the past are not always recognized or valued, we especially wish to acknowledge our debt to the scholars of the twentieth century who put forth such great effort to learn about learning. Our modest contribution has been to conceptualize a framework for thinking clearly about seven distinct ways of learning and to gather a rather sizable pool of resources for effective teaching into a comprehensive and usable guide.

Although we have referenced each example in our endnotes, we wish to thank once again those who have generously shared an example of their teaching practice to illustrate the ways of learning in this book. We know these examples have helped us see more concretely how the seven ways of learning work when applied, and we are certain readers will also find them illuminating.

We also wish to thank employees on the instructional quality team at University College at the University of Denver for reading, throughout seven consecutive weeks, chapters 4 through 10 in draft form. Although the goal for what came to be known as "Jim and Bridget's book club" was training in ways of learning, the collateral result was a huge amount of valuable feedback that enabled us to make each of those chapters clearer and more focused after trying them out on actual readers. In addition to ourselves, the participants in the book club were Jason Wyrick, Associate Dean; Paul

Novak, Senior Instructional Designer; Terri Johnson, Instructional Support Specialist; Allison O'Grady, Instructional Support Specialist; and Molly Smith, Instructional Support Specialist.

We wish to thank a number of people for supporting us in writing this book. Acquisitions editor Susan Slesinger provided continuous insight and commentary as well as many good suggestions. Early in the process, research support was provided by Jason Wyrick, Brian Elizardi, and Michelle Kruse-Crocker. Michelle provided continuing support in keeping track of and shuttling various versions of drafts back and forth between us electronically, making print copies, helping with errant endnotes, and making on-the-spot additions. Pete DeLong of Pete DeLong Design created the visual images throughout the book. Surely we could not have done this without the patience and support of our spouses, Jim's wife, Adelaide, and Bridget's husband, Chris, and their children, Zach and Chloe. Writing a book, as we have acknowledged to each other frequently, simply takes every spare minute for two years of your life.

Notes

1. Derek Bok, *Our Underachieving Colleges: A Candid Look at How Much Students Learn and Why They Should be Learning More* (Princeton, NJ: Princeton University Press, 2006), 8.

2. Examples include Barbara G. Davis, *Tools for Teaching* (Hoboken, NJ: Wiley, 2009); William McKeachie, *Teaching Tips: Strategies, Research, and Theory for College and University Teachers* (Boston: Houghton Mifflin, 2002); and Linda B. Nilson, *Teaching at Its Best: A Research-Based Resource for College Instructors* (Hoboken, NJ: Wiley, 2003).

3. Robert Leamnson, *Thinking about Teaching and Learning: Developing Habits of Learning with First-Year College and University Students* (Sterling, VA: Stylus, 1999); Carolyn Lieberg, *Teaching Your First College Class: A Practical Guide for New Faculty and Graduate Student Instructors* (Sterling, VA: Stylus, 2008).

4. As the following books demonstrate respectively, Maryellen Weimer, *Learner-Centered Teaching: Five Key Changes to Practice* (San Francisco: Jossey-Bass, 2002); L. Dee Fink, *Creating Significant Learning Experiences: An Integrated Approach to Designing College Courses* (San Francisco: Jossey-Bass, 2003); Susan A. Ambrose, Michael W. Bridges, Michele DiPietro, Marsha C. Lovett, and Marie K. Norman, *How Learning Works: Seven Research-Based Principles for Smart Teaching* (Hoboken, NJ: Wiley, 2010); Ken Bain, *What the Best College Teachers Do* (Cambridge, MA: Harvard University Press, 2004).

PART ONE

UNDERSTANDING TEACHING AND LEARNING

THE LECTURE PARADIGM
AND THE NEW CONTEXT OF
TEACHING AND LEARNING

Conscientious teachers want to make intelligent and creative choices about their teaching, but sometimes they don't know how to do so. They know what teachers are supposed to do—lecture—but if that option is taken away, they are not sure what to put in its place. They suspect that what they do may no longer be appropriate, but they are not sure exactly where to turn. They alternate between feeling guilty and feeling bombarded.

What is it that keeps people from making intelligent and creative choices about anything? What forces confine us in old ways? Habit? Comfort? Lack of knowledge about alternatives? Social norms? Fear of reprisal? Potential for embarrassment? These are some of the constraints that militate against any choice that involves a new or different dimension. For college teachers, the chief obstacle to teaching in more creative and effective ways is a strong but obsolete operative paradigm that sets the rules for acceptable collegiate-level instruction.

Trapped in a Paradigm

What is a paradigm? As an academic concept, *paradigm* has its roots in Thomas Kuhn's work *The Structure of Scientific Revolutions*.[1] He used it to describe the acknowledged bodies of belief and theory that undergird the activities of science. A paradigm is a way of looking at the world, a model, or a pattern accepted by an academic community. Newton and Einstein used different paradigms for doing physics.

A paradigm, more generally, is that array of normative beliefs and attitudes that support a particular endeavor. Because a paradigm is a cultural construct, it *is*, but has not always *been*, and thus may not always *be*. As Kuhn documented, a paradigm can shift. When a paradigm is very strong, those who are controlled by it may not even be conscious of it, may not understand that it has been constructed in response to certain historical circumstances, and may not realize that it can change. A strong paradigm confines us, convinces us of its absoluteness, and diminishes our awareness of alternatives. It also helps us get our work done because we don't have to ask troublesome questions about what we are supposed to do. College teaching has a strong operative paradigm.

Every paradigm started out as a new idea; it was itself a change to the usual way of doing things. It turned out to be such a good idea that it became a commonplace and widespread practice. A paradigm starts out as a good idea, gets overtaken by changes in society and institutions, becomes obsolete, and then gets replaced with a new and presumably better idea. The paradigm for college teaching has not always been what it is today.

In the colonial era, during the infancy of American higher education, students learned by making recitations to tutors. Students would read selected texts, try to understand them (or memorize them), and recite the ideas back to the tutor, who would guide them in their studies. Sometimes students engaged in formal debates with other students or their tutors called disputations. That is one paradigm for teaching and learning: recitation and disputation.[2] It dominated collegiate learning until a paradigm shift occurred in the nineteenth century.

Since that time, the dominant paradigm for teaching and learning has been and for the most part continues to be lecture and discussion. Although laboratory sections are also employed in the sciences to supplement lectures, and although case studies and group projects are sometimes used in professional schools, the dominant operative paradigm for postsecondary teaching is the lecture.

Lecturing emerged as the new teaching method, replacing recitation and disputation, which held sway during the seventeenth and eighteenth centuries. Lecturing was not new; it had its origins in the medieval university when there was a scarcity of books, and lectures were delivered very slowly so that students could copy them down verbatim. The lecturing that emerged as the dominant teaching method at the end of the nineteenth century was a German import. As Brubacher and Rudy note in their historical work, *Higher Education in Transition*: "Pre-eminent in scholarship, the

German professors were lecturing to their students as the means par excellence for informing them of the latest research, for helping them organize wide ranges of information, for giving them an overview of the domains yet to be conquered, and finally for electrifying them with the professor's enthusiasm for their specialties."[3]

The lecture method coincides with the initiation of graduate education in the United States. It was not a stand-alone innovation; rather it was part of a larger paradigm that included professors engaging in original research and teaching graduate students about what they had discovered.

Some teachers who recognize the dominant paradigm as a paradigm might ask: What is wrong with it? It has worked fairly well, hasn't it, for many years? True. But is it still relevant to the educational needs of today's students and twenty-first-century society? Has the traditional way of teaching been overtaken by social change? By new knowledge about learning? By technology?

The Lecture Paradigm in the Twenty-First Century

Today when most college teachers lecture, they stand alone in front of an entire class, occupying about one-fourth of the classroom space, while students seated in rows or in a tiered lecture hall designed for this purpose take notes—key words or short summaries of the important information and ideas that will appear on the exam or be useful in writing a paper. If there is enough time at the end of the lecture, after the essential information has been covered, the faculty member will ask for questions and guide a discussion of the material. Everybody knows what to do. Lectures are delivered, and oddly enough, even when other teaching methods are used in a class, students will often refer to it as a lecture: "Nice lecture today!"

The arrangement of the curriculum in distinct disciplines and professional fields of study with their specialties and subspecialties produces and reinforces the use of the lecture paradigm. The accumulation of knowledge produced by the disciplines (surely one of their great strengths) beckons a pedagogy of telling, of sharing a body of knowledge through textbooks and lectures, and insisting that the content of the discipline be "covered," remembered, and recounted.

Is this still the dominant paradigm for postsecondary teaching? Surely many exceptions exist. They do indeed, and finding examples of each of the ways of learning for this book has been a stimulating exercise. Exceptions are evidence that the dominant paradigm is being challenged, but there is also evidence that the lecture paradigm is still strong and widespread. In fact, it appears that lecturing may be even more prevalent than its prevailing stereotype. Even though there has been an explosion of literature about alternate teaching methods over the past few decades, studies during this same time frame have shown the predominance of the lecture method and minimal class participation by students. In the 1980s researchers in different studies observed classes across disciplines at public and private undergraduate institutions and found that the use of the lecture ranged a bit by class type, but the amount of class time devoted to lecturing averaged between 80 and 96 percent.[4] A few years later another researcher surveyed more than eighty universities and found that lecturing was the predominant instructional method for 89 percent of physical science and mathematics courses and 81 percent of social science courses.[5] In the 1990s a study of classroom discussion revealed that less than 6 percent of class time was devoted to discussions, and typically only 25 percent of students actually participated in discussions.[6] Later studies showed that things had not changed significantly after the end of the second millennium. Economics professors in 2000 spent 83 percent of their time lecturing, a percentage virtually unchanged from that of an identical national study five years earlier.[7] And yet another study revealed that in 350 upper- and lower-division class sessions, only 9 percent of students made two or more comments during a class discussion. In this study the instructors defined class participation as "showing up for class, keeping up with the reading, and paying attention."[8]

Is it that college instructors do not know what else to do? One hears from time to time stories of obsessive lecturers, and the tendency is to discount them as part of a body of mythology that lies beyond substantiation. Shelley Johnson Carey, Editor of *Peer Review*, a publication of the Association of American Colleges and Universities, cites her own experience as a student with a professor who knew of no alternative to lecturing: "One day, midway through the semester, I found myself sitting alone in front of him. I was the only one of fifteen students registered for the class to show up that morning. Instead of taking the opportunity to draw me into the subject with a conversation, he proceeded to lecture from memory for an hour while I struggled to keep from yawning."[9] Apparently these things do happen.

The lecture paradigm is perpetuated from generation to generation of teachers and students. Students who aspire to be college teachers have participated in class after class using the lecture method. When they go to graduate school they may participate in graduate seminars, which often turn out to be lectures in smaller classrooms, but seldom do they experience significantly different ways of teaching and learning. Nor do their mentors intervene in this entrenched tradition to teach their students how to teach in different ways. Although the Preparing Future Faculty programs sponsored by the Council of Graduate Schools and the Association of American Colleges and Universities made some significant headway in this regard, the overall effort to prepare graduate students as teachers still has not caught on in most graduate programs in major universities. When graduate students become college teachers themselves, they do unto others what has been done unto them. They lecture, answer questions to clarify, and test as they were tested. Need we ask about the use of the dominant paradigm for teaching and training at most professional meetings and conferences? How long will the dominant paradigm perpetuate itself?

Signs of challenge to the lecture paradigm exist. In fact, others have also identified it as a paradigm and have attempted to describe its alternatives. Calls to change the dominant paradigm are not new. Barr and Tagg's much referenced 1995 *Change* article proclaimed a need to move from an "instruction paradigm" to a "learning paradigm." They also denounced current methods for the evaluation of teaching.

> Our faculty evaluation systems, for example, evaluate the performance of faculty in teaching terms, not learning terms. An instructor is typically evaluated by her peers or dean on the basis of whether her lectures are organized, whether she covers the appropriate material, whether she shows interest in and understanding of her subject matter, whether she is prepared for class, and whether she respects her students' questions and comments. All these factors evaluate the instructor's performance in teaching terms. They do not raise the issue of whether students are learning, let alone demand evidence of learning or provide for its reward.[10]

Others have made similar calls to first of all recognize that higher education is entrenched in an outdated paradigm and, second, to begin to change it. Peter Smith, in *The Quiet Crisis: How Higher Education Is Failing America*, sums it up.

> The higher education establishment largely ignores the science that already exists about how people learn best. We continue to substitute the traditional model of education for an informed, professionally based educational process. Our actions say that we are committed to a specific version

of how to do business that is uninformed—structurally and profession-
ally—by what we know about how people learn. . . . In a world where we
have insulin patches for diabetics, we ignore the science of learning, asking
students and workers to "tough it out," to succeed or fail, based on their
sheer will and effort. This attitude is outrageous and it is unnecessary.
America needs to organize its schools and colleges around what we already
know about learning.[11]

Barr and Tagg predicted that changing the paradigm would take decades. More than a decade has already passed.

Today the conversation about changing the paradigm for teaching has
taken on new urgency in the context of higher education reform. Although
many things about colleges and universities are targets for reform—admissions,
financial aid, athletics, pricing, the curriculum—none is more urgent than
teaching. Teaching, after all, is central to the mission of every type of college
or university, and through the knowledge and understanding it provides, students are either prepared well or poorly to cross the bridge into society. It is
not surprising, therefore, that the dominant paradigm is coming under fire
from many directions. Consider the following propositions:

- The dominant paradigm rests on an obsolete view of learning in light
  of what was learned about learning in the last century.
- New technologies provide attractive and challenging alternatives to
  traditional methods of teaching.
- Knowledge has taken on a new importance in society, carrying grave
  consequences for those unprepared to live in the information age.
- The changing workplace creates educational needs that go beyond
  those typically addressed by the dominant paradigm.

We examine next each of these propositions in more detail.

Learning About Learning

The greatest challenge to the lecture paradigm is the existence of a body of
knowledge about learning that casts doubt on the limited capacity of lecturing to bring about the broad range of intellectual abilities college graduates
should have today. During the last century, a great amount was learned
about learning, so much so in fact that it would not be inappropriate to call
the twentieth century the *learning century*. At the beginning of the century,

behavioral psychologists, elaborating on the earlier work of Watson and Thorndike, demonstrated a connection between what the learner does (and attempts to do) and the feedback (sometimes called reinforcement) associated with it. B. F. Skinner elaborated on this model in great detail, with huge implications for identifying objectives and outcomes, describing what the learner already can do (the baseline), breaking learning into carefully worked out steps (task analysis), and intentionally managing feedback.[12] By midcentury, cognitive psychologists, tired of the behavioral model and curious about the questions it left unanswered, began to study how people pay attention to information, process it, and remember it. Their contributions were varied and significant, resulting in new understandings of how learners need to be actively engaged in making meaning of new information and assimilating it into their own contexts. Meanwhile, another set of scholars, social psychologists, and communication theorists were studying how people learn in groups, particularly how participants in a group modify their opinions, attitudes, and beliefs, and how they learn to collaborate in teams. Other scholars studied critical and creative thinking processes and how this type of learning takes place through inquiry, that is, by encouraging learners to find and use appropriate questions to discover and acquire relevant knowledge. Other researchers added to the understanding of problem solving and decision making while still others explored the learning that comes from virtual settings through role play, dramatic scenarios, and simulations. Going off in a completely opposite direction from the behaviorists are the advocates of experiential learning—using all the senses simultaneously to learn from experience. Most recently, learning theorists are beginning to assimilate what is being learned about learning from brain research, more formally known as cognitive neuroscience.

College professors, with few exceptions, have had neither time nor opportunity to become acquainted with this learning about learning. This is surely not their fault, because the dominant paradigm for preparing college teachers has not, with few exceptions, included instruction about learning. In general, college teachers have not been exposed to what has been learned in the last century about learning; they have not been guided systematically in how to adapt that knowledge for teaching, and they have not been encouraged to use new methods that violate the current norms of the teaching and learning paradigm. Even worse, this omission of the serious study of learning in the graduate curriculum sends an unintended message: there is nothing to learn about learning; knowing one's subject is sufficient. As Derek Bok, former President of Harvard University put it: "In the eyes of most faculty members in research universities, teaching is an art that is either too simple to require formal preparation, too personal to be taught to others, or too innate to be conveyed to anyone lacking the necessary gift."[13]

If anything has been learned from this century of research on learning, it is that learning is not one thing but many things, that the various methods used to elicit learning produce quite different outcomes, and the focus on only one method of teaching will produce only the very narrow range of results associated with that method. What is wrong with the lecture method? Nothing in itself. It is good for introducing students to information and ideas, new terminology and theories, and accounts of how certain discoveries were made, but that is about all. It is not especially good for helping students develop skills, think critically or creatively, examine their own values, solve problems, make decisions, and so forth. Other methods of teaching based on different ways of learning are needed to bring about more varied results. In other words, students are being hugely shortchanged in their education by being exposed so continuously to one way of learning.

Can college teachers really afford not to know about learning when a major portion of what a teacher does is to facilitate learning? Not knowing about significant new developments in the subject matter of one's specialty is considered to be intolerable, but not knowing about learning is thoroughly excusable within the traditional paradigm, because after all a professor is expected only to lecture. It is the students' job to learn. One strong challenge, therefore, to the dominant paradigm for college teaching is the explosion of knowledge about learning. The old paradigm, a needed change when it was introduced more than a century ago, is now being challenged by a century of learning about learning.

Technology and Teaching

The traditional paradigm for teaching and learning is also being challenged by the widespread availability of various educational technologies. Technology has often been called a disruptive element in higher education since the introduction of the computer, the blackboard, the handheld slate, and even the book. Technological changes are often resisted, but when they do arrive in the academy they come slowly. In the mid-1990s Steven Gilbert spelled out a simple three-stage process explaining how technological innovations at the turn of the twenty-first century would change higher education: first, by automating common administrative operations; second, by enhancing current tasks; and finally, by changing the core functions of teaching and learning.[14] Gilbert argued that we have automated and enhanced our teaching tasks, but it would take a decade or more to move firmly into the third stage of fundamental change. In fact, most of the newer technologies in the past decades have been absorbed into the lecture and discussion paradigm. The use of PowerPoint slides to visually reinforce the spoken word, the use of images and video to liven up presentations, and even the use of handheld response devices (clickers) have enhanced, but not fundamentally changed, the current teaching tasks of lectures and discussions. Laptops have entered the classroom, and some colleges and universities even require them. Yet laptops are more often than not used by students to take notes.

Newer technologies provide many more challenges and opportunities. One important technological innovation has been the course management system, often called a learning management system (LMS). With this technology, a course shell provides an electronic place for a course to reside, accessible to the teacher and registered students by password. This electronic platform allows teachers to post and distribute information such as biographical information; the course syllabus; weekly assignments; e-books and digital articles; slides, graphs, and diagrams; video and film clips; assessment activities; tests and examinations; and, yes, even texts or videos of short lectures. The course shell, when properly used, contains all the necessary information associated with a particular course and makes it readily available to students for use in class on their laptops and for out-of-class study. This technology is currently used in ways that are primarily compatible with lecture and discussion, but some aspects of the technology are encouraging learning activities that do not fit into the traditional teaching paradigm.

The LMS, as well as other technologies, provides the mechanism for class discussion, in synchronous and asynchronous formats, and opportunities for one-on-one communication with the instructor and other students as well as for the class or small groups. Students can ask questions of each other, discuss issues outside class, and create collaborative projects. Unlike the classroom-based discussion, online discussions, especially asynchronous threaded discussions, allow students to control and take ownership of the content and direction. Other tools like wikis, blogs, and quickly produced videos are allowing students to create their own content. Content and applications are now available on mobile devices, allowing students to participate in learning activities from any location. Intelligent tutors are being developed to provide individual feedback to students, augmented reality tools are bringing simulations to life, and students are interacting with experts in virtual worlds. Some are predicting the end of a formal LMS, arguing that newer technologies will allow students to collaborate, discuss, and create content in ways that go beyond classroom walls and involve a worldwide audience. Massive Open Online Courses are being offered for free to hundreds, thousands, even hundreds of thousands of participants simultaneously by select universities. Such courses offer various avenues to receive credit, certification, or develop knowledge and skills, changing the very nature of what it means to take a college course.

Such efforts challenge the paradigm through the sheer accessibility of information on the Internet and the ability students have now to access information at any time. Information on nearly any topic is only a click away, and some colleges and universities are putting content online for free public consumption. Furthermore, the Internet has transformed from a static information exchange, a place to read or otherwise get content, into a dynamic, ever-changing space to collaborate, create, repurpose, evaluate, and share content. Although many of the advances in technology are currently being used to enhance the traditional paradigm, the varied opportunities provided by these advances call out for different ways of using class time and out-of-class study. Almost anything that once required class time can now be done outside class electronically, technologies can often perform educational tasks more efficiently than humans, and information is readily available for free to anyone with Internet access. So the fundamental question arises: What is class time for? Surely not exclusively for lectures! The question itself threatens the traditional paradigm of lecture and discussion and forces teachers to consider other ways of learning.

The Importance of Knowledge in Society

Another challenge to the traditional lecture paradigm is the greater and growing importance of knowledge in society. Knowledge has always been important throughout history, and the founding of universities has been a strong confirmation of that importance. But something happened at the end of the twentieth century to give knowledge a greater importance and urgency in society than it had previously.

We live in what has come to be called the *information age,* and although the term may be overworked, the reality it describes greatly affects the activities of organizations and individuals. Although new technologies have made information much more widely available, it is not so much the accessibility of information that is important, but rather the way information is acted upon to produce knowledge, especially new knowledge. Perhaps the best description of the enhanced status of knowledge in the life of organizations is found in Peter Drucker's *Post-Capitalist Society.* He traces the course of three revolutions: industrial, productivity, and management. In each, knowledge becomes increasingly important in different ways, but in the fourth and latest revolution, the transition to a knowledge society, knowledge takes on an entirely new meaning. Today, Drucker argues, "Formal knowledge is seen as both the key personal and the key economic resource. In fact, knowledge is the only meaningful resource today. The traditional factors of production—land (i.e., natural resources), labor, and capital—have not disappeared, but they have become secondary. They can be obtained and obtained easily, provided there is knowledge. And knowledge in this new sense means knowledge as a utility, knowledge as the means to obtain social and economic results."[15]

The crucial difference today, Drucker points out, is that knowledge is not only being applied to the physical world, production, and the management of organizations, but to knowledge itself; that is, knowledge is being applied to create systematic innovation.

Lester Thurow makes a similar case in *The Future of Capitalism*, contending that this is an era of man-made, brain-power industries that can be located anywhere on the face of the earth.[16] Knowledge is clearly the new natural resource, the iron ore and bauxite of the new millennium. Human capital development is the key to moving from mere survival to success. Those who have the particular knowledge needed for the activity of their organization will prosper and be effective, and those without it will be left behind.

Robert Reich, in his useful book *The Work of Nations* identifies jobs of the future as providing three types of services: routine production services, in-person services, and symbolic analytic services.[17] Those holding jobs in the symbolic analytic services include scientists, engineers, public relations executives, investment bankers, real estate developers, accountants, consultants, and planners. Jobs in this category require knowledge and the ability to manipulate information at high levels of abstraction and often require sophisticated forms of training.[18] We usually think of these as college graduates with strong preparation in information and communication technology as well as technologies related to production, delivery of services, and research.

Richard Florida has characterized those who provide symbolic analytic services as the Creative Class: "The distinguishing characteristic of the Creative Class is that its members engage in work whose function is to 'create meaningful new forms' . . . [to] fully engage in the creative process. . . .

People at the core of the Creative Class engage in this kind of work regularly; it's what they are paid to do. Along with problem solving, their work may entail problem finding: not just building a better mousetrap, but noticing first that a better mousetrap would be a handy thing to have."[19]

Knowledge has clearly taken on an enhanced importance and a new urgency in organizations, but the same is also true for the lives of individuals. Having information and being able to analyze it critically and creatively and turn it into useful new knowledge is just as important for individuals as they make complex choices about raising children; purchasing real estate, cars, or technology; taking care of their health; and participating in civil society.

Oddly enough, the information component of knowledge is widely available. What was once the professor's cherished "store of knowledge" is now at everyone's fingertips instantly. In a fascinating article titled "How Web-Savvy Edupunks Are Transforming American Higher Education," Anya Kamenetz described a bewildering array of sources of information now readily available electronically often for free.[20] Consider that in 2001 the Massachusetts Institute of Technology (MIT) began to post materials on the web gratis for all its courses: syllabi, lecture notes, class exercises, tests, assignments, and lecture recordings. Kamenetz wrote, "The 'open content' movement that started at MIT has spread to more than 200 institutions in 32 countries that have posted courses online at OpenCourseWare Consortium."[21] Flat World Knowledge "commissions professors to write open-source textbooks that are free online."[22] Less dramatic, but just as important, are the e-books, reference works, databases, and electronic periodical collections available through university libraries and their consortia, now easily located through sophisticated search mechanisms. One of the main purposes of a lecture—providing information—has now been superseded by a far more pressing need: to know how to find, evaluate, analyze, and use information to create new knowledge. Ironically, what the lecture paradigm does best is hardly needed anymore, and what it fails to deliver has become the most essential and urgent aspect of learning.

The Changing Workplace

Although the new importance of knowledge has greatly influenced the nature of work, the work setting itself has changed, creating additional demands on workers. Not only must they be creative and effective symbolic analysts, they are expected to have additional skills and abilities badly needed in today's organizations.

In most organizations today, work has global and multicultural dimensions and one encounters people from around the world, or who are culturally different from themselves, as customers, suppliers, coworkers, or managers. The multicultural nature of work sometimes requires language skills but more often intercultural sensitivity and cross-cultural communication skills. These skills go well beyond mere tolerance, to the abilities needed for true collaboration and the creation of positive synergies. Work today is project oriented and team executed. Knowing how to work together is essential, and this means not only knowing the basics of cooperation but also the more sophisticated processes of project management and teamwork. College graduates are expected to have had experience working on projects and in teams.

Furthermore, organizations themselves are changing; in fact, whole industries are changing. Large industries merge and divest, small business start-ups grow and get sold, government engages in new ownerships and regulatory functions, and not for profits find themselves in unexpected collaborations. Most organizations today are change oriented, and they need leaders of change and adaptable workers. This means that people who have more than one specialization, who can work simultaneously on diverse projects and adapt quickly to new ideas are in high demand. Although the traditional lecture paradigm has its virtues, an exclusive exposure to lecturing leaves students shortchanged in the skills and abilities most needed in the twenty-first-century workplace.

Confusion Reigns as the Paradigm Crumbles

Clearly, the traditional paradigm is being challenged, outrun now as it is by the needs of a changing society. What was once the dominant and exclusive pattern of instruction has perhaps seen better days. Keep in mind that the lecture paradigm came into being and achieved its dominant position before cell phones, laptops, television, jet air travel, radio, and even cars and trucks. The endurance of the traditional paradigm has been truly remarkable; in fact, it is hard to understand how it has lasted so long.

Many college teachers today sense the need for change, but they often don't know what to put in place of lecturing. Alternatives abound, and these sometimes make the lives of professors even more confusing. Many approaches to college teaching exist, and some of these descriptions have strong advocates who lead movements. Teachers are bombarded with "ideal" solutions, exclusive alternatives, and commercial products—what we describe as a vendor environment of confusing ideas and remedies for improving teaching. Some of these are attractive and make good sense; others are really quite unfounded. It is important for teachers to know what is being said about college teaching today, to understand what these ideas imply or propose, to know how to evaluate them critically, and to distinguish them from what we are calling *ways of learning*.

Notes

1. Thomas Kuhn, *The Structure of Scientific Revolutions*, 2nd ed. (Chicago: University of Chicago Press, 1970), 10–34.

2. John S. Brubacher and Willis Rudy, *Higher Education in Transition, An American History: 1636–1956* (New York: Harper & Row, 1958), 82.

3. Brubacher and Rudy, *Higher Education*, 86.

4. Carol P. Barnes, "Questioning in College Classrooms," in *Studies of College Teaching*, ed. Carolyn L. Ellner and Carol P. Barnes (Lexington, MA: Lexington Books, 1983), 61–81; Daryl G. Smith, "Instructions and Outcomes in an Undergraduate Setting," in Ellner and Barnes, *Studies of College Teaching*, 83–116.

5. Wagner Thielens Jr., "The Disciplines and Undergraduate Lecturing" (paper, American Educational Research Association, Washington, DC, April 1987), as quoted in Joseph Katz, "Does Teaching Help Students Learn," in *Teaching Undergraduates: Essays from the Lilly Endowment Workshop on Liberal Arts*, ed. Bruce A. Kimball (Buffalo, NY: Prometheus Books, 1988), 173.

6. Claudia E. Nunn, "Discussion in the College Classroom: Triangulating Observational and Survey Results," *Journal of Higher Education* 67, no 3 (1996): 243–66.

7. William E. Becker and Michael Watts, "Teaching Economics at the Start of the 21st Century: Still Chalk-and-Talk," *American Economic Review* 91, no. 2 (2001): 446–51.

8. Linda M. Fritschner, "Inside the Undergraduate College Classroom," *Journal of Higher Education* 71, no. 3 (2000): 354.

9. Shelley Johnson Carey, "From the Editor," *Peer Review* 11, no. 2 (2009): 3.

10. Robert B. Barr and John Tagg, "From Teaching to Learning: A New Paradigm for Undergraduate Education," *Change* 27, no. 6 (1995): 12–25.

11. Peter Smith, *The Quiet Crisis: How Higher Education Is Failing America* (Boston, MA: Anker, 2004), xi–xii.

12. B. F. Skinner, *Science and Human Behavior* (New York: Free Press, 1953).

13. Derek Bok, *Our Underachieving Colleges: A Candid Look at How Much Students Learn and Why They Should Be Learning More* (Princeton, NJ: Princeton University Press, 2006), 314.

14. Steven Gilbert, "Making the Most of a Slow Revolution," *Change* 28, no. 2 (1996): 10–13.

15. Peter Drucker, *Post-Capitalist Society* (New York: Harper Business, 1993), 42.

16. Lester Thurow, *The Future of Capitalism* (New York: William Morrow, 1996), 67.

17. Robert B. Reich, *The Work of Nations* (New York: Vintage, 1992).

18. Reich, *Work of Nations*, 178.

19. Richard Florida, *The Rise of the Creative Class* (New York: Basic Books, 2002), 68–69.

20. Anya Kamenetz, "How Web-Savvy Edupunks Are Transforming American Higher Education," *Fast Company*, September 1, 2009, http://www.fastcompany.com/magazine/138/who-needs-harvard.html.

21. Kamenetz, "Web-Savvy Edupunks," 2.

22. Ibid., 3.

2

ALTERNATIVE APPROACHES TO TEACHING AND LEARNING

M any college teachers are ready to examine alternatives to the traditional lecture paradigm, but the dazzling array of options they encounter is often bewildering. College teachers, like tourists on resort beaches all over the world, seem to attract vendors, not just vendors of actual products, though these are plentiful, but vendors of ideas. On a beach—in Mexico, Hawaii, California, or Florida—on any given afternoon, vendors will offer to sell you brightly colored hats, glare-reduction sunglasses, handcrafted shawls, loom-woven blankets, hand-painted bowls, carved whistles, ice cream sandwiches, beadwork purses, leather wallets, and silver jewelry. Not all these items are valuable, although not all are worthless. Rather, the challenge is finding the most valuable items because there are so many items to choose from. Similarly, college teachers are offered active learning, problem-based learning, learner-centered teaching, inquiry-based teaching, andragogy, learning styles, left- and right-brained thinking, cooperative learning, collaborative learning, communities of practice, hybrid and online teaching, Bloom's taxonomy, Mager's behavioral objectives, and— need we go on? Some of these are the genuine article, like a sterling silver ring, a good buy of proven worth. Others sound like good ideas but need elaboration and backing before they can become useful. Some may not be a useful choice. College teachers live in a vendor environment of ideas about teaching, and most teachers, as subject matter experts, are usually not well prepared to evaluate these ideas that are continually drifting into their world. That world is filled with advocates, and although there is nothing wrong with advocacy—we are presenting ideas here that we advocate—from the teachers' point of view, the vendor environment is quite confusing and difficult to navigate. We have gathered these various suggestions, arrangements, remedies, and interesting ideas about teaching under the more general term *approaches*. The focus of this chapter is on describing, categorizing, and critiquing today's most prominent and well-known approaches to teaching and learning. We thought we should do that before moving on to our own suggestions about teaching and learning in Part Two of this book.

Approaches Based on Student Engagement

College teachers today often encounter the terms *learner-centered teaching*, *active learning*, and *inquiry-based learning*, all of which put the focus and responsibility for learning on the student.

Learner-centered teaching refers to a shift in the role of the teacher. It employs practices that place the responsibility of learning on the student or *learner*, which is the preferred term. This shift puts more control of learning tasks and assessment methods in the hands of the learner.[1] Learner-centered teaching does not rely on a particular way of learning; rather, many ways of learning are compatible with this approach to teaching and are in fact needed if learner-centered teaching is to have meaning or generate actual learning.

Similarly, *active learning* has become a general term that encompasses many different teaching methods. It is an approach that taps the active learning processes of students and is usually thought of as the opposite of passive learning, as when students take notes in a lecture. It refers to teaching methods that get students actively involved, such as creating or designing something, solving problems, participating in inquiries, or reflecting systematically on an experience. Active learning has been the basis of many studies comparing active to passive learning situations, with the results overwhelmingly favoring active learning methods.[2] However, similar to learner-centered teaching, active learning could employ nearly any way of learning that actively engages students.

Inquiry-based learning, yet another term that has become popular and can convey many meanings, usually refers to instruction where students are actively questioning the materials, ideas, and content to be learned. In a general way, this means the teacher avoids teaching the answers and instead encourages students to ask questions. In another conception used mainly in the sciences, inquiry-based learning focuses on developing experimental and analytic skills in students by posing questions and using a variety of learning methods to investigate the answers. Again, similar to learner-centered teaching and active learning, inquiry-based learning has become an approach that can include many types of teaching methods and ways of learning.

Such approaches to teaching suggest that many different specific teaching methods can support the principles of active learning, learner-centered teaching, and inquiry-based learning. Yet the way students are active or engaged is important and helps determine what they actually learn. Almost any teaching method can be implemented in a passive teacher-centered way or in an active student-centered way. In fact, the effective implementation of each of the seven ways of learning in this book relies on some level of learner initiative and engagement. If someone wants to teach using an active learner-centered or inquiry-based approach, the study and effective use of these seven ways of learning will help determine the specific ways to do this.

Approaches Based on General Teaching Methods

Whereas active learning, learner-centered teaching, and inquiry-based learning can be viewed as approaches to teaching based on ideas about learning, other approaches to teaching and learning use the familiar language of general teaching methods, such as lecture, discussion, and laboratory instruction. What we have identified as ways of learning fit nicely under these general methods, but we prefer to get much more specific about what students are learning and what teachers and students are doing when these ways of learning are used. Ideas about facilitating discussions, including Socratic discussion, are incorporated in chapter 6, on learning through inquiry. Group discussion methods, such as cooperative learning, collaborative learning, and team-based learning—well-known and researched approaches to teaching in small groups—are sorted out and discussed in chapter 8, on learning through groups and teams. Problem-based learning, frequently used in science instruction, is discussed in detail in chapter 7, on using mental models for learning, a way of learning that provides students with systematic processes for solving problems. The difference is this: general teaching methods are vague and subject to many interpretations; ways of learning are specific and useful when matched to particular learning outcomes. Consider the general method commonly referred to as discussion. What, after all, is a discussion? *Discussion* is a term that college teachers use frequently, but a discussion can be focused in many different ways: as an inquiry, as problem solving, or as a small-group discussion involving attitudes and feelings. In each case the way of learning is quite different. We try to go beyond general teaching methods to more solidly grounded and carefully defined ways of learning.

Approaches Based on the Andragogy/Pedagogy Distinction

After World War II college and university campuses were filled with older students, mostly returning veterans. A few years later, students who were older than those in the typical eighteen- to twenty-one-year-old cohort were characterized as nontraditional students. In 1970 Malcolm Knowles, one of the pioneers of adult education, developed the concept of *andragogy*, which he believed was a more appropriate method for teaching adults.[3] Drawing on the work of a colleague in the former Yugoslavia as well as several scholars in the social sciences, Knowles outlined ideas for teaching adults that he contrasted sharply with pedagogy, ideas about teaching children. Because older adults have more experience, particularly work experience, they are less subject oriented and more problem oriented in their approach to learning.[4] He believed adults should be taught by methods that take into account their need for knowing, their experience, their preference for self-direction, and their desire to apply what they know to real-world tasks.[5]

Although andragogy was a useful concept for its time, calling attention as it did to the characteristics of nontraditional students, as the years passed, nontraditional students became the traditional students (there are truly more adult learners now), and pedagogy adapted to become more like andragogy. It turned out that the ideas expressed in andragogy were good principles for learning in general, not unlike active learning or student-centered learning. The question remains: To what specific learning outcomes can these progressive principles of andragogy be applied? For the most part, one might say the seven ways of learning described in this book are quite compatible with the principles of andragogy, but andragogy alone doesn't produce specific kinds of learning outcomes.

Approaches Based on Student Characteristics

Other approaches to teaching are based on differences in students as learners. Most teachers notice that students vary considerably in such characteristics as gender, cultural background, aptitude, achievement, intelligence, motivation, values, personality, and other factors. Conducting a class with mainly nonmajor, first-year students will certainly be a different experience from a seminar with graduate students or an online class with working adults. Current literature about student diversity, adult learning principles, and concepts such as universal design and culturally relevant pedagogy is useful for learning how to adapt ways of learning to a particular individual or to a diverse group of students. But the key word is *adapt*. Our suggested approach is to begin first with desired learning outcomes, choose the appropriate way of learning, and then adapt that way of learning to the students at hand.

Approaches Based on Learning Styles

Another set of popular approaches to teaching is based on understanding student preferences and differences, often referred to as *learning styles*. Learning styles were first popularized in the 1970s, and by now hardly any college teacher has escaped the admonition to change his or her teaching to accommodate student learning styles. In fact, it is puzzling how the concept of learning styles has become so omnipresent in discussions of college teaching. Teachers who know almost nothing else about what has been written about postsecondary teaching and learning have somehow heard about learning styles and have come to believe that knowing a student's learning style is important.

Part of the confusion has to do with the many different theories and taxonomies that fall under the general heading of learning styles. One comprehensive review of the learning style literature uncovered no less than seventy-one apparently separate approaches.[6] The many layers of learning styles have been characterized by the metaphor of the layers of an onion. More stable traits such as personality and cognitive structure are at the core, while adaptable preferences and learning approaches constitute outer layers. A more useful and accurate way of understanding learning styles is to think of them as a continuum of approaches ranging from theories of fixed attributes on one end and theories of acquired preferences that are adaptable based on teaching methods and contexts on the other end.[7]

For example, at one end of the continuum, some versions of the learning styles concept are based on a belief that there are core, unchangeable characteristics related to learning. The best known of these are likely Gregorc's styles of perceptual qualities or Dunn and Dunn's VARK model, which proposes individuals possess visual, auditory, reading/writing, or kinesthetic preferences in how they prefer to receive information.[8] This view of learning styles has become a tremendously popular way of understanding learning; however, these instructional preferences have not shown consistency in research studies over the decades. An ongoing debate in the literature concerns the fixed or mutable nature of these preferences and their ultimate usefulness in relation to learning.

Other theories of learning styles also reflect stable traits but are more related to personality or cognitive structure. The Myers-Briggs personality inventory and Gardner's theory of multiple intelligences fall into this category.[9] Similarly, Kolb's learning styles inventory is based on a preferred entry point on his experiential learning model.[10] All these approaches outline some relatively stable attributes that purportedly influence how people learn. These theories can be a useful means for understanding differences in students and adjusting instruction accordingly, but are not very valuable as guidelines for designing instruction intended to produce specific learning outcomes. To put it simply, no one is going to learn to drive a car successfully based only on auditory instruction.

Learning style theories create an awareness of students' preferences, strengths, and weaknesses and provide an easy-to-use language for discussing learning differences observed in students. However, this area of study has suffered from a lack of an agreed-upon theoretical base and variations in research quality. A branch of this research has turned into a profitable industry based on overreaching claims. There is a tendency to use learning styles to label or pigeonhole students and to forget what they are intended to learn. Many critics view learning styles as oversimplified descriptions or hypotheses and not as established theories. They provide a quick answer (correct or incorrect) for students and instructors on learning difficulties but do not provide the depth needed for more substantial guidance on how to correct these difficulties or achieve specific learning outcomes.

The most important thing to remember is that learning styles are not to be confused with ways of learning. Learning style theory may contribute to understanding learners; it adds almost nothing to the discussion of how to bring about specific learning outcomes through particular ways of learning. Gardner's multiple intelligences theory contributes to an understanding of the different ways students demonstrate intelligence, but Gardner himself has refrained from designing a specific teaching approach from the theory of multiple intelligences.[11] He sees it as a theory that describes student characteristics rather than a teaching method. In fact, recent analyses of learning styles have come to the same conclusion, that instruction should match learning objectives, not student preferences.[12] In study after study it appears that certain instructional techniques are more effective than others for specific types of learning, even if it takes students outside their comfort zones. It is a wasted effort, therefore, for a college teacher to use a lot of teaching methods one after the other to appeal to the varied learning style preferences of students with the elusive hope of reaching at least some of the students some of the time. Learning styles can help teachers understand student differences and adjust their teaching accordingly, but they should not be used as a prescription for how to teach. That is determined, or should be, by the desired learning outcomes for the subject and by the selection of an appropriate way of learning that will best achieve the designated outcome.

Approaches Based on Learning Strategies

Considerable emphasis is placed on what teachers do or think they should do as teachers, but as any experienced teacher knows, students themselves are continually making decisions about what to do as learners. They make decisions about what to study, how much to study, which topics to study more than others, and how deep to go into any one topic. Researchers call these *learning strategies,* and they exist at the far other end of the continuum from fixed learning styles. It has become apparent that students alter their approaches to learning based on instruction, motivation, and other contextual factors. The concept of learning strategies has been useful in determining the impact of particular instructional practices on students' approaches to learning. For example, Entwistle's learning strategy taxonomy is useful for determining the effectiveness of certain instructional practices on students' learning strategies and study habits.[13] A teacher can determine if a particular instructional variable results in deep- or surface-learning strategies for most students. In a nutshell, whether a student takes a deep or shallow approach has a lot to do with expectations and types of assignments. However, the concept itself needs to be understood in terms of a student's adaptive response to learning, not as a descriptor for different types of students. In other words, students should not be labeled as deep or surface learners but rather should be understood as varying their learning strategies based on different situations, expectations, and interventions. For each of the seven ways of learning in this book, students will in fact develop strategies for managing their own learning. They can be prompted to deeper learning through high expectations and effective methods of assessment.

Approaches Based on Technology Use

In the past few decades, college teachers on most campuses have been asked to incorporate greater use of technology in their teaching. Technology has meant electronic media of many types but especially those mediated by the computer. In some cases, asking has evolved into requiring, based on the belief that more extensive use of technology results in better learning. As we shall see, this may or may not be true.

The debate about the efficacy of media for learning goes back over many years, but one key chapter in that controversy includes the so-called "Clark-Kozma debate" centered on the question, Is the medium the message? In 1983 Richard Clark wrote an article titled "Reconsidering Research on Learning from Media" in which he argued there are "no learning benefits to be gained from employing any specific medium to deliver instruction."[14] Using the analogy of a delivery truck, Clark concluded that media are mere vehicles that deliver instruction and do not influence student achievement any more than a grocery truck influences nutrition. Robert Kozma responded to Clark's article with his own article, "Learning with Media," in which he argued that unique characteristics of the media interact with characteristics of the learner to promote high achievement.[15] The debate went on, with claims and counterclaims, but at stake was whether the media are simply a vehicle for supporting good teaching methods or whether the media in themselves enhance learning.

Although this debate was primarily concerned with studying the effects of technology use on learning, it is interesting background for considering the effects of technology on teaching. Considerable investment has been made in promoting the use of technology to improve and develop teaching. Often when teachers are faced with using technology—they are at a loss on where to begin. Their familiar tools of instruction, the whiteboard, the lectern, even the classroom—might be missing or replaced, and as a result they are forced to revisit their learning goals for students and question their established teaching practices fundamentally. In this sense, then, using technology improves, or at least upends, teaching. New and presumably more appropriate teaching methods are often adopted as a result.

This still leaves unanswered the question: What specific technologies should be used to support which types of teaching? Although technologies surely can enhance the learning activities of students, there is continuing confusion about which of the various technologies to use. Here the vendor environment becomes even more intense, as teachers are confronted incessantly with new products and tools while hype and overblown promises fill the air. Web conferencing, telepresence, interactive whiteboards, blogs, wikis, mobile devices, simulations, games—the choices are endless. Critical to making good choices is the way these technologies are used to support ways of learning. Although like Kozma, we feel technology itself can enhance some learning activities in unique ways, like Clark, we feel that the medium itself is not the message but the vehicle. Technology should be chosen appropriately as the vehicle to extend a particular way of learning. This is why we include in each chapter a discussion of the specific technologies most suited to supporting the way of learning being described.

Other Approaches

Many other approaches to teaching have surfaced over the last century. Some of these specific methods and models are woven into this book within the discussion of a related way of learning. For example, Mager's behavioral objectives are discussed in chapter 4 on behavioral learning. Neuroscience and constructivism undergird experiential learning. The concepts of prior knowledge and knowledge organization are discussed in chapter 5, on cognitive learning, and chapter 7 on learning with mental models. Metacognition, the ability to monitor one's own levels of understanding and performance and make the necessary adjustments, informs inquiry and the use of mental models as ways of learning. Assessment and educational technology are discussed in chapters 4 through 10, on the particular ways of learning.

Many complementary lenses are available for viewing college teaching, and they have many approaches and many advocates. We hope this book will help college teachers feel less overwhelmed by the vendor environment, be more able to distinguish what is useful and not so useful, and be able to see how the seven ways of learning presented in this book are a valuable way to approach teaching and learning because they address particular learning outcomes.

Beyond Confusion

What lessons can be learned from this brief review of alternative approaches to teaching and learning? A lot of ideas, theories, concepts, suggestions, frames, and commercial products are floating around in the vendor environment of college teachers. The alternatives have advocates, and deciding upon what is true or useful is not easy. Many of those who advocate for a particular idea lack a formal background in teaching and learning theory. Many approaches are promoted without clearly articulating what learning outcomes they best support. Moreover, a plethora of vague terms that lack conceptual clarity—let's call it a jumble of ideas that somehow sound important—makes it difficult for the uninitiated to know what to think. Learner-centered teaching? Who could be against it? Active learning? It has been around at least as long as the philosophy of John Dewey. Team-based learning, blogs, wikis, or Socratic teaching? Sure, why not? But what is the best approach to use for one's particular course or learning goals?

What college teachers truly need in the midst of this conceptual chaos is a clear and useful framework for thinking about and organizing teaching, as described in the following list. Is it really so complicated?

- Clear goals expressed as student learning outcomes
- A good match between student learning outcomes and the chosen ways of learning
- Well-organized teaching based on the concepts and practices inherent in each way of learning
- Engaging and stimulating materials and activities drawn from the subject being taught
- Technology that supports and enhances teaching where appropriate
- Assessment methods that actually measure if learning outcomes are being achieved

When these conditions are met, students are more likely to learn. When students learn, they are happier, society is better served, and teachers are better satisfied, having contributed to actual learning. Teaching that is purposefully aligned is more effective and, in the end, more enjoyable.

Notes

1. Maryellen Weimer, *Learner-Centered Teaching: Five Key Changes to Practice* (San Francisco: Wiley, 2002).

2. Charles C. Bonwell and James A. Eison, *Active Learning: Creating Excitement in the Classroom* (ASHE-ERIC Higher Education Report No. 1, Washington, DC: George Washington University, School of Education and Human Development, 1991).

3. Malcolm Knowles, *The Modern Practice of Adult Education: Andragogy vs. Pedagogy* (New York: Association Press, 1970).

4. Knowles, *Modern Practice*, 58.

5. Malcolm S. Knowles, Elwood F. Holton, and Richard A. Swanson, *The Adult Learner: The Definitive Classic in Adult Education and Human Resource Development*, 7th ed. (Burlington, MA: Elsevier, 2011).

6. Frank Coffield, David Moseley, Elaine Hall, and Kathryn Ecclestone, *Learning Styles and Pedagogy in Post-16 Learning: A Systematic and Critical Review* (Trowbridge, Wiltshire: Learning & Skills Research Centre, 2004).

7. Coffield et al., *Learning Styles*.

8. Anthony F. Gregorc, *Gregorc Style Delineator: Development, Technical and Administration Manual* (Columbia, CT: Gregorc Associates, 1982); Rita Dunn, Kenneth Dunn, and G. E. Price, *Learning Style Inventory* (Lawrence, KS: Price Systems, 1984).

9. Isabel Briggs Myers and Mary H. McCaulley, *Manual: A Guide to the Development and Use of the Myers-Briggs Type Indicator* (Palo Alto, CA: Consulting Psychologists Press, 1998); Howard Gardner, *Frames of Mind: The Theory of Multiple Intelligences* (New York: Basic Books, 1993).

10. David Kolb, *Experiential Learning: Experience as the Source of Learning and Development* (Englewood Cliffs, NJ: Prentice Hall, 1984).

11. Howard Gardner, *Intelligence Reframed: Multiple Intelligences for the 21st Century* (New York: Basic Books, 1999).

12. Harold Pashler, Mark McDaniel, Doug Rohrer, and Robert Bjork, "Learning Styles: Concepts and Evidence," *Psychological Science in the Public Interest* 9, no. 3 (2008): 105–19.

13. Noel Entwistle and Velda McCune, "The Conceptual Bases of Study Strategy Inventories," *Educational Psychology Review* 16, no. 4 (2004): 325–45.

14. Richard E. Clark, "Reconsidering Research on Learning from Media," *Review of Educational Research* 53, no. 4 (1983): 445–59.

15. Robert Kozma, "Learning with Media," *Review of Educational Research* 61, no. 2 (1991): 179–211.

3

USING THE SEVEN WAYS OF
LEARNING FOR TEACHING

A colleague asked his eight-year-old son to help out the family by teaching his younger brother how to tie his shoes. Several weeks later, when the older son was asked why his little brother still couldn't tie his shoes, he replied, "I taught him; he just didn't learn." The young lad had no idea, of course, about how profound his comment was, nor did he know how widely those words, spoken and unspoken, are used to explain teaching gone astray.

Reconnecting Teaching and Learning

Teaching succeeds when learning occurs. Without learning, teaching is "sound and fury, signifying nothing."[1] Or to put it less dramatically, it can be fairly frustrating when so much effort goes into teaching, and students don't learn. Knowing as we all do, as even an eight-year-old knows, that there is an inherent and obvious connection between teaching and learning, why is there so often a disconnect?

Teaching is frequently viewed as an entity unto itself, a set of discrete behaviors that can be described and discussed in great detail, that can be evaluated, and that can even have a philosophy, yet all quite separate from student learning. Isn't it odd that so much of the writing about teaching is focused on what teachers do or should do? Tips are given for preparing a syllabus, getting through the first class, delivering a lecture, guiding a discussion, setting up a laboratory as if one were cooking a dinner without regard for the guests who will eat it. Wouldn't all this conversation about teaching go deeper, and perhaps in a different direction, if the focus was on learning? What do teachers do to facilitate learning? Isn't that the key question?

31

Well-Established Theories of Learning

College teachers, primarily oriented to subject matter, may become jittery at the mention of learning theories, perhaps because the word *theory* carries the connotation of unsubstantiated, but also because there is a deep-rooted suspicion that the research by scholars on learning has little to do with what takes place in college classrooms. Although there is legitimate concern for wariness, turning one's back on what was learned about learning in the last century is not appropriate either. The challenge is to sort out these theories, identify their origins, describe their basic principles, and make the big stretch of application to specific subjects. This is what we attempt to do in Part Two.

That the twentieth century produced a significant amount of research and theory building about learning is now well established. Sorting that scholarship into categories is a challenge, and not everyone will agree on the names or the boundaries of the categories, but fairly obvious groups do exist. The first historically and most easily defined is behavioral learning theory. It satisfies those who like to see grounded empirical study that results in clear principles as well as identifiable cause-and-effect connections. Its findings can be easily crafted into principles that guide learning. Likewise, cognitive learning theory is based on scholarship but of a somewhat different order. Although numerous studies have been done on such topics as attention, information processing, and memory, there is more inference used in the research about mental operations, and the task of drawing out and synthesizing principles applicable to college teaching is more challenging. The literature on critical and creative thinking that supports learning through inquiry is less empirical but derives its credibility from analysis of reasoning and studies of thinking processes. A deeper understanding of how people organize knowledge, solve problems, and make decisions was gained through advances in problem-solving and decision-making theory. As one moves to the study of learning in groups, the research comes not from psychology but from the literature on group behavior and teamwork, largely from the field of communications. Similarly, the related work on role play, dramatic scenarios, and simulations comes from offshoots of communication theories such as psychodrama, sociodrama, and game theory. Advances in neuroscience, along with theories of constructivism, have informed an understanding of experiential learning.

Well-established theories of learning rely on different sources of explanation and substantiation. Some are more empirical, others more inferential, but each has its own rules of evidence, boundaries, and case for support.

After years of studying the literature and analyzing the research trends on learning, we believe it is possible to delineate clearly seven discrete areas where research and theorizing have taken place. We prefer to call these areas simply *ways of learning*. Would people who work in the field agree that exactly seven categories exist? Perhaps not. Is there some variation and overlap in interpreting learning theories? Likely so. Is it possible to fit the complex world of human learning into seven neat and tidy categories? We think there is value in making this attempt. The names of the ways of learning and the titles of the chapters of this book reflect the learning outcomes college teachers typically try to achieve. The categories have evolved and have been refined over time, and like all intellectual constructs they are defensible and assailable. The important points are that learning is not one thing, that different ways of learning can be distinguished from each other and can be given names, and that enough is known about these different ways of learning to regard them as well established. These well-established ways of learning are the key to effective and satisfying teaching and are described and illustrated in this book.

Establishing Learning Outcomes

The path to more effective and more satisfying teaching is crowded with vendors of attractive options, but the key to success is to think clearly about the learning intended for students and to associate those outcomes with a way of learning most likely to bring them about. Effective teaching will be informed, first and foremost, by the goals of learning. The first question a teacher asks is: What am I trying to teach? The next question is: What kind of learning does that involve? Teaching—what the teacher does—needs to be firmly grounded in goals and aligned with a particular way of learning.

The first essential task of the teacher, therefore, is to think systematically about the intended learning he or she hopes to bring about through teaching, that is, the goals of instruction. This is typically referred to as establishing *learning outcomes*. Learning outcomes move beyond the subject matter of the curriculum. They are not a list of topics to cover. They are what the learner is supposed to get from or do with the subject. Learning outcomes can be quite varied, and this is not a problem because learning itself is quite varied and can be facilitated by drawing upon quite different ways of learning.

Instructors sometimes become confused about level and specificity when writing learning outcomes. Scholars in this area often use the term *objectives* and suggest three levels of objectives: global objectives, which are written at the college or program level; educational objectives, written at the course level; and instructional objectives, written at the session, lesson, unit, or task level.[2] All three levels of objectives should be aligned with each other, but it is this last category, instructional objectives, that is the main concern of this book. The instructional objectives dictate the ways of learning to be used.

To think systematically about instructional objectives, it is useful to project very specifically what the learner will know or be able to do after learning has occurred. This is often aided by very specific infinitive verb forms such as *to explain, to demonstrate,* or *to apply,* followed by some description of what the learning looks like. For example, "Students will be able to compare and contrast the theories of Adam Smith and Karl Marx on four key points: role of the market, degree of planning, long-term outcomes, and social equity" is a more adequately expressed objective than "Students will learn about Smith and Marx" or "Students will understand the free market and Marxism." It is only in the first example that you get a real sense of what students are being asked to do.

Bloom's taxonomy of educational objectives for the cognitive domain, which classifies six types of cognitive abilities, has been a very useful guide for college teachers when writing outcomes for different types of learning.[3] Bloom's taxonomy remains popular and has lasted over fifty years because it is an easy to understand and useful framework. A revision of the taxonomy by several scholars has provided additional specificity to the original framework. These authors have separated knowledge dimensions from cognitive processes, and it is in the cognitive process dimension where helpful verbs to describe learning can be found.[4] The cognitive processes—remember, understand, apply, analyze, evaluate, and create—have been used by many to design their instruction for more than just knowledge transfer.

However, it is important to remember that this popular taxonomy is written only for the cognitive domain, and that other kinds of learning do occur and are important in higher education. Skill development, attitude shaping, and self-discovery, to name a few, are all part of the education of college students. Luckily, other taxonomies do exist and perhaps need to be revisited. Bloom and his colleagues also began work on psychomotor and affective domains, which has been further developed by other scholars. Seven levels of a psychomotor domain have been proposed for the development of physical movement and the use of motor skills.[5] Similarly, but more difficult to articulate, five levels for an affective domain—receiving, responding, valuing, organizing, and characterizing—spell out an awareness and growth of attitudes, beliefs, and feelings.[6]

College teachers have found L. Dee Fink's taxonomy of significant learning goals to be a useful reference when determining course objectives.[7] Fink's categorization is based on a series of questions for creating significant learning goals and goes beyond the cognitive processes of Bloom's taxonomy to include other aims of college teaching. His questions begin with a focus on foundational knowledge (What key information or ideas are important? What do students need to remember or understand?), application (What types of thinking are important to develop? What skills do students need to learn? What complex projects do they need to learn how to manage?), and integration (What connections should students recognize and make?). The questions also include areas not always considered by instructors: What can or should students learn about themselves? About interacting with others? What changes would you like to see in their interests or values? What would you like students to learn about learning?

All these categorizations and guides are useful tools for college teachers to examine when they are trying to articulate their teaching goals, but eventually it comes down to each instructor's having to establish his or her own goals and find the precise language that expresses them most clearly. We have gathered a collection of useful verbs in the following table to help teachers with this process. We have refrained from trying to attach verbs to specific ways of learning, as most verbs can be used for multiple purposes.

The task of spelling out learning outcomes may be challenging and feel foreign at first, but with a little practice facilitated by talking them through with a colleague and writing them down, the process will come to be second

recognize	value	detect
interpret	be aware of	react
classify	characterize	respond
summarize	originate	assemble
infer	demonstrate	construct
compare	justify	sketch
explain	share	adapt
execute	integrate	revise
implement	question	build
differentiate	display	compose
organize	engage	generate
attribute	judge	plan
determine	critique	produce

nature. Just ask yourself for each class: What do I hope the students will learn from this class, and how will they show me they have learned it?

Selecting a Way of Learning

Once learning outcomes have been thought through very carefully, the next step is to associate those outcomes with a particular way of learning. Although professional judgment will need to be used in making this match, we try to make clear in this book which way of learning is best suited to bringing about what desired outcomes.

The learning outcomes, or instructional objectives, for teaching are the very precise specifications for a class or segment of a class often referred to as a lesson. If a class (either on campus or online) is thought of as being divided into segments, each with its own specific learning outcomes, the challenge is to select for that segment the way of learning that is most likely to produce the desired learning outcome. When outcomes are matched to a particular way of learning, the teacher then asks: How do I facilitate that way of learning? The chapters in Part Two provide extensive guidance on selecting and facilitating each of the seven ways of learning.

The following list contains a series of questions to help identify the way of learning to be used. The questions serve as a useful checklist for selecting the way of learning that will be most useful in bringing about the desired learning outcome. Chapters 4 through 10 begin with the questions from this list that pertain to the way of learning discussed in the chapter. The table on page 38 summarizes these seven ways of learning.

- Is this learning that involves a procedural or physical skill? Is this something concrete and observable that a student performs? Is it a routine (though not necessarily easy) set of mental or physical operations that can be broken into steps and observed? Is there one best way to perform this skill? Is this a task a student attempts and through feedback can get better at it? These are learning outcomes that are well served by *behavioral learning* (chapter 4).
- Is this learning that involves information acquisition? Does it involve new ideas, new terminology, or useful theories? Does it require understanding of how something works or functions? Is this information that might be presented through an explanation? Is it possible to identify key concepts, main ideas, or points to be understood and

remembered? These are learning outcomes that are well served by *cognitive learning* (chapter 5).

- Is this learning that involves being aware of and improving one's thinking processes? Does this involve criticizing information, evaluating arguments and evidence, or reasoning to arrive at conclusions? Does this learning involve creative thinking by actually producing unusual but relevant new ideas? Does it involve appreciating what other people think? These are learning outcomes that are well served by *learning through inquiry* (chapter 6).

- Is this learning that involves solving problems or making decisions? Does it involve challenges for students to organize their knowledge into systematic strategies? Do students need to learn how to find and define problems, how to generate solutions, and how to evaluate and choose among solutions? Does this learning require students to deal with issues they need to make choices about, weigh the values of different options, and predict outcomes as probabilities? These are learning outcomes well served by *learning with mental models* (chapter 7).

- Is this learning that involves changing opinions, attitudes, and beliefs? Does it involve creating understanding from an awareness of multiple perspectives? Does it deal with feelings? Does it cultivate empathy? Is teamwork or collaboration being addressed here? These are learning outcomes that are well served by *learning through groups and teams* (chapter 8).

- Is this a kind of learning that involves developing professional judgment in a variety of different contexts? Does the development of judgment need to be practiced in a safe environment? Does this learning involve activities that could cause damage, expense, or even loss of life? Will students feel more confident and be more competent if they have been able to work first in a simulated environment before going into the real world? These are learning outcomes that are well served by *learning through virtual realities* (chapter 9).

- Is this a kind of learning that bubbles up out of experience? Is this learning that occurs when students go out and get immersed in a real-life work, service, or travel experience? Could students learn more from the experience if they have a chance to reflect on it and make meaning of it? Is there a potential here for learning to see something in a new way? These are learning outcomes that are well served by *experiential learning* (chapter 10).

Intended Learning Outcomes What students learn	Way of Learning Origins and theory	Common Methods What the teacher provides
Building skills Physical and procedural skills where accuracy, precision, and efficiency are important	**Behavioral learning** Behavioral psychology, operant conditioning	Tasks and procedures Practice exercises
Acquiring knowledge Basic information, concepts, and terminology in a discipline or field of study	**Cognitive learning** Cognitive psychology: attention, information processing, memory	Presentations Explanations
Developing critical, creative, and dialogical thinking Improved thinking and reasoning processes	**Learning through inquiry** Logic, critical and creative thinking theory, classical philosophy	Question-driven inquiries Discussions
Cultivating problem-solving and decision-making abilities Mental strategies for finding solutions and making choices	**Learning with mental models** Gestalt psychology, problem solving, and decision theory	Problems Case studies Labs Projects
Exploring attitudes, feelings, and perspectives Awareness of attitudes, biases, and other perspectives; ability to collaborate	**Learning through groups and teams** Human communication theory, group counseling theory	Group activities Team projects
Practicing professional judgment Sound judgment and appropriate professional action in complex, context-dependent situations	**Learning through virtual realities** Psychodrama, sociodrama, gaming theory	Role playing Simulations Dramatic scenarios Games
Reflecting on experience Self-discovery and personal growth from real-world experience	**Experiential learning** Experiential learning, cognitive neuroscience, constructivism	Internships Service-learning Study abroad

Relationships Among the Seven Ways of Learning

Some readers may question our methods of organizing and presenting these seven ways of learning. One might ask: Why is behavioral learning presented as the first way of learning, as if this gives it greater emphasis? Actually, we are not prioritizing one way of learning over another; our hope is to describe and value them equally. The chapters are presented in more or less historical order, so that by reading all of part 2, one has taken a journey through one hundred years of research about learning. Behavioral learning is first because it came first. We recognize that some college teachers think they are engaged in something far more sophisticated than training a pigeon in a box, and they assume this way of learning has already been discredited and replaced. We have put the behavioral learning chapter first because it characterizes the first attempt historically to study learning empirically. Although behavioral principles work best for skill development using practice and feedback, the underlying principles of behavioral learning *do* work and are present at some level in nearly all learning interactions. Cognitive research was a reaction, in part, to the limits of behavioral learning. The other chapters are presented more or less historically, up to recent developments in cognitive neuroscience, presented in support of the seventh way of learning.

Other readers may ask whether the ways of learning may be used in combination with each other or for purposes beyond those we describe. Keep in mind that these ways of learning are focused at the lesson or class level, not on the smaller minute-by-minute events within a lesson. For example, when engaging students in role play, the class might begin with a brief presentation; during a lecture, a teacher might have students chat in small groups for a few minutes to explore their feelings about a controversial issue. We do not see these small deviations from the general strategy as a problem but rather as techniques for making each way of learning more effective. For the most part, however, the ways of learning have a greater effect when used independently with sufficient time in between for each to make its impact.

Sometimes the ways of learning appear to overlap. For example, students might be involved in an online simulation using problem solving in small groups. Is this learning through virtual realities, mental models, or groups and teams? In this situation the teacher needs to ask: What is the primary learning outcome targeted here and which way of learning is to be emphasized most? It might seem interesting to use inquiry for the purpose of knowledge transfer, but this is not the most effective or efficient route to the goal. Students recognize when appropriate ways of learning are being used to bring about the intended outcomes, and they get restless when the match is bad. Don't confuse them with a smorgasbord.

Consider the following example.

Coauthor Bridget Arend teaches a course about educational program evaluation at the University of Denver. This course has several course-level educational objectives, including helping students develop the ability to

- identify when and how to use five levels of evaluation: reaction, learning, behavior, results, and Return On Investment (ROI);
- design evaluations that match learning objectives and evaluation goals;
- develop appropriate quantitative and qualitative assessment measures;
- refine skills for conducting interviews and focus groups; and
- design a comprehensive evaluation plan for an educational program.

When designing instruction for this course, it becomes apparent that several skills and abilities need to be developed and practiced, each of which involves a different way of learning. The course is based on a five-level model to organize an approach to evaluation, which students use to create a program evaluation plan. Knowledge about the model itself and related topics is transferred through readings and occasional short explanations and presentations by the instructor, following the guidelines of cognitive learning. A basic level of quantitative statistical skill is needed, and this is achieved through practice and feedback in class and through an online tutorial system using behavioral learning. Context-dependent abilities for conducting interviews and focus groups are developed and practiced through role-play activities, as supported by learning through virtual realities. The final project of the course, where students use the five-level model to design a comprehensive evaluation plan, is based on learning with mental models. Students practice working with the model on sample problems and hypothetical scenarios during the course as they develop their own project. Arend comments, "Before thinking through the framework of the final project as a mental model, I was often surprised to find that some students worked very hard on their projects but didn't end up using the five-level concept appropriately. Now I conceptualize it as a mental model—as solving a complex evaluation problem—and I spend time explicitly walking through the model and providing opportunities for students to practice solving related problems. I rarely encounter this issue with their final projects anymore." Having precise learning outcomes and a clear idea of when and why to use a particular way of learning makes the process of teaching this course more purposeful, effective, and enjoyable.

Choosing and Using the Ways of Learning

By now it should be clear that the main criterion for deciding to use a particular way of learning is the learning outcome (objective) itself. The goal is simply to match the way of learning best suited to the objective. Three precautions are in order.

First, it is inappropriate to select ways of learning randomly and use a lot of them so at least some students will find a way that works for them.

The uncoordinated use of a variety of ways of learning is not the goal. On the contrary, as described previously, ways of learning need to be precisely matched to outcomes. When you select a particular way of learning, you are doing so to bring about stated objectives.

Second, it is inappropriate to choose a way of learning based on a student learning style. As noted in the previous chapter, the whole notion of learning styles is quite precarious to begin with, and although understanding the characteristics of groups of students and individual students is an important aspect of adapting one's teaching, it should never be the basis for selecting a way of learning. Selection is based solely on the desired learning outcome.

Third, it is inappropriate to select a way of learning based on one's comfort with that way. Most college teachers will, indeed, feel more comfortable and confident with certain ways of learning than with others, but with practice a diligent teacher can become more effective, and therefore more comfortable, at using them all. In fact, using the wrong way of learning just because one feels comfortable using it can result in not achieving the desired learning outcomes and serious confusion for everybody.

Many of the ideas presented in this chapter will become clearer as the specific ways of learning are understood, selected, and used. As different ways of learning are explored, it will become clear how they differ from the dominant lecture and discussion paradigm and from each other. As new ways of learning are encountered, the power of these ways will come to be appreciated, and neglected learning outcomes in one's teaching will be obvious and can be addressed. The process of developing learning outcomes will become more comfortable, and matching the right ways of learning to them will appear more natural. The proof in the pudding, however, is actually trying to facilitate a specific way of learning using the extensive guidelines described in each chapter, selecting the appropriate technologies to support that way of learning, and using appropriate assessment techniques. Teachers who can do this will have a rational framework for organizing their teaching, will be more effective, and will enjoy seeing students learn. They will be able to say, "I taught them, and they learned."

Notes

1. William Shakespeare, *Macbeth* (New York: David Longworth, 1816), 55.
2. Lorin W. Anderson et al., *A Taxonomy for Learning, Teaching, and Assessing: A Revision of Bloom's Taxonomy of Educational Objectives* (New York: Longman, 2001).

3. Benjamin S. Bloom et al., *Taxonomy of Educational Objectives: The Classification of Educational Goals; Handbook I: Cognitive Domain* (New York: Longmans, Green, 1956).

4. Anderson, *A Taxonomy for Learning.*

5. Elizabeth J. Simpson, *The Classification of Educational Objectives in the Psychomotor Domain* (Washington, DC: Gryphon House, 1972).

6. David R. Krathwohl, Benjamin S. Bloom, and Bertram B. Masia, *Taxonomy of Educational Objectives: The Classification of Educational Goals. Handbook II: Affective Domain* (New York: David McKay, 1973).

7. L. Dee Fink, *Creating Significant Learning Experiences: An Integrated Approach to Designing College Courses* (San Francisco: Jossey-Bass, 2003).

PART TWO

ORGANIZING TEACHING
AND LEARNING

4

BUILDING SKILLS

Behavioral Learning

Intended Learning Outcomes What students learn	Way of Learning Origins and theory	Common Methods What the teacher provides
Building skills Physical and procedural skills where accuracy, precision, and efficiency are important	**Behavioral learning** Behavioral psychology, operant conditioning	Tasks and procedures Practice exercises

Is this learning that involves a procedural or physical skill? Is this something concrete and observable that a student performs? Is it a routine (though not necessarily easy) set of mental or physical operations that can be broken into steps and observed? Is there one best way to perform this skill? Is this a task a student attempts and through feedback can get better at it? These are learning outcomes that are well served by behavioral learning.

A nursing teacher guides students step-by-step in developing the skill to insert a tube in the patient's nose that goes to the stomach. Nasogastric tube insertion is a basic skill taught in a Fundamentals of Nursing course. How does the teacher use principles of behavioral learning to teach this skill effectively and efficiently?

College teachers are often called upon to help students develop specific skills. Sometimes these skills involve physical movements such as playing a musical instrument or hitting a tennis ball. These are physical skills, sometimes called *psychomotor* skills by psychologists. Other

45

skills may be procedural in nature such as making routine mathematical calculations or following basic grammar and punctuation rules. These are called *cognitive* skills because they require mostly mental effort.

Many basic skills are taught in secondary school but are often not learned and need to be retaught at the postsecondary level. Teaching skills in higher education, however, is not limited to basic skills. It also includes many advanced physical and cognitive skills such as learning to operate an electron microscope, calculating certain statistics, programming computer functions, or operating ultrasound equipment. Skills can be simple or complex. In any case, we use the following definition: a skill involves a patterned set of operations requiring routine—though not necessarily easy—physical activity, mental activity, or both. Most of these skills have a right way and a wrong way. They need practice for mastery, and once mastered they can be recalled and revived. In teaching skills there is often a concern about results and efficiency, seeing that the skill can be performed with a high level of accuracy and getting the skill taught in the most efficient manner possible. When this is the case, teachers use the way of learning best suited to teaching skills called *behavioral learning*.

Unfortunately, teaching skills is often looked down on as an inferior activity, and the word *training* is sometimes used to designate a kind of teaching that occupies a rung on the status ladder somewhat below its more lofty cousin, *educating*. Because many college teachers believe, and for good reason, they are primarily engaged in higher-order learning, they sometimes dismiss any need for skill development. But in fact, nearly every discipline involves some need for skill development, from writing to math to neurosurgery. The focus on skills is obviously greater in some courses than others, yet an awareness of skill development and the way of learning that best supports it can be valuable to anyone who teaches skills of any kind. Consider the following examples:

- Foreign language teachers make arrangements for students to practice pronouncing new words over and over while giving them feedback on accuracy.
- A voice student listens carefully to the feedback from her voice coach to make sure the vowels are open and consonants are clear but not exaggerated.
- Nursing students learning to draw blood refine their technique through small improvements such as changing the angle of the needle, adjusting the tightness of the tourniquet, and altering the speed of inserting the needle.

All these efforts to teach skills can be improved when teachers draw on a way of learning with deep historical roots in behavioral psychology. Although behavioral learning has many applications, the main focus as we have defined it is on using behavioral principles to teach skills. It is important to understand how this way of learning works to facilitate skill building most effectively.

Shaping Random Behavior Into Skills

Psychologists first learned about behavioral learning and elaborated on it as a theory through a series of very clever experiments performed with animals in laboratory settings. Just as new medicines are tested first on animals, so were some of the earliest approaches to learning, and we should be grateful for and not offended by these early efforts with animals to establish the principles of behavioral learning theory. There is no better way to understand how to teach simple skills, through a process known as *shaping*, than to return to these early laboratory experiments.[1]

Suppose the research objective is to teach a pigeon to turn clockwise in a complete circle. First the researcher must clearly describe (operationalize) the objective as observable behavior so everyone can agree the pigeon is doing the job. Next, the pigeon is put into a specially designed box and observed to see whether it is already able to turn in clockwise circles. Psychologists call this measuring the operant level or taking the subject's base rate. Educators might call it measuring present performance or seeing what the student already knows. Assume that the pigeon does not turn in circles and that it just walks around poking its beak into every nook and cranny of the box. How will the researcher get it to turn in clockwise circles? Likewise, how does the teacher move from random behavior to skills?

The answer is to break the objective into a series of small steps called *tasks*, or *successive approximations* of the objective. Thus, when the pigeon makes its first move—it may simply shift its weight to the right foot—the action is reinforced by dropping food into the box at just the right moment through a device controlled by the researcher. Next the pigeon steps to the right and leans to the right. Accidental? Who cares? More food appears. Then the pigeon takes two steps to the right and twists its neck back and to the right. Food drops into the tray again. The shaping process continues over time through a series of steps until the objective is attained. The pigeon learns through a shaping process by making connections with the reward, and this process is called *operant conditioning*.

Although we are certainly not training pigeons in colleges and universities, additional research has shown that the process of shaping works for many kinds of human learning, and this shaping process can be used to inform the teaching of skills. The procedures are relatively simple:

1. A clear agreed-upon observable objective (skill) is identified and described.
2. A measure of existing skill or present performance is established.
3. The skill is broken into steps of appropriate size and difficulty.
4. Successive approximations of the goal are reinforced, providing incentive and feedback until the skill has been shaped.

Behavioral learning has its foundation in this theory drawn from laboratory experimentation. This way of learning can be used for different types of procedural or physical skills. Consider the following example.

At the University of Alabama, Instructor Jamie Glass teaches Intermediate Algebra. In this course students learn various algebraic principles, including working with linear inequalities. To solve advanced algebraic problems, students must understand inequalities, and to understand inequalities, students must see how sets of numbers work together. Examples and problems are used to first allow students to grasp the smaller aspects related to this concept. For example, objectives include (1) find the intersection of two sets, (2) solve compound inequalities containing "and," (3) find the union of two sets, (4) solve compound inequalities containing "or," and (5) write the solutions both in interval notation and graph them on a number line. Jamie explains, "In compound inequalities, the first several homework problems deal with set notation and how to find the union and intersection of two sets. This is preparing them for the algebraic compound inequalities they will see in later problems. After the problems dealing with sets, they are given basic algebraic problems to work on dealing with the intersection and union of the solution sets of two inequalities. The problems progressively get more difficult as students become more confident in their work." Students work through the homework problems using a commercial software program that provides instant feedback for each answer. Students are encouraged to work through the homework until they solve all the problems correctly and then take a quiz to see how well they learned the concept. If they still have not mastered the concepts, students are allowed a second attempt at the quiz after seeing what they missed. Jamie concludes, "This process gives students a lot of practice, which in my opinion, is key for learning mathematics."[2]

This is a somewhat complicated cognitive skill, but notice that the task involves steps performed in a specific way, mastery of certain steps before moving on to others, and a considerable amount of practice. Does the teacher in this example know about behavioral learning theory and call it that? Perhaps, but keep in mind that behavioral learning theory has influenced many educational movements and goes by many different names today. For example, direct instruction, self-paced instruction, and intelligent tutoring owe a debt to the well-established field of behavioral psychology. Does the teacher in this example use behavioral learning intentionally? Perhaps, but the principles of behavioral learning are there working, whether we know it or not. When we understand it, we can use it intentionally to improve results. Like most ideas that have become second nature to us, someone had to get the insight, develop the theory, and put it into a usable form. For behavioral learning, we look to B. F. Skinner.[3]

Origins of Behavioral Learning

Next to Sigmund Freud, Burrhus Frederic Skinner was perhaps the world's most famous psychologist before his death in 1990. Behaviorism became completely identified with Skinner, and he was its foremost spokesperson.[4] Skinner did not invent behavioral learning, nor did he discover it. But he described it so thoroughly as one of the ways people learn that we can now call it a well-established theory.

Skinner was indebted to John B. Watson for establishing psychology as a science of human behavior, hence, the term *behaviorist* applied to Skinner and his colleagues. Skinner was perhaps even more indebted to E. L. Thorndike, who at the beginning of the twentieth century had already outlined the basic relationship (connection) between response and consequence that is the foundation of operant conditioning. By examining behavior, Thorndike was able to identify the relationships between rewards and learning.[5] Thorndike is remembered for his law of effect. If the consequence (reinforcement) that follows a response is satisfying, the behavior is likely to be repeated. If the *aftereffect*, as he called it, is annoying, the behavior is not likely to be repeated.

Skinner followed through on the work of Watson and Thorndike by conducting extensive research to establish the principles of operant conditioning experimentally.[6] He investigated how the rate and persistence of learning are affected by different schedules, wrote a text on operant conditioning, developed teaching machines, cowrote a programmed text on conditioning techniques, and in his later years began to speculate on how behavioral principles could be used to form a more just and humane society.

What We Know About Behavioral Learning

After years of research, behavioral psychologists were able to describe precisely and in great detail a way of learning that boils down to specifying objectives, measuring present performance levels, performing task analysis, and providing appropriate feedback. Let us consider these components of behavioral learning in more detail.

Specifying Instructional Objectives

When behavioral learning is used for the development of skills, it is necessary to get very specific about learning outcomes, and these outcomes are usually called *instructional objectives.* They are like other learning outcomes, but for skills they need to be precise and observable. Where do objectives come from? They are derived from the competencies needed to perform a given skill. A broader discussion about objectives is in chapter 3, but they are discussed further here because of their crucial importance for behavioral learning. When involved in building skills, actual learning cannot begin until the teacher has worked out and usually written down an adequate list of desired instructional objectives. Instructional objectives by themselves won't take you very far if you don't use other aspects of this way of learning, but without them you probably won't even get started.

Instructional objectives have been formally defined as "relatively specific statements of learning outcomes expressed from the learner's point of view and telling what the learner is to do at the end of instruction."[7] Note that the emphasis in the definition is not on what the teacher does but on what the learner is able to do when the learning has been completed. The classic specifications for formulating behavioral objectives were developed by Robert F. Mager, and these always focus on the observable behavior of students.[8] To help teachers write objectives that are precise and specific, Mager distinguished between using words open to many interpretations, such as *to know* or *to understand,* and words open to few interpretations, such as *to identify* or *to construct.*

Instructional objectives describe the skill and usually include what the student will be doing when the objective has been achieved, as well as a statement of the standards of acceptable performance. The following is how an instructional objective might be written for a two-week-long unit of a business software applications class:

> The student will demonstrate the ability to gather and organize data and use a spreadsheet to display results. The spreadsheet table will be named, rows and columns will be labeled clearly, and an interpretive statement will be included to describe the conclusions drawn from the data displayed.

Some college teachers may balk at the thought of writing such specific behavioral objectives for their lessons, but consider the alternative: "Students will learn about developing a spreadsheet."

The terminal behavior? *Learn about.* The standards of performance? *What standards?* How do we know the students have learned it? Does learn about mean they can simply describe a spreadsheet or actually use one? If instructors don't know how to establish measurable objectives, it will be difficult for them to know what, if anything, students have learned. Consider how objectives are stated in the following example.

> At Massachusetts Institute of Technology all courses in the Department of Aeronautics and Astronautics list their instructional objectives online as part of the OpenCourseWare project. The developers of each course have created what they term *learning objectives* and *measurable outcomes*: "Learning objectives describe the expected level of proficiency with syllabus topics that a student should attain. To complement the learning objectives, measurable outcomes describe specific ways in which students may be expected to demonstrate such proficiency."[9] In Mark Drela's Fluid Mechanics course, the course-level educational learning objective reads:
>
> Students will learn to:
>
> - Explain the physical properties of a fluid and their consequence on fluid flow, expressed in terms of Mach and Reynolds numbers
> - Apply the basic applied-mathematical tools that support fluid dynamics
> - Create conceptual and quantitative models of inviscid, steady fluid flow over simple bodies (airfoils, wings) and in channels
>
> However, measurable instructional outcomes are also stated up front. Students will be able to:
>
> - Explain the basic concepts of aerodynamics to a high-school senior or non-technical person

- Apply the conservation principles of mass, momentum, and energy to fluid flow systems with emphasis on aerodynamics
- Model inviscid, steady fluid flow over simple aerodynamic shapes, and compute or estimate the associated forces and moments[10]

For Mark, the benefits of spelling out course objectives include having explicit expectations for students and teachers, having an explicit basis for evaluating educational success, and in essence allowing for truth in advertising.[11]

For those who teach skills, well-written instructional objectives are beneficial in planning instruction and essential in designing and evaluating instruction. For students they are useful as a guide to what is expected and how to study. When instructional objectives are used effectively they link the goals of instruction with the means of evaluation and the teacher with the learner, so that everyone is clear about the desired outcomes. When teaching skills in which accuracy and efficiency are important, the case for clear instructional objectives is hard to refute.

Measuring Present Performance

Once an objective is clear, the teacher needs to find out whether a student can already perform the skill. The nice thing about this way of learning is that it is usually easy to establish present performance simply by asking the student to perform the skills to be taught. If students can do them perfectly, there is no need to teach them. The chances are, however, that students will give a less than perfect performance. In some cases they won't be able to do the skills at all and will need to start from the beginning. But where is the beginning? If the prospective student can't learn the first step needed to achieve the objective and has little success with the initial stages of learning, there may be some prior skills—prerequisite skills—that must be learned.

Sometimes a group of students will be ready to start at the beginning, and others will not. This is an opportunity to provide extra instruction to those who are not succeeding or to refer them to the growing array of technological applications designed for teaching foundational skills rather than letting these students fall further behind. Knowing present performance— where the learners are initially—helps the teacher prevent repeating things already known and avoid beginning at a level that is too high for most students. Establishing present performance levels can save time and frustration for everyone.

Performing Task Analysis

It is important to specify the objectives of instruction and determine present performance, but an objective is seldom achieved in one leap. As a destination or an end, an objective is logically distinct from the means of getting there. The objective may be to perform a surgical procedure, but the steps involved in actually performing the skill are something different. Most skills involve a multitude of tasks and subtasks. Thus, most people who are learning new skills need to advance in small steps toward the objective. The process used to break a skill into its parts is called *task analysis*.[12]

The key to task analysis is in gathering all the tasks and subtasks and getting them in the right order. One difficulty for college teachers is that as experts in their area they may be able to perform their skills automatically without being able to describe the steps that go into them. It's easy to say cook until the sauce thickens, but novice cooks might not know what a thick sauce looks like. It is important to walk through the process of any skill to be taught, carefully taking note of all the tasks and subtasks. These subtask areas are often where students get confused or led astray.

When the task analysis has been completed, decisions still need to be made about which parts of the skill to teach first and how to coordinate the various parts of the task into one smoothly functioning whole. The order for teaching the task may not be the same as the order for performing the task. For example, if one were teaching parachute jumping, it might be wise to teach landing before teaching jumping. The order for teaching is sometimes referred to as a *learning hierarchy*.[13] The development of a learning hierarchy involves asking what students have to know first to perform X, and what they need to know next to perform Y. One skill may come before another, like steps in an algebra problem.

Such structuring is called instructional scaffolding, where the instructor provides a temporary structure or framework to assist the student in getting to the next level. Russian psychologist Lev Vygotsky became famous for his theorization of the zone of proximal development, defined as the space between what a student can accomplish without help and what he or she needs help to accomplish.[14] It is in this zone where learning occurs. Depending on the nature of the task and characteristics of learners, less structured or more structured scaffolding might be necessary.[15]

Once a task analysis and learning hierarchy have been developed, it is sometimes useful to demonstrate or model the task to be performed and to talk about it. The commonsense inclination to demonstrate and describe the activity is supported by research on modeling.[16] The classic studies reported by Albert Bandura suggest that learners who watch a task being performed actually benefit simply from having been able to watch.[17] Of course, this does not mean that a novice student watching an expert will suddenly be able to perform the task. It does mean that some gains in learning may occur that might not happen in the absence of modeling. Variously known as imitation, observational learning, or vicarious learning, modeling tends to augment the shaping process through visual and verbal mediation that takes place within the learner. Furthermore, it has been found that by watching others who are being reinforced for learning, students are not only more likely to do better with the skill, but they are better able to overcome their fear of the task. Consider this example of how a task is divided into steps:

> At Aims Community College in Colorado, students learn a variety of basic nursing skills in the Fundamentals of Nursing course taught by Christy Nibbelink. Medication administration, tracheostomy care and suctioning, and catheter insertion are all skills that Christy says "cannot be learned solely from a textbook. Instead learning primarily occurs in the nursing lab when they are practicing." For each skill, students are given instructions, watch videos, and practice with a checklist of the steps of the skills. For example, nasogastric tube insertion involves first measuring and lubricating the tube before students insert it into the patient's nasal airways. When the tube is inserted, it has to be directed down and back through the nasal cavity and into the throat. At some point, the patient needs to be encouraged to swallow or is given water to prevent gagging so the tube can travel into the stomach. If one of these steps is forgotten or done incorrectly, it can be very difficult for the patient, and the entire process might even have to be repeated. "Primarily mistakes are caught while practicing the steps of the skill during the lab time," says Christy. "The students spend a lot of time practicing with their lab partners where they are closely observed and corrected by instructors and each other."[18]

Providing Appropriate Feedback

After the instructional objectives have been determined, a baseline has been established, and the skill has been broken down into its tasks, it is time to have students try the skill. As indicated, this may involve some explanation and modeling, but the essence of this way of learning is *action*, having students try to perform the actual task involved. The learner tries something, and the teacher responds. This is the point in the learning where feedback comes in.

What is feedback and how does it work? Recall the pigeon learning to turn in clockwise circles in a laboratory setting. The pigeon tries something, actually many things, but only certain things bring food. Learning occurs at that crucial moment when a specific action gets linked with a particular consequence. The process of linking behavior to consequences is called *reinforcement*. In teaching, where students are involved in making their first awkward efforts to learn a skill, we simply call it feedback. Managing feedback is one of the most important things a teacher does to facilitate behavioral learning.

Feedback can be divided into two basic classes: rewards and punishments. Behavior that precedes a reward is likely to be repeated; hence, a reward is often referred to as a positive reinforcer. Positive reinforcers are anything an individual is willing to put forth an effort to obtain, sometimes referred to as an incentive. Punishment, on the other hand, consists of those things an individual is willing to work hard to avoid. But how do we know what people find rewarding? It varies, but a careful observer can find out. The process of feedback does not depend on the intrinsic properties of the reward or punishment itself. In fact, a reinforcer probably has no intrinsic properties. Consider why. When people have just pushed themselves away from the holiday dinner table, they probably will not find food to be rewarding. But at other times, when hungry, they might. The degree to which something is reinforcing depends on the internal state of the organism, its relative hunger and satisfaction. Furthermore, there will be considerable variation in tastes. For a consequence to work as a positive reinforcer, it must be satisfying to that particular individual. What works as feedback for some won't work for others. It is not accidental, therefore, that reinforcement is defined in terms of the behavior it produces.

There are four types of feedback—two simple methods to initiate, speed up, or maintain desired behavior, *positive reinforcement* and *negative reinforcement*, and two simple methods to slow down or stop undesirable behavior, *extinction* and *punishment*. (Negative reinforcement is often confused with punishment, but the differences between the two will become clear as they are further discussed.) This terminology originated from laboratory research, so it may appear impersonal and controlling to educators; however, the terms have taken up familiar meanings in the modern lexicon. To keep these simple feedback methods in mind, see the following figure.

Methods for Initiating, Speeding Up, and Maintaining Desirable Behavior

Positive Reinforcement Giving a reward	**Negative Reinforcement** Threatening something unpleasant

Methods for Slowing Down and Stopping Undesirable Behavior

Extinction Withholding all reinforcements	**Punishment** Doing something unpleasant

Positive Reinforcement

This method of feedback is used as a reward for tasks to be learned. Depending on the age or personality type of the student, positive reinforcers are likely to be things such as

- praise, attention, and recognition
- confirmation of right answers
- positive comments on a test or an assignment
- successful completion of a skill or task
- points or grades
- certificates or awards
- honor roles or dean's lists

Positive reinforcers are anything that might convey approval or generate satisfaction. The best positive reinforcement comes naturally from the task itself, when the student gets things right, finds out how something works, or successfully performs a skill. Sometimes this is called knowledge of results.[19] Positive reinforcement may be reminiscent of the choices and rewards commonly used in parenting, implying, "If you do this, you get . . ." The teacher's role in using positive reinforcement is to provide incentive for the student to complete each step and to reward correctly performed approximations of the objective.

Negative Reinforcement

This method of feedback involves setting aversive conditions an individual will work hard to avoid. It is like punishment in that the prospect is unpleasant, but it is unlike punishment because it is never applied. It is best thought of as the threat of punishment, because the emphasis is on avoidance. Like positive reinforcement, it can be used or it can occur naturally. Typical types of aversive conditions are those things students will work hard to avoid, such as

- doing something wrong
- having to repeat the task
- becoming unhappy with poor performance
- working longer at the task
- low or failing grades
- critical remarks on papers or assignments
- reprimand or embarrassment
- failing a class or academic suspension

Although negative reinforcement is unpleasant, the possibility of avoiding it controls the behavior. Working hard in a class is often motivated by the threat of negative consequences. The problem with threats, of course, is that they are negative, and sometimes they must be carried out, at which point they turn into punishment, which carries its own associated problems.

Extinction

A third method of feedback, known as extinction, is the process of withholding reinforcement selectively. Behavior is neither punished nor rewarded but is passed over with the hope that it will slow down or go away. Sometimes a teacher will ignore certain mannerisms associated with a particular skill, knowing that wasted motions will cease when the student discovers they are nonfunctional. If a teacher withholds attention from a student who consistently disrupts the class with off-topic comments, the annoying behavior should go away naturally unless the student is receiving social reinforcement from peers. Not all behavior needs to be accompanied by consequences. Any of the things normally used as rewards or punishments can be withheld. Extinction functions as the absence of positive reinforcement.

Punishment

A final method of feedback is the direct application of an unpleasant stimulus. Most people need no further definition of punishment.[20] All the forms of aversive feedback listed under negative reinforcement become punishments when applied. The basic research on punishment shows that it works, if by works one means that it will stop the associated behaviors. A behavior that is punished is not likely to be repeated. In certain situations a sharp reprimand or warning may be used in teaching, especially when matters of safety, basic rights, or human dignity are involved. This kind of feedback may be used occasionally where something must be stopped, but in most cases the goal is not stopping behavior but getting it started in the right direction and continuing it. The research is clear; punishment is good for stopping behavior but not for establishing it. Positive reinforcement, in generous quantities, is needed to establish new patterns of behavior, such as learning new skills.

The effects of punishment are not easily contained. Punishment has a way of generalizing and escalating, and it produces a conditioned (associated) emotional response in the learner. Although the teacher may have meant to provide a carefully targeted punishment to stop a specific behavior, the student will often associate other things with that punishment. A student who is punished can learn quickly to dislike the teacher, the course, the topic, and the entire institution, because each has become associated with the punishment. Effective teachers use punishment sparingly, if at all, and focus their energies instead on imaginative ways of using positive reinforcement. After all, college students are adults, and they respond better to the carrot than the stick. With the exception of punishment, which poses a special problem, the four types of feedback can be mixed and used generously.

It is important to remember that for behavioral learning, a great deal of feedback should be provided—much more than usual in typical teaching situations—and it needs to be well timed, that is, as close as possible to the occurrence of the desirable behavior. To contribute to learning, feedback also needs to be specific. A student who receives vague comments, such as "incorrect" or "poor work," days or weeks after a test or an assignment is completed is probably not going to learn much from that feedback. Alternatively, if the student is given precise feedback about specifically why an answer or assignment is incorrect or needs to be rewritten, if the feedback is received fairly soon after the work is completed, and if specific suggestions about how to improve are included, the resulting learning can be expected to be much more significant. When students are given an opportunity to try again or revise their work, they usually learn from specific feedback and improve their performance.

Timely feedback results in learning because it reinforces the connection between the task (effort) and the feedback (reward). Without appropriate, well-timed feedback, the student just stumbles along, never sure whether anything is right or wrong. Students need timely feedback to know when and how to move on to the next step. Without it, they are left hanging. The shaping process functions by providing appropriate, timely feedback for small steps accomplished as well as for the overall goal. It may even be necessary to provide different types of feedback for each student depending upon the different ability levels and stages of skill development. Consider the following example:

Jill Pearon teaches the course Studio Voice at State University of New York at Potsdam, where, among other outcomes, students are expected to demonstrate healthy vocal production. One of the many subskills needed in vocal production is breath support. In addition, there are many different substeps involved in breath support, including proper inhalation, awareness of the muscles involved, and engaging the appropriate muscles. Students can undertake different types of exercises to support proper breath support, but much of the skill development happens through repetition with the teacher present to give feedback. "Helping the students become aware of these sensations that are so internal is a real challenge," says Jill. "Particularly early on in the process, when students are still learning these sensations as they are trying to produce them, they need to hear from an external reliable source as to when the support was engaged and when it was not." Jill also asks questions such as, "Can you describe the sensations you are feeling?" to help students develop awareness of the sensations. "Because we can neither feel all of these muscles nor pay attention to all at once, I usually focus on a sensation or two the students experience when the support has engaged." Students then need replication, repetition, and lots and lots of practice. Jill often finds that she needs to give feedback on different subskills at different times. "No part of the whole will work at its full potential if another part is not up to par. You can work on breath support all you want, but if body alignment isn't good, the breath support won't work as well as it can." She also has to be adept at determining where each student is developmentally and working with him or her individually. "Students approach each of these skill sets with different abilities and challenges. While I can break down any element of singing into a logical sequence of steps, the steps required for each student to succeed are sometimes different. Just when I think I could not possibly break something down into more steps, a student struggles with a step and I find a way to help them do a *part* of what we need to achieve—a smaller step."[21]

It is also important to consider when and how often opportunities for practice are designed. Researchers have explored massed practice in which students are asked to practice a skill repeatedly in a short time frame, and spaced practice in which longer sessions of practice are conducted with longer intervals in between. Although many factors have to be taken into account, it appears that massed practice is better for mastering simple routine tasks or those that require close attention to detail, whereas spaced practice is better suited for more complex tasks and more mature learners.[22]

Assessing Behavioral Learning

Assessment should occur throughout the teaching and learning process, not just at the end. This is true for most ways of learning, but it is especially important for behavioral learning, because this way of learning progresses in steps. Assessing behavioral learning is fairly straightforward. A teacher with carefully established instructional learning objectives simply wants to know if and how well the student is progressing toward performance of the skill. If learning objectives are measurable, the teacher simply measures the student's ability to perform the skill, or subskills, according to specified standards.

A distinction is often made between *summative assessment*, which is evaluation at the end of teaching and often at the end of the course, and *formative assessment*, evaluation conducted along the way while learning is taking place. Although it is important to know at the end of instruction whether a student can actually perform the skill in order to establish a grade or certify a competency, summative evaluation doesn't contribute much, if at all, to the actual process of learning.

In the past two decades, researchers have focused on the impact of formative assessment practices to improve learning. Formative assessment includes activities and practice exercises completed in class or conducted for purposes other than a grade or an evaluation measure. The focus of these studies is on the effect of the quality and quantity of feedback given by instructors. In the United Kingdom, a government-sponsored initiative in the late 1990s reviewed studies on formative assessment for a better understanding of this practice. It was found that formative assessment had more influence on learning than all other types of educational interventions.[23] Teachers should realize that the time-intensive process of giving individual feedback to students is time well spent.

Behavioral learning also fits naturally with what is called *criterion-referenced assessment*, with its focus on measuring proficiency or competency rather than comparing students to each other, a practice called *norm-referenced assessment*.[24] The central question with norm-referenced assessment is: How well is the student doing compared with most of the other students? What most students do on a test becomes the norm or standard. If most students get 60 percent of the problems correct, then those become the Cs, and the rest of the grades are determined accordingly. The reference is set by other students, thus the familiar concept known as grading on a curve. There is one serious fallacy to this method, however. With regard to the stated criteria for performance, all the students could be missing the criteria. Criterion-referenced assessment, on the other hand, places the focus on the stated criteria: How many students can actually perform what is called for in the objective?

The use of criterion-referenced assessment has led logically to the idea of mastery learning.[25] The concept of mastery learning was elaborated originally by Benjamin Bloom and his colleagues at the University of Chicago in the 1960s.[26] Bloom felt that a normal distribution in grading is actually what occurs without instruction, and that the goal of instruction is to change this distribution. Mastery learning is an effort to deal with the practical problem of getting most of the students to master most of the material most of the time.

Bloom argues that students vary widely according to aptitude, ability, and motivation when they enter a classroom. The mistake teachers make is treating all students the same, in effect, giving them the same instruction, when in fact what is needed is *differentiated instruction* (differing amounts and types). Students with less aptitude need more instruction. Students who are slower need more time. With the right instruction, Bloom argues, a very high percentage of students, as high as 80 to 90 percent, can master the material. The most important ingredient in mastery learning (after setting clear objectives and determining acceptable levels of mastery) is the quality of instruction and feedback.

Mastery learning in the classroom requires a redefinition of equal opportunity. Throughout the history of American education, equal opportunity has generally meant giving all students the same chance, which usually means the same instruction. Bloom's suggestion is that equality of learning should become the goal, not just equality of opportunity for learning. This means that teachers must find ways of giving each student not (just) equal treatment but what each student actually needs to be successful. Thus, inequality of treatment may be necessary—in materials, time, instruction, reinforcement—if equality in learning is to result. This is a new concept of fair treatment: those who need the most get the most. Behavioral learning, with its emphasis on stated outcomes and stepwise reinforcement of learning, leads naturally toward the criterion-referenced approach, and greater numbers of students achieve mastery when it is used effectively.

Useful Technologies for Behavioral Learning

A particular type of computer-based instruction sometimes used for drill and practice is clearly associated with behavioral learning principles. The development of what was once called computer-assisted instruction has a fascinating history and illuminates how behavioral learning theory produced some of the very first uses of technology for teaching.

In 1961 B. F. Skinner's article "Why We Need Teaching Machines" marked the beginning of efforts to use various forms of technology to extend the principles of behavioral learning theory, long before the word *technology* came to be associated with computers.[27] Skinner's teaching machines drew upon a format for carefully developed textbooks called programmed instruction, a system for presenting lesson materials through small steps. The student responds to questions by selecting an answer from the ones provided. By referring either to the bottom of the page or to the back of the book, students are able to get immediate confirmation of right and wrong answers and move through the material at their own pace.[28] The steps contain clues that have the proper information systematically embedded so students can learn something new and not just be tested.[29] Skinner and his colleagues developed the concept of programmed instruction into teaching machines using disks, cards, and tapes. The students scrolled through questions and, by turning the material in the machine upward, compared their responses with the correct answer. Obviously, teaching machines are no longer used, but they were the precursor to computer applications that employ step-by-step instruction accompanied by immediate feedback. Today one can find drill-and-practice and tutorial lessons online that are based on behavioral learning theory.

In addition, behavioral learning often works best when all the variables in the learning process can be applied systematically to one student at a time. In the late 1960s a specific form of self-paced learning known as the personalized system of instruction (PSI) was developed by Fred Keller, one of B. F. Skinner's graduate students.[30] Using PSI, also known as the Keller Plan, students are expected to work through self-paced learning modules, progressing at their own pace. Some students might master material faster than classroom-based instruction, while others might take longer because completion is based on individual mastery. Designing self-paced modules takes tremendous work on the part of the instructor but is greatly assisted by advances in computer programs that handle the administrative aspects of such designs.

Today's college students have grown up with sophisticated computer software that uses drill and practice, immediate feedback, and self-paced instruction. In elementary schools, spelling can be conducted in an individualized manner without the tremendous work it would take for one teacher to accomplish with a group of students at different ability levels. An entire class of students can spend fifteen minutes with computer software each week, with each student receiving individualized quizzes using spelling words that are at the right level of challenge. Stars, points, and video game–like interfaces act as positive and negative reinforcers designed for young students. Most college students today have experience with such programs, in school and from personal use. In fact, let us return to the example of teaching Intermediate Algebra from p. 48 at the beginning of this chapter.

Jamie Glass's Intermediate Algebra course is not taught in the traditional classroom method. As Jamie explains, "Students do not have a 'lecture' class. Instead, they report to the Mathematics Technology Learning Center (MTLC) once a week for a working lab session where they work on assignments that are required of them in the course." They are also required to put in three additional hours each week in the lab, working on the concepts for that particular week. Students are expected to have an active role in this course by independently completing the homework and quizzes, not, as Jamie says, "by sitting and listening to an instructor talk about math." The MTLC was set up as a means for the students to learn via the software provided, but also receive personal help when they need it. The software program is tied to the students' textbook and provides videos, practice problems, and demonstrations related to each lesson. If they don't understand how to work a problem, students can use the software to guide them through the process. At each step students are asked to input an answer, and the program provides immediate feedback. A positive message such as "Good Work" might appear, or a suggestion or explanation about how to look for the correct answer, along with the opportunity to retry the problem. If students run into difficulty they can ask the staff at the MTLC for help. The center is open more than seventy hours per week and typically has anywhere from three to eight instructors or tutors on hand to help students individually when they begin having difficulty. Jamie feels this process has been successful. "Ultimately the students have to take personal responsibility in learning the concepts, but we are always there to help along the way."[31]

Such integration of computer applications and instructor support is becoming more common in college classrooms that focus on building skills. Large lecture courses across the country are being redesigned into modules in which individual instructor feedback is replaced or supplemented by sophisticated software programs.[32] The Open Learning Initiative uses teams of learning scientists, content experts, human-computer interaction experts, and software engineers from Carnegie Mellon and the University of Pittsburgh to develop intelligent tutoring systems for introductory college courses.[33] These systems focus on the ability of web-based applications to conduct ongoing assessment and feedback to provide students with individualized instruction as they progress through online content materials. Students are given frequent opportunities to assess their own learning and receive immediate feedback and further instruction. Students can work through these courses independently, or in a course an instructor can use aggregate feedback about student progress to adjust instruction based on common patterns or areas of confusion. As technology advances, behavioral learning continues to provide a robust theoretical base for sophisticated efforts such as these.

Behavioral learning is an area ripe for technological advancements because of its focus on practicing steps and providing immediate and individualized feedback, guidance that is very time and labor intensive for teachers. Many advances have been made, and newer materials are being developed by publishers and private companies. Some of these drill-and-practice exercises, quizzes, and numerous other study materials developed by publishers are amazing accompaniments to behavioral learning; others involve a lot of activity but run the risk of becoming drill-and-kill exercises. They may not incorporate the right type of practice, the right type of feedback, or the right type of tasks to be truly effective. The level of thought put to task analysis, sequencing, and appropriate feedback—the essential components of behavioral learning—varies widely in the programs that are available, but well-developed tools can greatly assist the college instructor. Teachers need to evaluate, select, and effectively use such technologies to determine when and how personal feedback is best used in conjunction with individualized software programs, and to find the appropriate mix of self-paced and group instruction.

Final Thoughts

Behavioral learning theory has been criticized because it was strictly based on observable behavior. Learning is a complex process, and observable behavior does not always adequately reflect internal thought processes. Behavioral learning lost some of its popularity because of the "cognitive revolution" in the past fifty years; however, many of the basic concepts behind this way of learning—task analysis, feedback, and self-pacing—are alive and well today. Studies of behavioral learning live on under the term *behavior analysis*, and behavioral learning has helped to support great advances in elementary and secondary schools in such areas as autism and whole-school discipline issues.[34]

This way of learning works best with physical or procedural skills, when the goal of learning is something tangible and observable, and where accuracy and efficiency are important. Most college-level subjects contain some type of physical or procedural skill development challenge. Behavioral learning is not particularly helpful in learning underlying principles, complex ideas, critical thinking, or problem solving. The most telling criticism of behavioral learning is that its emphasis on steps can become cumbersome, confining, and boring. There is little room for spontaneity in behavioral learning, and it can also present problems for student motivation. Extrinsic motivation can be very effective for physical and procedural skill development when observable changes in behavior are at play but is not as effective for other ways of learning described in this book. Extrinsic motivators can create an unhealthy dependence on the system of reinforcement itself, thus interfering with the cultivation of the inner motivation that students require to be able to manage their learning at advanced levels.

While it is especially valuable for teaching skills, behavioral learning can also be thought of as a master model of learning. Although we have focused on skill development, its principles are broadly applicable in the design and delivery of other types of instruction. Learning outcomes, present performance, steps, feedback—these are broadly applicable concepts for almost any way of learning. Behavioral learning provides the theoretical base for the overall design of instructional settings. Even classroom management and the most basic communication exchanges between teacher and student are fraught with behavioral overtones related to feedback. Behavioral learning is presented first in this book not only because it represents the first effort to study learning in a systematic way, but also because it has the most far-reaching applications and long-lasting relevance. This way of learning is never obsolete. It is not something to be accepted or rejected, selected or dismissed, because it is a built-in component of nearly every learning environment, producing, whether the instructor knows it or not, what might be called the inevitable consequences of consequences.

Points to Remember

Teachers who want to use behavioral learning effectively should do the following:

✓ Clearly define observable, measurable learning objectives.
✓ Perform task analysis to break complex learning activities into steps and substeps, arranged in hierarchical or sequential order if necessary.
✓ Measure students' present performance level.
✓ Identify and remediate prerequisite skills as needed.
✓ Model the task or tasks to be performed.
✓ Allow sufficient time and opportunities for students to practice.
✓ Use various forms of well-timed and specific feedback to shape students' behavior.
✓ Find appropriate motivation for students in the form of positive and negative reinforcers.
✓ Use positive reinforcers to establish behavior; avoid the use of punishment unless necessary to stop harmful behavior.
✓ Assess actual learning throughout instruction according to the stated objectives.
✓ Carefully select and use technologies that allow students to practice skills and subtasks while receiving timely and specific feedback.

Notes

1. The shaping process is described by B. F. Skinner in *Science and Human Behavior* (New York: Free Press, 1953).

2. Thanks to Jamie Glass, Instructor and MTLC Lab Coordinator, Department of Mathematics, University of Alabama, for granting permission to use her example. E-mail message to author, June 17, 2011.

3. The discussion of behaviorism is based on the writings of B. F. Skinner. Most textbooks on educational psychology summarize his work. The clearest introductory explanation of behavioral learning theory is found in the work of his student Fred S. Keller, *Learning: Reinforcement Theory,* 2nd ed. (New York: Random House, 1969). The most accessible work by Skinner is *About Behaviorism* (New York: Knopf, 1974).

4. Skinner was an enormously productive scholar. The basic principles of behaviorism are outlined in *The Behavior of Organisms* (New York: Appleton-Century-Crofts, 1938). The relationship between behavior and reinforcement is described in *The Contingencies of Reinforcement* (New York: Appleton-Century-Crofts, 1969). The effects of various systems of rewards and punishments are spelled out in *Science and Human Behavior* (New York: Free Press, 1953) and in *Schedules of Reinforcement,* cowritten with Charles Ferster (New York: Appleton-Century-Crofts, 1957). Skinner's essays on education are collected in *The Technology of Teaching* (New York: Appleton-Century-Crofts, 1968). His article "Why We Need Teaching Machines" appeared in *Harvard Educational Review* 31 (1961): 377–98. His texts on operant conditioning are *About Behaviorism* and *The Analysis of Behavior,* cowritten with J. Holland (New York: McGraw-Hill, 1961). For his work on languages, see *Verbal Behavior* (New York: Appleton-Century-Crofts, 1957), *Walden Two* (New York: Macmillan, 1948), and *Beyond Freedom and Dignity* (New York: Knopf, 1971).

5. Edward L. Thorndike, *The Psychology of Learning* (New York: Teachers College, 1921), 237. Thorndike understood the relationship between consequences and learning and referred to "associative learning," "connection forming," and "laws of habit" (Ibid., 17). The law of effect is explained in Thorndike's *Human Learning* (New York: Century, 1931), 58–61. See also Thorndike's *The Fundamentals of Learning* (New York: Teachers College, 1932).

6. Skinner discusses punishment in *Technology of Teaching,* 96. For a review of forms of corporal punishment, see Adah Maurer, "Corporal Punishment," *American Psychologist* 29 (August 1974): 614–26.

7. Richard Burns, *New Approaches to Behavioral Objectives* (Dubuque, IA: Brown, 1972), 5.

8. Robert F. Mager, *Preparing Instructional Objectives* (Palo Alto, CA: Fearon, 1962), 11.

9. Mark Drela et al., "16.01 Unified Engineering I, II, III, Fall 2005–Spring 2006," Massachusetts Institute of Technology: MIT OpenCourseWare, accessed July 13, 2012, http://mitocw.aucegypt.edu/OcwWeb/Aeronautics-and-Astronautics/16-01Fall-2005-Spring-2006/Syllabus/index.htm.

10. Mark Drela, "Fluid Mechanics," Massachusetts Institute of Technology: MIT OpenCourseWare, accessed June 9, 2011, http://ocw.mit.edu/courses/aeronautics-and-astronautics/16-01-unified-engineering-i-ii-iii-iv-fall-2005-spring-2006/fluid-mechanics/learningobjectives.pdf.

11. Thanks to Mark Drela, PhD, Professor of Fluid Dynamics, Department of Aeronautics and Astronautics, Massachusetts Institute of Technology, for granting permission to use his example. E-mail message to author, June 10, 2011.

12. The discussion of task analysis is based on chapter 5 in Robert H. Davis, Lawrence T. Alexander, and Stephen L. Yelon, *Learning System Design* (New York: McGraw-Hill, 1974).

13. Robert M. Gagne, "Learning Hierarchies," *Educational Psychologist* 6 (1968): 1–9.

14. Michael Cole, Vera John-Steiner, Sylvia Scribner, and Ellen Souberman, *Mind in Society: The Development of Higher Psychological Processes/L. S. Vygotsky* (Cambridge, MA: Harvard University Press, 1978).

15. Patricia L. Smith and Tillman J. Ragan, *Instructional Design* (Hoboken, NJ: Wiley, 2005), 130.

16. The classic research on modeling and modeling effects is by Albert Bandura, *Principles of Behavior Modification* (New York: Holt, Rinehart and Winston, 1969).

17. Bandura, *Principles*.

18. Thanks to Christine Nibbelink, Nursing Faculty at Aims Community College, for granting permission to use her example. E-mail message to author, September 12, 2011.

19. David Premack, "Toward Empirical Behavior Laws: 1. Positive Reinforcement," *Psychological Review* 66, no. 4 (1959): 219.

20. Gary C. Walters and Joan E. Grusec, *Punishment* (San Francisco: W. H. Freeman, 1977).

21. Thanks to Jill Pearon, PhD, Assistant Provost and Associate Professor of Voice at the State University of New York at Potsdam, for granting permission to use her example. E-mail message to author, February 1, 2012.

22. Smith and Ragan, *Instructional Design*, 276.

23. Assessment Reform Group, *Assessment for Learning: Beyond the Black Box* (Cambridge, UK: University of Cambridge School of Education, 1999). See also Paul Black and Dylan Wiliam, "Assessment and Classroom Learning," *Assessment in Education* 5, no. 1 (1998): 7–74.

24. The discussion of norm-referenced and criterion-referenced assessment is based on Robert Glaser and David Klaus, "Proficiency Measurement: Assessing Human Performance" in *Psychological Principles in Systems Development*, ed. Robert M. Gange (New York: Holt, Reinhart and Winston, 1962), 419–74.

25. James Block, *Mastery Learning* (New York: Holt, Reinhart and Winston, 1971).

26. Benjamin Bloom, *Human Characteristics and School Learning* (New York: McGraw-Hill, 1982). See also Benjamin Bloom, *All Our Children Learning* (New York: McGraw-Hill, 1981).

27. Skinner, "Why We Need Teaching Machines."

28. Lawrence Stolurow, "Programmed Instruction" in *Encyclopedia of Educational Research*, ed. Robert Ebel (London: Macmillan, 1969), 1017–21.

29. C. Thomas, I. Davies, D. Openshaw, and J. Bird, *Programmed Learning in Perspective* (Chicago: Educational Methods, 1964).

30. Keller's description of PSI can be found in "Good-Bye Teacher," *Journal of Applied Behavioral Analysis* 1, no 1 (1968): 79–88. See also K. Johnson and R. Ruskin, *Behavioral Instruction: An Evaluative Review* (Washington, DC: American Psychological Association, 1977); Ohmer Milton, *Alternatives to the Traditional* (San Francisco: Jossey-Bass, 1972).

31. Jamie Glass, e-mail message to author, June 17, 2011.

32. See the National Center for Academic Transformation for advances in this area, for example, "Course Redesign Recommended Readings," accessed June 20, 2011, http://thencat.org/Rec_Reading.htm.

33. Open Learning Initiative, "Get to Know OLI," accessed November 28, 2009, http://oli.web.cmu.edu/openlearning/initiative.

34. William L. Heward et al., *Focus on Behavioral Analysis in Education: Achievements, Challenges, and Opportunities* (Upper Saddle River, NJ: Pearson, 2005).

5

ACQUIRING KNOWLEDGE

Cognitive Learning

Intended Learning Outcomes What students learn	Way of Learning Origins and theory	Common Methods What the teacher provides
Acquiring knowledge Basic information, concepts, and terminology in a discipline or field of study	**Cognitive learning** Cognitive psychology: attention, information processing, memory	Presentations Explanations

Is this learning that involves information acquisition? Does it involve new ideas, new terminology, or useful theories? Does it require understanding of how something works or functions? Is this information that might be presented through an explanation? Is it possible to identify key concepts, main ideas, or points to be understood and remembered? These are learning outcomes that are well served by cognitive learning.

A political science teacher uses sports analogies to help students draw on prior knowledge to understand new information. How is the U.S. Constitution like the rules of the game in sports? How does this comparison help students acquire knowledge about politics?

I n the information age, having the right knowledge, understanding it, and being able to use it is of prime importance. Although information is available through a multitude of electronic sources today, not all information found digitally is of equal worth, and much of it needs to be evaluated, combined with other information, and turned into knowledge.

Sometimes knowledge needs to be in our head. Many times students need a base level of knowledge or background information before group work, critical thinking, problem solving, or other ways of learning can be attempted. Factual information is often the building block of other types of learning. Some of the knowledge we need is basic and uncomplicated, but more often the essential knowledge used today is quite complex, involving technical language, difficult concepts, and complex relationships among ideas. To acquire knowledge is still one of the key reasons students give for going to college.

Acquiring Knowledge

As established in chapter 1, lecturing is the dominant teaching paradigm in higher education—some would call it the default college teaching method—and it is certainly overused.[1] Lecturing is not only common, it is commonly misused. A famous quote, attributed to R. K. Rathbun, among others, shares the common complaint: "A lecture is a process by which the notes of the professor become the notes of the students without passing through the minds of either." Why the criticisms? In some cases, lectures are disorganized and poorly presented. In other cases, essential knowledge is already transmitted through readings or multimedia presentations, and the classroom lecture becomes redundant or otherwise unnecessary. As many years of studies have shown, lectures are effective for transmitting information but not for most other learning outcomes.[2] In spite of its limitations, lecturing is not obsolete nor should it be totally discarded. Lecturing can be very efficient for transmitting information to receptive audiences, as is the case for many academic conferences. There is usually a need to present information at some point in nearly every college course. Lecturing could profit from a name change, however, so let's call it presenting information. We call this way of learning *cognitive learning*.

Cognitive psychology is now a broad subfield in the discipline of psychology, and its findings range across an array of topics related to perception and cognition. We draw upon three sets of concepts from cognitive psychology, which we believe are the most applicable and useful to the teacher who wants to make effective presentations: attention, information processing, and memory. These are the focus of this way of learning.

As with any teaching, the best place to begin is with learning outcomes. Because lecturing is the dominant paradigm in higher education, there is temptation to turn every class into transmission of knowledge. A college teacher today needs to determine the overall need in a course for various learning outcomes such as developing skills, encouraging thinking processes, or changing attitudes and then identify the areas where knowledge transfer really is necessary. When that is clarified, the instructor asks: What exactly is it that students are supposed to learn from a presentation of information? Is the emphasis on stimulating interest in new ideas, introducing unfamiliar terminology, explaining how something works, or creating a deeper understanding of key concepts? Once purposes have been clearly established in a way that confirms not only what will be presented but what students will be able to do with what is presented, three important questions need to be addressed:

1. Why will students be motivated to pay attention to the presentation, and how much mental effort will it take for them to focus on understanding what is essential?
2. How will students receive and process the information, and what will help them to do that more readily?
3. What information should students remember from the presentation, and how can the presenter facilitate that process?

Every teacher knows from prior experience as a student that a presentation can be brilliant or dull, engaging or boring, enlightening or deadly. What makes it so? Some would say it is the personality of the presenter. Others say it is the subject or the media. We believe that where learning is the key criterion, the most important factor in an effective presentation is the use of a well-designed communication process attuned to the listener. How is it that people come to learn when they are listening to or watching a presentation? What actually takes place when students attempt to pay attention to, process, and remember information? How do they acquire knowledge?

Origins of Cognitive Learning

Cognitive psychology has no B. F. Skinner, no single figure who can be said to be its foremost spokesperson. The study of mental processes has its roots in the work of Wilhelm Wundt, William James, F. L. Bartlett, and the European movement known as Gestalt psychology. But from the turn of the nineteenth century until the end of World War II, the behaviorists dominated psychology, insisting that human consciousness was a black box and that behavior was the only appropriate subject of scientific psychology. What occurred in the period from 1950 to 1980 in the area of cognitive psychology was nothing short of an intellectual revolution. An area that had been beyond the proper domain of study for psychologists—human consciousness—now became the focal point for an outpouring of scientific investigation and theory building. Although some psychologists continued to study communication processes in animals, such as the fascinating work on apes and sign language, the focus of the research was on human information processing. The field attracted some of the best scholars and became an area of intense and exciting activity.

Behaviorism had reached its zenith. But more important, an increasing number of psychologists found the behavioral theory inadequate for fully describing human learning. Although learning is certainly influenced to some extent by behavior and consequences, human beings, they argued, tend to act upon and reorder the stimuli that constitute their environment, largely through the uniquely human instrument of language. Through language and other symbolization processes, humans engage in complex, covert mental activity called mediation. A new breed of psychologists became convinced that the behaviorists were wrong about not being able to study the black box of the human mind. They came to believe that covert mental processes are the key to understanding human behavior. It was as if the behaviorists were leaving out the most important aspect of human behavior just because it was hard to study.

Other forces combined to stimulate new interest in cognitive psychology. A science of human engineering was emerging from military applications of psychology. Verbal learning theorists and linguists were developing new models to explain language behavior.[3] Communications engineering developed as a new science, and systems analysts began to describe what took place between input and output in a computer. As cognitive psychologists began to speculate about the processes that occur between human input and output, it was only a short leap from thinking of the computer as a complex information processing system to conceptualizing the human mind as a complex symbol manipulation system. If one was to attempt to assign a date for the emergence of cognitive psychology as a recognized field, the year would probably be 1958, the date of the now famous conference of the leading psychologists of the day sponsored by the Rand Corporation from which emerged the influential pretheoretical ideas of Newell, Shaw, and Simon, providing an overview of elementary information processes needing further study. Their work stimulated a flurry of research.[4]

What We Know About Cognitive Learning

Picture the typical classroom: a teacher is speaking in a strong voice and using supportive media; the students are sitting in rows and taking notes, trying to understand what is being shown and said. What is known about this kind of learning? The processes we use for communicating through presentations have been investigated extensively by cognitive psychologists, scholars who study the mental activity of attending to, processing, and remembering information. After years of research, they have developed basic information processing models to illustrate how cognitive processes work. The following figure is a composite and simplified version of models that appear commonly in the literature.[5]

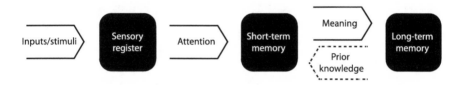

According to these models, information passes through any of our five senses and impinges on a sensory register. Filters are activated and selectively let pass or screen out what a person will pay attention to based on stimulation and motivation. The main features of the information are analyzed, abstracted, and encoded. They are held in short-term memory for a few seconds while the information is organized and a decision is made about what to do: respond directly, think about the information, integrate it with other information, forget it, or store it in long-term memory. Prior knowledge and past experiences from long-term memory help us decide what to do with the information in short-term memory. If information has meaning, emotional value, or makes sense based on our prior knowledge, it is more likely to be integrated into long-term memory. Although the process is enormously complex, there appears to be general agreement about the functions called attention, information processing, and memory. These are not places in the brain, of course, but are rather sets of interrelated processes in the mind to facilitate the symbolic manipulation of information.

Attention Processes

When a teacher is presenting information, the first challenge is to get the attention of the students. This may sound obvious, but some teachers don't think this is their responsibility. Why should students pay attention? How many things can they pay attention to at the same time? For that matter, why does anyone pay attention to anything? Some cognitive psychologists describe attention as the ability to concentrate, a process influenced by external stimulation and internal motivation.[6] The internal aspects may be outside the control of the instructor, but much of the external aspects can be influenced. How can an instructor help students focus on the most important aspects of a presentation? What about distractions—laptops, mobile devices, computer games, and text messaging?

Some of the earliest experiments on attention were designed to examine what happens when people try to listen to more than one thing at a time. Cherry called this the cocktail party phenomenon.[7] Most people have had the experience of standing around at a party listening in on one conversation but then being drawn off to another. What do people hear in another conversation that tends to make them lose what they hear in the first? Cherry and others simulated the party situation by having subjects listen to two separate but comparable messages through earphones, one message in one ear, another message in the other ear. In these dichotic presentations the subjects were directed to shadow (repeat aloud) the message they were hearing in the designated ear. It is not surprising that subjects usually could report in great detail afterward what they heard in the designated ear, but when asked what they heard in the unattended ear, they floundered. Sometimes they could not even tell if the message had been switched to another language or played backward. In other words, their attention was relatively undivided.

Experiments like these became the basis of *switch theories of attention*. If two messages arrive at the same time, one will get through and the other won't, as if there were a switch to turn one channel on and another off. Apparently when attention is focused on something, it is focused there almost exclusively. Notice the word *almost*. Additional studies suggested that attention is not so much like a switch that is on or off but is instead like a filter that selectively lets through the important information while screening out most (but not all) the rest. Attention has also been said to be like a spotlight that either focuses intently on one thing or spreads out, shining light and awareness on many things at once, but here the light is dimmer and attention is diffused and at a surface level. In a now famous video experiment from the late 1990s, individuals were asked to count how many times students wearing white shirts pass a basketball around. Most viewers are so intent on counting the passes among moving players they do not notice a person dressed as a gorilla walking through the middle of the scene.[8] When the video is replayed most people are shocked that their selective attention allows them to miss such an obvious and dramatic sight. Today, our need to not miss out on anything, spurred by the accessibility of nearly everything through technology, has created what Linda Stone calls *continuous partial attention*.[9] While this is especially prevalent with younger generations, many of us seem to be walking around in a state of dim attention and need direction and guidance to focus selectively on certain tasks or information.

Other experiments have dealt with the amount of attention required and available for different kinds of activities. Some activities simply require more attention than others, and when that is the case, more mental energy is used for paying attention. Capacity for attention, though limited, is not a fixed entity; it varies with the difficulty of and familiarity with the activity. Some activities when sufficiently practiced are almost automatic; others require deliberate attention. It may be possible to carry on a heated debate while driving on an open highway but nearly impossible to speak at all while negotiating a vehicle through a crowded and unfamiliar intersection. Some activities use similar cognitive processes and cannot be done simultaneously. Reading, talking, and writing use similar processes, and an individual simply cannot read or write while carrying on a conversation.

Students have always daydreamed and lost attention during lectures. But in this age of laptops and portable mobile devices, teachers have even more competition for attention during presentations. Naturally there is some debate about the efficacy of multitasking. Many students believe they can pay attention to a lecture while sending messages to their friends and looking up websites on the Internet. This is partially true and partially untrue. Students can accomplish all these things during a class period, but they cannot do them at the same time. They actually shift their attention between each activity, losing processing time and effort each time they shift back and forth—a very ineffective process. Students often don't understand the limits of their attention and need some guidance in understanding these limits, along with making them aware that their use of mobile devices can distract others around them.

Many instructors take a hands-off approach to managing the use of such devices, whereas others try intentionally to integrate such technologies into the presentation, asking students to participate in Twitter feeds, back-channel discussions, and Internet searches during presentations. College teachers today need to design intentionally how such technologies are used during presentations. Just as an effective presenter would carefully arrange the chairs and tables in a room, today's presenter needs to arrange carefully the way participants interact with technology during live events.[10] Students' attention is influenced by the design, or lack of design, of what they can do and access on their mobile devices during presentations.

Another area of research has focused on the attention persistence of students in a typical college lecture. Given a typical uninterrupted lecture class period, students have predictable periods of attentiveness and attention lapses, typically being inattentive for the first five minutes, attentive for the next ten to fifteen minutes, inattentive for another five minutes, and so on, bouncing back and forth but with attentiveness declining as the class progresses.[11]

The bad news is that our capacity for attention is limited, perhaps far more limited than intuition would suggest or multimedia-oriented students would admit. The good news is that when it is necessary to attend closely to something, we have a rather remarkable capacity for focusing almost exclusively on what we want and need to see or hear. Although some aspects of attention are based on internal motivation, external aspects can be influenced when giving a presentation. Of the following sixteen rules that we provide in this chapter for using cognitive learning, teachers may find this first set, rules 1 through 5, to be useful guidelines while thinking about the importance of attention when making a presentation.

Rule 1: Whatever it takes, get their attention. Students won't learn much of anything from a presentation unless they are first inspired to pay attention to it. This may mean beginning with something sensational—a fascinating story, a strong visual image, or three good reasons why the participants will not survive without this essential information.

Rule 2: Tell students what to focus their attention on. It is encouraging to know that students can be well focused and single-minded in their attention if they know what to pay attention to, so it helps to tell students directly to focus on certain things, such as the three main points, the essence of the model, or the key process being discussed. An effective teacher uses advance organizers, previews the lesson, shares the purpose and goals, and helps students to distinguish between the trivial and the important.

Rule 3: Don't overload the system. Because students have a limited capacity for attention, effective teachers use media serially, that is, one thing at a time. If they distribute a handout, they know participants will start reading it and stop listening, so they give them time to do this. If they show an image, they make sure it is relevant and supports the message, and they show images only when they are being described. They never talk, pass out handouts, and show irrelevant images at the same time.

Rule 4: Slow down and regain attention when necessary. Effective teachers also know that some things are harder to pay attention to than others. They recognize they may need to slow the pace, cover material more than once, or refocus attention for difficult concepts. The harder the material, the more likely the mind will wander. Effective teachers take breaks, use dramatic pauses, and use changes in pace, format, and style to help renew attention.

Rule 5: Don't try to compete with distractions. Most teachers know that when a student comes in late, starts a private conversation, or plays games on a mobile device, the other students will lose their focus. If the distraction is a strong competitor, the presenter may need to stop, wait, and repeat what was being covered at the time the distraction began. Don't be apologetic about telling students to turn off electronic devices or to pause for some screen downtime if the devices are not actually being used in support of the presentation.

Attention is a limited resource, and effective presenters work to create sustainable learning environments for processing information. If attention is never gained or breaks off, all else is lost. Consider the following example:

> Chemistry Professor Brent Iverson teaches large classes of up to five hundred students at the University of Texas at Austin, but he tries to keep a sense of whether his students are tuned out or tuned in. "Sometimes you just need to call a break and launch into a discussion of a relevant topic that connects what we're talking about in class to something they are familiar with. It captures their attention and reenergizes the class." In Brent's class the students are asked to learn up to fifty chemical reactions in the first forty-five days of the course, "but only a few of those are carbon-carbon bonds, and those are the ones that are most important." And that's when Brent brings out his trumpet. When he plays a few notes on his trumpet and announces, "This is a mind-blowing turn of events," you'd better believe students pay attention. "Sure it's a gimmick, but it's memorable. It keeps the class on their toes and demonstrates the importance of the material, and that is the whole point."[12]

Information Processing

Assuming the teacher has captured and focused the attention of the students, what can be done to help students comprehend what is being said and shown to them? Once information has begun to come in through sight and hearing, how is it processed?

A traditional, commonsense view of perception is that a person simply sees or hears what is out there. Philosophers have struggled for centuries with the problem of the relationship of the mind to the objective world. Cognitive psychologists have joined those in this debate who emphasize the importance of what the mind does in information processing. They say there is no one-to-one correspondence between what is out there and one's perception of it; rather, perceptions involve a highly complex mental interpretation of what is being said or shown.[13] Think about it: What is the real world, interpreted by a sniffing dog or, for that matter, a flitting butterfly? Doesn't it depend on the equipment the organism has for making perceptions and interpreting them?

What is involved in this process of interpretation? How does a person come to recognize and make meaning of the sounds, words, sentences, and images that are the building blocks of communication? As with many other breakthroughs in cognitive psychology, the story begins with the computer. In developing the technology for scanning, now widely used to read zip codes and bank checks, it became necessary (before bar codes) to learn how to develop programs that would read letters and numbers. A process known as template matching was developed to search for and match a predetermined shape, such as an electronic template for the number 3 to correspond to the shape of the Arabic number 3. But the problem becomes more complex when the scanner must read a variety of stimuli, such as the typography from many different printing styles or even handwriting. For example, what does a scanner have to do when it is asked which of the following characters are *A*s?

$$A \triangle V A a F a$$

In this situation the electronic device does not have a template but rather a bank of features, all of which have characteristics of *A*s. For example, *A*s have some of the typical features shown in the next set of characters.

$$/ \; / \; \wedge \; a \; \urcorner \; r$$

This more complex scanner looks for features, not an exact template; it looks for the abstract characteristics of *A*, not just a specific *A*. Selfridge and his colleagues developed an electronic scanner for hand-printed characters that could identify key features, count them, and decide whether the letter had enough characteristics to be called an *A*.[14] This became a useful model for describing human information processing as well. Humans apparently have a highly complex, feature-based pattern recognition system for information processing. Recognizing key features and patterns is important in biology, for example, for studying cells under a microscope; in art history for recognizing styles such as impressionism and cubism; and in music for discriminating between major and minor chords and keys.

Up to this point, this description of information processing has centered on what cognitive psychologists call bottom-up processing, those aspects of the system that are data driven and guided by the features of the stimulus coming into the system. Operating simultaneously with this bottom-up system is a top-down system, which is more concept driven or hypothesis driven and seems to come more from within the individual than from outside stimuli.[15] While processing outside stimuli, the individual simultaneously marshals ideas, thoughts, and meanings from prior knowledge and tests the new inputs against experience. Top-down theorists emphasize what the individual brings to the information during processing. These researchers have found that *context*, *meaning*, and *prior knowledge* affect information processing directly and deeply.

Context

Drawing on the work of the Gestalt psychologists who preceded them, cognitive psychologists have been able to establish that perception is greatly influenced by context. In the following figure, for example, groups of dots in five rows of four tend to be perceived as rows or columns, depending on the way they are arranged.

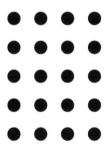

In the previous figure they tend to look like columns, especially if you cover up the last column, thus reducing the length of the rows. In the following figure, like elements tend to be perceived together (even though they are all the same distance apart) so that the rows tend to dominate instead of columns.

The legacy from Gestalt psychology is that individuals organize their perceptions according to the whole configuration (*gestalt*), and therefore context is very important. The perceiver puts individual perceptions into the big picture and sees things as part of a larger whole. What does this mean for educators? Consider the following example. In a classic "if p then q" experiment called Wason's selection task, researchers ask participants to solve this logic problem:

> Each card has a letter on one side and a number on the other. Turn over the minimum number of cards to verify this rule: If there is a vowel on one side, there must be an even number on the other side.[16]

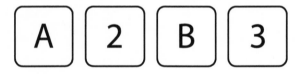

This problem may seem easy at first glance, but very few people solve it correctly. The answer is two, turning over A and 3 will satisfy the rule; turning over the 2 card is not necessary as the rule does not state what is necessary for an even-numbered card. Still confused? Try this next problem:

> Each card represents a student in a bar and shows the student's drink on one side and age on the other. Turn over the minimum number of cards to verify this rule: If the student is drinking beer, the student must be twenty-one years of age or older.[17]

Most college students can easily answer this second problem, which is based on the same logic as the first. The second problem is much easier to solve because it is presented in a context most young adults can easily relate to and figure out.

Meaning

Top-down processing theory also emphasizes the importance of meaning making in the processing of information. Individuals work hard to discover the meaning of what they are seeing and hearing, especially semantic meaning, and then process that information as part of an overall pattern of meaning. For example, for processing the word *ice* in the sentence, "The car slid on the *ice*," a great deal of help is provided by the earlier part of the sentence, "The car slid on the." That part of the sentence almost cries out for the word ice. Less help is provided if the sentence ends with the words *banana peel*. Even though a person might slide on a banana peel, a car usually would not, and the statement begins to border on nonsense, causing the listener to slow down and take a second look.

Research bears out the importance of semantic meaning in information processing. Word pairs that are meaningful, such as *nurse-doctor*, are processed and pronounced more rapidly than nonmeaningful pairs such as *nurse-tree*. Similarly, lists of words presented in a meaningful order, such as *dog, chased, cat, tree*, are more rapidly processed than unrelated words presented in random order such as *tree, boat, pickles, sheep*.

The place of semantic meaning making has been widely examined by cognitive psychologists interested in the study of reading. Although to some degree reading surely involves the bottom-up functions of learning the alphabet and certain phonic rules, there is growing evidence that readers also depend to a large extent on context for establishing meaning. For example, it is not necessary to have every letter of every word to read a sentence: Thix example xhould proxe xhe poixt.

Sometimes the reader interprets the same symbol as different letters as needed according to the context, as shown in the following figure.

THE CAT

Clearly, when people read they process words, groups of words, and phrases—chunks of information, not individual letters. In fact, once one has learned to read at a satisfactory rate, it is very difficult to process individual letters accurately. Consider the point by counting the number of *f*s in the following passage:

> Finished files are the result of years of scientific study combined with the experience of many years.

A count of less than six requires more careful reading. As most writers know, proofreading goes much slower than reading for meaning, and most cognitive psychologists would agree that different processing activities are involved. The point of all these examples is, whether we are aware of it or not, information that has meaning is processed more easily.

Prior Knowledge

In most processing of information, an attempt is made by the individual to make sense of what is being processed, but meaning does not come out of thin air; it comes from prior knowledge. What the person knows already about the information being presented has a great effect on the speed and ease of processing. For example, when subjects are given a very brief glimpse of a flash card containing three rows of nonsense letters such as

GBY

QOP

LZV

they have a great deal of difficulty processing the information quickly and accurately. They may get one row or a few letters in a couple of rows. But when exposed for the same length of time to another set of letters

IBM

SOS

IOU

the processing is rapid, easy, and accurate. Of course, most subjects would have a high degree of previous knowledge of the second set of letters.

Cognitive psychologists have tried to describe how previous knowledge is stored and called forth to assist in information processing. What previous knowledge does it take, for example, to understand a simple passage like the following, adapted from an example by Daniel Willingham: Oscar gained strength overnight with wind speeds over one hundred miles per hour. Forecasters predict the eye will hit the already battered coast of Belize tomorrow.[18]

Most American students know that Oscar is neither a person nor a Hollywood award but a named hurricane and that the eye is the central part of the storm, not a part of the body or the top of a sewing needle. Elementary-aged students without the knowledge of weather forecasting gained over the years might not understand this statement at all. A college student from Japan might have difficulty as well because tropical storms, called typhoons there, are given numbers in Japan and are not named after people. Some expert students might even recognize that Oscar is a hurricane and not a tropical storm because the wind speeds are over seventy-four miles per hour. Some may know where Belize is located, others may not. Think of the various levels of comprehension possible and the disastrous results of a presentation about Oscar if students do not have the appropriate context, meaning, or prior knowledge.

Cognitive psychologists (with some help from linguists) suggest that individuals organize their prior knowledge into scripts, frames, and schemas and that they call up this knowledge in preorganized knowledge packets when they encounter new information. For example, when a person is learning about going to a Chinese restaurant, the restaurant script is called into play. It already contains information about general restaurant experiences such as getting seated, reading a menu, ordering, being served, and paying the bill, as well as the proper sequence for doing these things. When one learns something new about how this is done in a Chinese restaurant, the basic restaurant script is used and serves quite well for making sense of the new learning that takes place. If there is no restaurant script to begin with, then problems will arise in learning about sharing main dishes, eating with chopsticks, and limiting dessert to a fortune cookie. Effective information processing involves relating new information to old (previously learned) information. Consider the following example:

> Tom Knecht teaches political science at Westmont College. He has created one class in particular, Politics and Sports, to help certain students grasp the abstract and complex concepts of political science. The kinesiology and physical education students who make up the majority in this course generally have poor background knowledge and low interest in American politics. Tom uses these students' prior knowledge of sports to help explain political science concepts and put them in a context they can relate to.

He explains that the American Constitution makes politics possible and determines the laws, similar to the rules of the game in sports. "In a basketball game, if your team is losing by five points, there are no time-outs remaining, and the other team has the ball, what do you do? Most sports fans know the best option is to foul the other team to stop the clock. It doesn't matter who the team is or who the players are, this is the optimal strategy given the rules of the game." He explains that in the same way optimal strategies in politics are dictated by the rules of the political and legal system. It doesn't matter who the politician is or which political party he or she represents. Given the rules, most political behavior can be predicted. "Students can learn a lot about politics and see that much of political behavior is predictable by relating it to the rules of the game."[19]

Prior knowledge can be greatly beneficial in learning new information, but sometimes prior knowledge can be inappropriate, insufficient, or downright incorrect and can actually interfere with new learning.[20] Everyday prior knowledge might get in the way of learning when common terms are used in a different way or when misconceptions or partial knowledge predominant. Students may know how to write a term paper, but this knowledge is not appropriate for writing a creative essay or a lab report. Even when prior knowledge is present and accurate, it often lies dormant and needs to be activated, and teachers are wise to try to determine the prior knowledge of their students and remind students what they already know.

In addition, teachers need to be aware of their own prior knowledge. A common problem with the cognitive strategy is because of presenter expertise, or the "expert blind spot."[21] It can be difficult to remember what it was like to be a novice in the field without the immense background knowledge acquired by those who teach at the college level. College teachers often make incorrect assumptions about students' background knowledge, context, and awareness of meaning because their own scholarship as teachers is so extensive. This can result in a confusing and hard-to-follow presentation. Without a base of knowledge and guidance from the instructor, students are likely to organize information sequentially or in random order rather than in a conceptual, meaningful order that seems obvious to experts in the field.

Receiving information is not a passive process for the participant. To "get it" the learner needs to be actively involved and fully engaged in trying to perceive and understand the information being presented. Students who are actively involved can receive and understand impressive amounts of new information from effective presentations when principles of cognitive learning are employed. The second set of rules, 6 through 12, addresses the question: What does the presenter need to do to increase the likelihood that information will be processed as intended?

Rule 6: Recognize that interpretation will always occur. It is important to remember that there is no one-to-one connection between what the teacher says and what the student hears or sees. What students process is not the information but their perception of the information. In this sense it is never possible to tell any student anything directly because it is always being acted upon and interpreted by the learner. Effective presenters make an attempt to know their audience, their likely prior knowledge, or lack thereof, and any common preconceptions about the material.

Rule 7: Help students discover the overall structure in the information being presented. Students seldom process individual pieces of information—sounds, words, images—as isolated bits but rather as parts of larger structures and patterns. However, when information is very new to students, they often lack any structure to understand it. If students are searching for overall structures, why not offer them some? Present the material in an organized way and explain the organization to students. Use mental and graphic organizers to help them see how information fits together. When the trees are part of a forest, give students the forest, name it, and then look at the trees. Details take on importance when they fit into overall patterns.

Rule 8: Present information in context. Because context makes processing smoother, information should always be presented in its larger context. Where did this information come from? How is it related to similar or different information? How can this information be used? Especially if the information is abstract, put it in a context that makes sense not only to you but to your audience.

Rule 9: Help students with meaning making. Because students are trying to find meaning to process information more effectively, the teacher needs to provide interpretations of the meaning of the information along with the information. How do things work? Why do they work? What are the best words and phrases to carry the meaning? Is there a good story that can be used to illustrate a key point? Recognizing that different people make meaning in different ways, the teacher does not assume the meaning is obvious but states explicitly the meaning of the information and asks students to share their different ways of making meaning.

Rule 10: Build strong bridges from prior knowledge to new information.
Because new information needs to be understood through prior knowledge,
the teacher needs to have a good grasp of the prior knowledge most students
in the class have. Pretests, open-ended knowledge probes, or even just a raise
of hands can shed light on students' prior knowledge. If students have little
prior knowledge to use as a base for processing new information, the teacher
may need to go very slowly or back up and build that knowledge base.
Assuming adequate prior knowledge exists, the teacher then needs to help
activate this knowledge and make connections to it. Sample problems, content reviews, or short discussions can remind students that they already know
certain processes, techniques, and procedures and already have the scripts for
certain activities. Sometimes prior knowledge is misinformation and needs
to be unlearned and relearned.

Rule 11: Use visuals and images to aid with memory. Richard Mayer, a
leading researcher in multimedia learning, explains that we have separate
channels in different parts of our brain for processing verbal and visual information. We retain information better if we are processing words and pictures
rather than just words.[22] But the images need to be relevant and supportive
of the content and words. If the images are irrelevant, students spend valuable cognitive processing time trying to figure out the image rather than
letting it support the message. Effective presenters use just the right amount
of relevant visual stimulation to help students process the content of the
presentation.

Rule 12: Devise ways to ensure that students are actively involved. Because
this kind of learning requires active participation, which is contrary to common assumptions about presentations, teachers find ways to engage students
with activities and exercises interspersed to stimulate involvement. Effective
presenters may ask for volunteers to demonstrate a concept, use clickers to
ask periodic comprehension questions, or ask pairs of students to summarize
and explain concepts to each other in their own words. Teachers may stop
once in a while to ask students which point is still muddy or unclear.

> Leslie Reid teaches a course called Intro to the Geosciences at the Univer-
> sity of Calgary in Alberta, Canada. She has focused this class to center
> around a number of big ideas that represent the main concepts of the
> course. Even though these big ideas are revealed to students in the syllabus,
> Leslie and her colleagues found that students didn't know how to use this
> as a resource for their understanding and processing of the course content.
> Now Leslie uses concept mapping to get students to see the big picture.

On the first day of class students are asked to create a concept map of the big ideas. Most students simply list the ideas at the top of a page or don't even know what to write down. After she walks around for a while and observes the students working individually and in small groups, Leslie models her own concept map on her tablet computer, drawing connections and engaging in a discussion about the various ways different students see the concepts relating to each other. At various points in the course she asks the students to pull out their concept maps or to create a new one to continually make this connection between the current information and the big ideas. "We're always asking them to review their concept maps and visually see where we've been, where we are now, and where we are going." Leslie is constantly referring to the concept maps and the big ideas as a way of reinforcing what information is important to learn.[23]

Memory

Like Leslie, most teachers would like students to remember what they learn, but unlike Leslie, they seldom identify what students should remember or how they should remember it. Retaining information over long periods of time involves memory. How do we remember things, and is it possible to improve our memory or the memory of others?

Short-Term Memory

Cognitive psychologists make a distinction between *short-term memory* and *long-term memory*. Short-term memory, as the term implies, doesn't last very long, and it doesn't hold very much. It is used to keep information temporarily in mind to act on it.

In looking up an unfamiliar phone number, a person uses short-term memory to keep the numbers in mind long enough to dial them, and, alas, even then it is often necessary to take a second peek at the source, especially if there has been an interruption. How short is short-term memory? Estimates vary on the exact length of storage time. Visual images last in the sensory register for less than one-half of a second, and sounds last only one-fourth of a second, but their features can be extracted and retained in short-term memory for somewhere between fifteen and thirty seconds.[24] Unless the information is rehearsed (repeated over and over mentally) or unless something else is done with the information to fix it in long-term memory, rapid decay sets in—hence the name *short term.*

Short-term memory is also limited in capacity; that is, it doesn't hold very much. In a now famous and influential article titled "The Magical

Number Seven, Plus or Minus Two: Some Limits on Our Capacity for Processing Information," George Miller established that most people are limited to retaining between five and nine bits of information in their short-term memory.[25] In his experiments and in those conducted subsequently by others, the magical number seven kept popping up. In tests of the number of sounds, digits, or words people could retain in short-term memory, the results were always similar—somewhere around seven, plus or minus two. The research that followed this original work is now centered on the theory of *cognitive load,* a concept not focused on a specific number but rather on the place where intended learning exceeds a person's cognitive capacity.

People forget what they have in short-term memory unless they do something with the information to establish it in long-term memory. Usually this means taking a longer string of information and grouping it into a smaller number of *chunks.*[26] It would be difficult, for example, to remember the number 3027429643 as a single number, but it can be chunked into 302 742 9643.

It is more likely these three chunks of numbers will be retained. If the chunks are further rehearsed, the numbers will be transformed, encoded, and sent on their way to long-term memory.

Experts, which most college teachers surely are, understand their area of expertise at a more sophisticated level and essentially can chunk larger groups of information. They have different levels of cognitive load than beginners. For example, beginning readers process one letter at a time, as each letter represents a chunk. As readers advance they process one word as a chunk and finally entire phrases as a chunk. Advanced readers are able to process cognitively more information with less effort. This is why experts can learn much more from lectures and are more tolerant of them than beginners in a subject area. Experts simply know more and have learned how to process more information at a faster rate.

What is the purpose of short-term memory, with its demonstrated lack of staying power and capacity? Short-term memory plays an important function in holding information temporarily in mind while other monitors and control mechanisms get to act on it. It is like hanging a picture. One person holds the picture in place while another takes a look and tries to decide whether to move it up or down, left or right, or whether to hang it, put it in another room, or put it in storage. In hanging pictures it is not wise to go too fast or to look at too many pictures all at once. *Working memory,* a distinct but closely related concept, provides a limited mechanism for holding up words, images, ideas, and sounds to look at briefly while a decision is made about what to do with them next.

Long-Term Memory

Long-term memory is what most people mean when they refer to memory, and this kind of memory is usually the concern of teachers and students. It picks up where short-term memory leaves off. If something is remembered after roughly twenty-four hours, it is considered part of long-term memory.

Cognitive psychologists have described various types of long-term memory and recognize that somewhat different processes are at work for remembering different kinds of things. Remembering the event of walking to school as a child is different from remembering what was learned about Pilgrims in sixth grade. Remembering images, such as the international driving signs, is different from remembering movements, such as skiing or riding a bicycle. Cognitive scientists make a distinction between *procedural memory*—remembering how to do something, such as a motor skill—and *declarative memory*—remembering what something is, such as factual information. Most teachers deal primarily with a form of declarative memory called *semantic memory*, the memory for information, ideas, and concepts mediated by words.

How does long-term memory work, and what can be done to assist it in its work? One commonly expressed view is that the mind records everything perfectly, like a human video recorder, but the trouble comes in playback. When individuals representative of the general populace are surveyed and asked how they think their memory works, three-fourths believe that all the information is in long-term memory; they just can't retrieve it.[27] This idea of a complete but inaccessible memory, while widely held, does not bear the scrutiny of research. Research suggests that the mind does not record everything and that what is recorded is subject to inaccuracy, distortion, and serious decay.[28] Attempts to unlock memory with hypnosis, truth drugs, and electrical stimulation result in as many false reports, fragments, and distortions as accurate memories. If long-term memory is not a digital record of experience, how does it work?

Memory work was first understood to be somewhat like storage on a computer. There are places where information is stored, like files, and it is necessary to enter that information in a systematic way so it can be retrieved. Similar kinds of information seem to be stored in the same files. Thus, the words *animal, bird, feathers, wing,* and *fly* are arranged in a hierarchy on networked files.[29] The structure of these networks has been mapped and tested, and we know that some things are easier to call up than others; for example, the concrete image of zebra is easier than the abstract concept of justice. Putting things into long-term memory and retrieving them involves associations among words, concepts, and ideas, and usually, but not always, semantic associations. Some models of long-term memory focus on the importance of word associations, hooking up one word with another word (or image or sound) to produce meaningful and memorable connections in the networked filing system. The human brain, with its potentially enormous and complex storage and retrieval system, relies heavily on language, and the associations of meaning conveyed by language and image, for its smooth functioning. Scientists now understand the brain works in an even more complex fashion than a computer; it's an organic network that is continually changing and growing but with connections still based on semantic associations.

Emotions also affect long-term memory. Sousa explains that we seem to remember things according to a hierarchy.[30] Our brain first remembers data affecting our survival. Any child who has touched an open flame needs no reminding that fire is hot. Next we remember data concerning emotions. The emerging field of neuroscience has shown us that the emotional system in the brain plays a strong role in memory. Self-concept and past experiences influence what data is allowed into the memory system. If a student has previous negative experiences related to a new learning situation, the sensory register in the brain "is likely to block the incoming data, just as venetian blinds are closed to block light."[31] Teachers may reach out to such students with more focus on making sense of the information, but the problem is with the emotions.

After survival and emotional roadblocks, we are able to engage in new learning, but we remember more easily those things that make sense to us and that we feel have meaning. If these two conditions are not met, it's much more taxing for us to integrate the information into long-term memory. Simply wanting to remember something does not lead to better memory.[32] For students, being told that certain information will be on the test has some meaning but not the type of meaning that makes it easier for their brains to remember.

Giving students information that makes sense and has meaning in an emotionally supportive environment is the best way to ensure retention. However, certain information can be hard to tie to meaning and sometimes just plain has to be memorized. The alphabet, multiplication tables, and the periodic table of elements are bits of information that if stored in long-term memory allow for more complex processing using less cognitive load. If it is known that memory depends on building associations between and among words, images, concepts, and ideas, what are some of the ways teachers can help students store information so it can be retrieved as needed? Five categories of techniques are especially useful for enhancing the storage and retrieval of information in long-term memory: rehearsal, encoding, imagery, method of loci, and semantic association.

- *Rehearsal.* The most frequently used and least effective memory technique is rehearsal, sometimes referred to by educators as rote learning. Rehearsal involves repeating information over and over again (out loud, to oneself, or using online quizzes or memory games) until it sinks in. It is possible, for example, to memorize a difficult list of words if sufficient time for rehearsal is allowed between the presentation of each word. Rehearsal, however, is not very efficient, and when it does work another technique is often being used (perhaps unconsciously) besides pure repetition.

- *Encoding.* Far more efficient and productive is the memory technique known as encoding. At its simplest level, encoding means associating a key word with the word to be remembered; at its more complex level encoding means transforming the information to be remembered into a new semantic unit or form. Using a synonym is a form of encoding, as is placing a word in a meaningful and memorable sentence. More complex encoding involves developing mnemonic devices known as acronyms, such as HOMES to remember the Great Lakes (Huron, Ontario, Michigan, Erie, Superior), or catchy sentences, such as "Every good boy does fine" to remember the lines on the treble clef (E, G, B, D, F) in music notation. Research on encoding suggests, oddly enough, that more elaborate and distinctive devices work best.[33] One of the more useful forms of encoding is chunking. Long strings of information can be subdivided or transformed into chunks so the number of individual units to be remembered is smaller and more manageable.

- *Imagery.* Images are mental pictures. Research has shown that people generally find it easier to remember pictures than words.[34] When subjects were shown 1,000 vivid pictures, 1,000 ordinary pictures, and 1,000 words, on the average they remembered (identified correctly from test pairs) 830 vivid pictures, 770 ordinary pictures, and 615 words. One picture may not be worth a thousand words, but vivid images may be useful in storing information in long-term memory. One way to remember a new piece of information is by associating it with vivid, preferably ridiculous and even bizarre, images. Suppose, for example, a person is asked to learn a list of words that includes airplane, tree, and envelope. You may wish to picture an airplane with trees growing from the wings and with envelopes hanging from the trees like leaves. Apparently, bizarre and elaborate visual associations work well as memory devices.[35]

- *Method of loci.* Another memory technique involving the use of imagery is known as the method of loci, or the place method. The object is to place items to be learned into a pattern of familiar locations, such as the rooms of a house, the corners of a classroom, or the shops along a familiar street. A grocery list, for example, might be learned by placing each item on the list mentally at a different place in the kitchen: the milk in the refrigerator, the paper towels on their rack, a can of soup at the stove, and so forth. While shopping, one mentally walks through the kitchen and retrieves the items to be purchased.[36]
- *Semantic association.* Information that has meaning is remembered more easily than nonsense. Language has what linguists call surface structure, properties of the words themselves, and deep structure, the underlying meaning the words convey.[37]

What people do when they read a passage or listen to a presentation is look for the underlying message of the information, the gist of the content. What people often put into long-term memory are not the exact words but the message, and the message, in turn, is also what they recall. When subjects were given a passage to read about the performance of exploratory surgery, they later recalled a host of words, such as *doctor, nurse,* and *scalpel,* that weren't in the passage at all. Apparently they remembered the general theme of the passage and made decisions on the basis of which words should have appeared in such a passage.[38]

If this is how people remember, why do they forget? There are many explanations for forgetting. Forgetting can involve interference from previously learned material; repression, as in the classical Freudian sense; failure in the retrieval system, as with tip-of-the-tongue forgetting; or actual memory decay, as with aging.[39] More likely than not, however, what is called forgetting is really a matter of not learning the information in the first place. People don't forget names; more likely they don't learn them initially. Memory usually involves active processing that requires significant intentional effort. When subjects were asked to recall the head of a penny, most could not describe what was on it and could not distinguish real pennies from fake pennies that were presented even though they dealt with pennies every day. Did the subjects forget? Unlikely. One must learn something before it can be forgotten. When students say, "I forgot," their more accurate admission might be, "I didn't learn it in the first place."

Rules 13 through 16 suggest what a teacher can do to increase the likelihood that the information presented will be remembered by the students.

Rule 13: Allow time for short-term memory to function. It is important for teachers to move slowly enough to allow time for students to deal with new information. Students need to be able to project the words and images on their own private short-term memory screens long enough to decide what to do. It takes some time for the raw material of the presentation (words, images, or ideas) to register, and as soon as it does, beware, because it will start to be lost. The students have to scramble to decide what to do with this material, whether to take notes, relate the visuals to the spoken words, or search their memory for something familiar before they lose it.

Rule 14: Explode the myth of automatic memory/faulty recall. Let students know they need to get actively involved in trying to remember. To facilitate long-term memory, it is useful for teachers and students to stop acting as if students were like video cameras, remembering what took place because they were fortunate to have been in the same room at the same time with the teacher. Tell students bluntly they won't remember much from the presentation unless they get actively involved in fixing the information in their memory, and help them with structures, concept maps, or other organizational frameworks that will assist their retention.

Rule 15: If needed, provide students with mnemonic devices. Because we know information will be lost unless it is actively transformed into something memorable, teachers should play a role in facilitating the storage and retrieval process. One can, of course, take the position that presenting is the teacher's job and remembering is the student's problem, but it makes a huge difference in learning if the teacher assumes at least some of the responsibility for helping students remember the material. This means being selective in telling students what is essential—if you don't know, how can they?—and helping them create mnemonic (memory) devices when something just simply has to be memorized.

Rule 16: Let students know that rehearsal alone doesn't work well. Work with students to use the techniques of encoding, imagery, and semantic association to remember essential information. Usually this means providing a synonym, an acronym, a set or chunk, a diagram, a bizarre image, a simple routine, or fresh metaphor for remembering the material. Or when possible, help students make sense and meaning out of new information. Cramming for a test might work for short-term memory but not for long-term retention.

Assessing Cognitive Learning

Cognitive learning is primarily concerned with knowledge transfer, so assessment of cognitive learning is focused on the students' recognition, basic comprehension, and recall of information. Objective tests fit this strategy because they primarily test these cognitive processes. Multiple-choice and fill-in-the-blank questions can be effective for testing recall of information, and true/false and multiple-choice questions can be used for recognition of information. Asking students to summarize or paraphrase information, while not as easily graded, involves students' demonstrating some level of understanding beyond basic recall. Sometimes teachers present information to students and then assess them on application, critical thinking, problem solving, or other ways of learning. When this is done, the teacher is assessing a different kind of learning from what was actually taught, which is not exactly fair. Teachers need to understand the limits of learning when presenting information.

Research has focused on the role of testing itself as a means of increasing recall and memory, what is being called the testing effect.[40] Studies are showing that repeated testing on material increases long-term retention better than studying the material alone. It appears the attention given to the material during testing and the feedback given during the process identifies incorrect answers and reinforces correct answers.[41] Many technologies support rehearsal of material through quizzes and simple games that reinforce recall of information. In addition, the use of student response systems or clickers, described in the following example, illustrates the benefits of quizzing and taking time to help students make meaning out of information.

> At Cleveland State University, Conor McLennan's presentations about statistics are interspersed with questions about the content he is presenting. Periodically he will pose content-based questions through his presentation slides, and students use handheld clicker devices to choose their answer. Conor, as well as the rest of the class, can immediately see the percentage of students who got the question right. He can adjust his presentations accordingly, reviewing information that many students get incorrectly, or skipping ahead through information the class seems to have mastered.

"When students see immediately if they got a question right or wrong, it allows them to understand what they know and what they don't know, and where and how to focus their studies later on." Conor also uses techniques such as Think-Pair-Share to turn the quiz questions into learning activities.[42] After students vote on a question, they turn to their neighbor to talk about the question, and vote again before the correct answer is revealed. "This helps them process the information, attempt to explain it in their own words, and hear the information explained in different ways by other students. Almost all of the time, the percentage of students who get the correct answer goes way up." Whenever possible, Conor tries to make time to review all the responses in his clicker questions, correct as well as incorrect responses. "It's one thing to confirm correct responses, but I also want to correct any misunderstandings and explain why some answers are wrong. Discussing the incorrect answers is an effective way to reinforce students' understanding."[43]

Useful Technologies for Cognitive Learning

Supportive media and technologies, such as clickers, can enhance acquisition of knowledge. Clickers are commonly used to break up a presentation, determine prior knowledge, or test comprehension. Like Conor, many teachers ask students to talk with a neighbor or complete some other activity before and after responding to questions, allowing them time to make meaning of information and move it from short-term to long-term memory. Although clickers have been shown to improve information recall, their effective use is as much about using appropriate teaching methods as about the technology itself.[44] Effective use of clickers relies on the quality of the questions. In addition, the number of clicker questions used during a presentation can affect student learning; questions should not be so frequent that they are not taken seriously but not so infrequent that they are ignored.

Other forms of technology can also assist presentations, and sometimes having to make decisions about supportive media can help with the organization of the presentation itself. It can be incredibly useful to think, "What visual captures the message I'm trying to send?" There is no better exercise for shaping and ordering a presentation than having to design the slides, frames, images, or handouts used to support the main ideas. Many technologies exist to support presentations, PowerPoint remaining the most well known and widely used. There are certainly limits to using PowerPoint, and unfortunately the ease of this technology has led to its overuse and misuse. Many instructors use PowerPoint for their own benefit to act as digital notes.

However, notes are nothing students need to see. Students bemoan the thought of sitting through lectures with the presenter reading the text off PowerPoint slides (that sometimes simply cover the material already covered in the book). Instead, PowerPoint should be used to support the visual processing of the audience. Thinking through how PowerPoint presentations are received by students rather than how useful they are for the teacher can result in much more effective presentations.

Another common complaint about PowerPoint is its linear and rigid design. Newer presentation technologies are offering alternatives for nonlinear and flexible presentations. For example, Prezi allows teachers to create different paths through a presentation, or no path at all, and to zoom in and out of a presentation, providing students with visual reminders of the overall structure and the specific details of the presentation. The continual development of technology options for supporting presentations will offer even more choices in the future.

Recording presentations is popular and relatively easy to do with the availability of lecture capture technology. Such recordings can be useful for students who miss a class, for second language learners, or for those with learning disabilities, all of whom would benefit from being able to replay a presentation at their own pace or as many times as needed. However, recorded presentations can certainly be misused. Sitting through a redundant or poorly delivered presentation is only made worse when watching it via a recording. Such technology should be used only when the purpose outweighs the disadvantages. One increasingly popular and promising approach is to record presentations to create what is called an inverted, or flipped, classroom, where students watch presentations as their homework, gaining this information outside class and then spending in-class time on other ways of learning.

With these trends and the increasing availability of user-friendly technologies, entire presentations can be created to be offered online or via audio, video, voice-over slides, or other interactive presentation methods. Such presentations are common in online and hybrid courses and can also be used in on-campus courses. A talking head approach, in which the teacher simply videotapes a presentation, is popular and easy, but is not usually the most effective. Studies have shown the lowest levels of stimulation are attributed to watching a talking head. Watching two people talking results in higher stimulation for the student, and the addition of visual stimulation increases attention further.[45] All the same rules for live presentations about attention, information processing, and memory apply to multimedia presentations. It is best to present related words and images together simultaneously, use memorable and relevant images, provide students with a structure of the presentation, and keep presentations short and in manageable chunks. Studies from educational TV programming in the 1960s show that fifteen to twenty minutes is the maximum time someone pays attention to video for learning.[46] Most recommendations about time limits for online multimedia presentations today are closer to ten minutes or less.

Final Thoughts

Presentations have their place in college classrooms, but they have a specific and limited purpose: for students to acquire knowledge. Because so much knowledge and information is widely available through multiple venues today, spending large amounts of class time conducting presentations is a questionable practice. Often course readings or Internet searches provide the needed information most efficiently. However, when presentations are necessary, there are ways to make them effective.

Obviously the best way to conduct effective presentations and explanations is to follow rules 1 through 16 as closely as possible. Knowing the subject, of course, is essential, but knowing the theory derived from cognitive psychology and applying it can greatly enhance any presentation and get better results. What is often the case is a preoccupation with content, and sometimes the presenter needs to ask fundamental questions about outcomes. After all, what are participants expected to take away from this presentation and remember? What learning is to take place, and what knowledge is to be acquired?

Brilliant people often forget what it is like not to know anything about their subject and can have difficulty paring down a complex subject into a few well-organized points. That is why it is important to think of the students as learners and to structure the presentation in such a way that the students can attend to, process, and remember it. The best way to encourage this structuring is for teachers to ask themselves tough questions persistently during the preparation of the presentation: What do I need to do to get the students' attention? What do I want them to focus on? What are the main ideas and concepts? How can I relate new material to what is already known? What do I want them to remember?

Above all, the teacher needs to keep in mind that the purpose of a presentation is to help students acquire knowledge. Heavy, formal presentations conducted in the traditional manner without benefit of cognitive learning principles do not work. Formal speeches are like throwing the shot put.

The speaker spends a lot of time getting together a very heavy message, usually a written script. When the athlete flings the shot, no one would think of trying to catch it. Onlookers may admire the form or measure how far it went, but they would be crazy to try to catch it. Formal speeches are usually received the same way. On the other hand, an effective presentation is like throwing a Frisbee: the presenter has a lighter message that is attention catching, relevant, and understandable and throws it in such a way that it can be caught, examined, and thrown back.[47]

Points to Remember

Teachers who want to use cognitive learning effectively should do the following:

- ✓ Recognize that presentations are effective only for transmitting information.
- ✓ Gain students' attention.
- ✓ Tell students what to focus attention on.
- ✓ Do not overload the system.
- ✓ Do not compete with distractions, regain attention when necessary.
- ✓ Slow down for new or difficult material.
- ✓ Realize that interpretation is always taking place.
- ✓ Help students discover the overall structure in the information being presented.
- ✓ Present information in context.
- ✓ Help students with meaning making.
- ✓ Build strong bridges from prior knowledge to new information.
- ✓ Use visuals and images to help with processing.
- ✓ Devise ways to ensure that students are actively involved.
- ✓ Allow time for short-term memory to function.
- ✓ Get students actively involved in remembering.
- ✓ Provide mnemonic devices if needed.
- ✓ Let students know rehearsal alone doesn't work.

Notes

1. See Donald A. Bligh, *What's the Use of Lectures?* (San Francisco: Jossey-Bass, 2000), 3, for studies and reports about the overuse of lectures in higher education.

2. Bligh, *What's the Use of Lectures?*

3. In an interesting twist of fate, Noam Chomsky, a young linguist, was asked to review B. F. Skinner's *Verbal Behavior*. The result was more than a book review; Chomsky emerged as a leading psycholinguist. See Noam Chomsky, "A Review of Skinner's *Verbal Behavior*," *Language* 35 (1959): 26–58.

4. A. Newall, J. C. Shaw, and H. A. Simon, "Elements of a Theory of Human Problem Solving," *Psychological Review* 65 (1958): 151–66.

5. Based on Richard E. Mayer, *Applying the Science of Learning* (Boston: Pearson, 2011); David A. Sousa, *How the Brain Learns: A Classroom Teacher's Guide* (Thousand Oaks, CA: Corwin Press, 2001); and the original model by Robert Stahl, "Cognitive Theory within the Framework of an Information Processing Model and Learning Hierarchy: Viable Alternative to the Bloom-Mager System," *Instructional Development: The State of the Art* (1984): 149–68.

6. Bligh, *What's the Use of Lectures?* 44.

7. Colin Cherry, *On Human Communication* (New York: Wiley, 1957).

8. Research by Christopher Chabris and Daniel Simons, of Harvard University, led to the book *The Invisible Gorilla* (New York: Crown Archetype, 2010). Original video, accessed September 5, 2011, http://www.theinvisiblegorilla.com/videos.html.

9. Linda Stone, "Continuous Partial Attention," accessed September 5, 2011, http://lindastone.net/qa/continuous-partial-attention/.

10. Eric Gordon and David Bogen, "Designing Choreographies for the New Economy of Attention," *DHQ: Digital Humanities Quarterly* 3, no. 2 (Spring 2000), accessed September 12, 2011, http://www.digitalhumanities.org/dhq/vol/3/2/000049/000049.html.

11. A. H. Johnstone and F. Percival, "Attention Breaks in Lectures," *Education in Chemistry* 13 (1976): 49–50.

12. Thanks to Brent Iverson, PhD, University Distinguished Teaching Professor, Faculty Warren J. and Viola Mae Raymer Professorship at the University of Texas at Austin, for granting permission to use his example. E-mail message to author, September 21, 2011.

13. Roy Lachman, Janet Lachman, and Earl Butterfield, *Cognitive Psychology and Information Processing: An Introduction* (Hillsdale, NJ: Erlbaum, 1979).

14. Oliver Selfridge and Ulrich Neisser, "Pattern Recognition by Machine," *Scientific American* 203 (1960): 60–68.

15. The following discussion of top-down processing draws heavily on the excellent summary of research in Anthony J. Sanford, *Cognition and Cognitive Psychology* (New York: Basic Books, 1958), 51–62. Some of the ideas for the illustrations are drawn from the basic psychology text by Phillip Zimbardo, *Psychology and Life* (Glenview, IL: Scott, Foresman, 1985), 196–99.

16. Peter C. Wason, "Reasoning about a Rule," *Quarterly Journal of Experimental Psychology* 20, no. 3 (1968): 273–81, as quoted in Daniel T. Willingham, *Why Don't Students Like School? A Cognitive Psychologist Answers Questions about How the Mind Works and What It Means for the Classroom* (San Francisco: Jossey-Bass, 2009), 29–30.

17. R. A. Griggs and J. R. Cox, "The Elusive Thematic-Materials Effect in Wason's Selection Task," *British Journal of Psychology* 73, no. 3 (1982): 407–20.

18. Willingham, *Why Don't Students Like School?* 76.

19. Thanks to Tom Knecht, PhD, Assistant Professor of Political Science at West-mont College, for granting permission to use his example. In discussion with the author, September 15, 2011.

20. Susan A. Ambrose et al., *How Learning Works: Seven Research-Based Principles for Smart Teaching* (San Francisco: Jossey-Bass, 2010), 10–39.

21. Ibid.

22. Mayer, *Applying the Science of Learning*.

23. Thanks to Leslie Reid, PhD, Tamaratt Teaching Professor, Department of Geoscience, University of Calgary, for granting permission to use her example. In discussion with the author, September 20, 2011.

24. Lloyd R. Peterson and Margaret J. Peterson, "Short-Term Retention of Indi-vidual Verbal Items," *Journal of Experimental Psychology* 58, no. 3 (1959): 193–98.

25. George A. Miller, "The Magical Number Seven, Plus or Minus Two: Some Limits on Our Capacity for Processing Information," *Psychological Review* 63, no. 2 (1956): 81–97.

26. R. Lachman, J. L. Lachman, and E. C. Butterfield, *Cognitive Psychology and Information Processing: An Introduction* (Hillsdale, NJ: Erlbaum, 1979), 52.

27. E. F. Loftus and G. F. Loftus, "On the Permanence of Stored Information in the Human Brain," *American Psychologist* 35 (1980): 409–20.

28. Elizabeth Loftus, *Memory* (Boston: Addison-Wesley, 1980).

29. R. C. Oldfield and A. Wingfield, "Response Latencies in Naming Objects," *Quarterly Journal of Experimental Psychology* 17, no. 4 (1965): 273–81.

30. David A. Sousa, *How the Brain Learns: A Classroom Teacher's Guide* (Thou-sand Oaks, CA: Corwin Press, 2001).

31. Ibid.

32. Willingham, *Why Don't Students Like School?* 46.

33. Roger N. Shepherd, "Recognition Memory for Words, Sentences and Pic-tures," *Journal of Verbal Learning and Verbal Behavior* 6, no. 1 (1967): 156–63.

34. Lionel Standing, "Learning 10,000 Pictures," *Quarterly Journal of Experimen-tal Psychology* 25, no. 2 (1973): 207–22.

35. Harry Lorayne and Jerry Lucas, *The Memory Book* (New York: Stein and Day, 1974), 25–27.

36. Loftus, *Memory*, 181.

37. Noam Chomsky, *Aspects of the Theory of Syntax* (Cambridge, MA: MIT Press, 1965).

38. K. F. Pompi and R. Lachman, "Surrogate Processes in the Short-Term Reten-tion of Connected Discourse," *Journal of Experimental Psychology* 75, no. 2 (1967): 143–50.

39. Phillip Zimbardo, *Psychology and Life* (Glenview, IL: Scott, Foresman, 1985), 327–30.

40. See Jeffrey D. Karpicke et al., "The Critical Importance of Retrieval for Learning," *Science* 319, no. 5865 (2008): 966–68.

41. Andrew C. Butler, Jeffrey D. Karpicke, and Henry L. Roediger, "Correcting a Metacognitive Error: Feedback Increases Retention of Low-Confidence Correct Responses," *Journal of Experimental Psychology: Learning, Memory, and Cognition* 34, no. 4 (2008): 918–28.

42. F. Lyman, "The Responsive Classroom Discussion," in *Mainstreaming Digest*, ed. A. S. Anderson (College Park, MD: University of Maryland College of Education, 1981), 109–13.

43. Thanks to Conor McLennan, PhD, Assistant Professor of Psychology at Cleveland State University, for granting permission to use his example. In discussion with the author, September 15, 2011.

44. For more about the effective use of clickers, see Derek Bruff, *Teaching with Classroom Response Systems* (San Francisco: Jossey-Bass, 2009); and Douglas Duncan, *Clickers in the Classroom: How to Enhance Science Teaching Using Classroom Response Systems* (San Francisco: Pearson, 2005).

45. Mayer, *Applying the Science of Learning*, 70.

46. Bligh, *What's the Use of Lectures?* 48.

47. The shot put/Frisbee metaphor is borrowed from a conversation with Alton Barbour, Professor Emeritus of Human Communication Studies, at the University of Denver.

6

DEVELOPING CRITICAL, CREATIVE, AND DIALOGICAL THINKING

Learning Through Inquiry

Intended Learning Outcomes What students learn	Way of Learning Origins and theory	Common Methods What the teacher provides
Developing critical, creative, and dialogical thinking Improved thinking and reasoning processes	**Learning through inquiry** Logic, critical and creative thinking theory, classical philosophy	Question-driven inquiries Discussions

Is this learning that involves being aware of and improving one's thinking process? Does this involve criticizing information, evaluating arguments and evidence, or reasoning to arrive at conclusions? Does this learning involve creative thinking by actually producing unusual but relevant new ideas? Does it involve appreciating what other people think? These are learning outcomes that are well served by learning through inquiry.

An English teacher encourages critical thinking about a text by asking students to respond in writing to a question she poses. After ten minutes or so, students pass what they have written to another student, who seeks to identify what is powerful or interesting in what the student is reading on that paper. The papers continue to rotate, and eventually the instructor asks students to share what they regard as the most compelling ideas. Then she uses these ideas to build a class discussion involving further inquiry about the text.

Teachers want their students to be able to think. Although many teachers identify teaching students to think as one of the most important goals of instruction, they often lament that they don't have enough time to do a better job of it because there is so much to cover. Teaching is more than dispensing information, and learning is more than acquiring it. Students also need to develop the ability to sort through and make sense of the deluge of information they encounter, especially in this digital age of information overload. But what is the process of thinking, and why is it important that students be able to think? What is the type of thinking that is the focus of this way of learning?

The classic argument for teaching people to think is that clear thinking is necessary for effective citizenship in a democracy.[1] Thinking has also been seen as a liberating force, freeing the individual from the ignorance that characterizes prejudice and ethnocentrism, from narrow self-interest and small-mindedness. One of the main purposes of a liberal education is to free students from "their biases, stereotypes, distortions, illusions and misconceptions."[2] Paul and Elder, scholars in the field of critical thinking, remark that "thinking, left to itself, is biased, distorted, partial, uninformed, or downright prejudiced. Yet the quality of our life and that of what we produce, make, or build depends precisely on the quality of our thought. Shoddy thinking is costly, both in money and in quality of life."[3] Perhaps the most practical argument for teaching thinking is that the work increasingly required in organizations is intellectual, which is to say it is analytical and employs symbolic manipulation. Intellectual work requires an inquiring mind, an approach to learning that involves asking a lot of questions.

Critical thinking is usually high on the list of the stated outcomes of education at most colleges and universities. Although teaching critical thinking appears to be one of the main goals of higher education, many studies have indicated that students, unfortunately, are learning only at rote and shallow levels in many colleges and universities.[4] As Paul Ramsden summarizes, "It has been clear from numerous investigations that: many students are accomplished at complex routine skills . . . many have appropriated enormous amounts of detailed knowledge . . . many are able to pass examinations . . . but many are unable to show that they understand what they have learned when asked simple yet searching questions that test their grasp of the content. . . . Conceptual changes are 'relatively rare, fragile, and context-dependent occurrences.'"[5]

The development of thinking is an internal process and is the creation of a habit of learning.[6] It is not something that is taught once a week or mastered in one course but is in continual development throughout the college years.

We must clarify our use of the word *inquiry*, to provide more detail than we did in chapter 2. The term *inquiry* is commonly used in education today to refer to nearly any kind of teaching approach that is based on getting students involved in actively questioning what they are studying. For example, in *Teaching and Learning Through Inquiry*, Virginia Lee defines inquiry-guided learning as "an array of classroom practices that promote student learning through guided and, increasingly, independent investigation of complex questions and problems, often for which there is no single answer."[7] Although active, curiosity-enhancing learning is certainly a worthy goal, in this book we intentionally use the term *inquiry* to refer to a specific way of learning that uses questions to teach critical, creative, and dialogical thinking. That is our focus for this way of learning—facilitating thinking by asking questions. Consider the following example.

Mary Reda teaches English at the College of Staten Island (City University of New York). She uses various forms of discussion to teach students to think critically about a text or piece of writing, sometimes using class discussions, small discussions, journals, or starting class with quick writing responses. A few times each semester, when she wants to dig deep into a piece of writing like an Austen novel or a text that challenges her students' values, such as *The Awakening* by Kate Chopin, she will use a freewriting technique in which students engage in a conversation about the work through silent writing. For example, she might pose a specific question like, "Why does Morrison employ multiple narrators in *The Bluest Eye?*" and give students ten minutes to respond in writing. Or she may simply ask students to begin by examining their own unanswered questions about a text. Then she redistributes the papers among the students and asks them to mark what is powerful or interesting in the response in front of them and to respond to those ideas. After a few rounds of this, she writes on the board what the students think are rich or compelling ideas and begins a verbal discussion to interpret the text based on the students' questions. "The discussions take off incredibly quickly from there," says Mary. "Comments that are not very fruitful or appropriate get weeded out in the process, and the discussions we have are often much more complex and richer than those shaped around my questions about what students 'should know' about the text." Mary's role is to encourage students to look for connections among ideas and to use carefully placed follow-up questions to guide the discussion, such as "Where else do you see this happening in this text?" or "What is the effect of this narrative structure?" She will also ask questions such as, "Why might the author have chosen to use a metaphor here?" to introduce terminology or to keep the discussion focused on technical and interpretive aspects. "I want to respect the role of silence in the thinking process. And I've found not only does this process give a voice to the quiet students, but those who offer many, perhaps shallower, responses often talk less, think and listen more, and develop richer interpretations of the text."[8]

Thinking About Thinking

What is thinking? The random thoughts that pass through our heads as we shower or drive along the highway are called nondirected thinking, which is different from purposeful directed thinking. Directed thinking includes asking questions, analyzing arguments, identifying reasons, formulating hypotheses, seeking and weighing evidence, distinguishing facts from opinions, judging the credibility of sources, classifying data, making definitions, using analogies, making value judgments, and weighing alternatives. Directed thinking also involves certain dispositions or habits of mind, such as trying to be well informed, being open-minded, being willing to consider opposing viewpoints, respecting evidence, suspending judgment, tolerating ambiguity, being curious and skeptical, as well as revering the truth.[9] There are three main types of thinking that are developed in students through the use of inquiry: *critical thinking, creative thinking,* and *dialogical thinking.*

Critical thinking has been defined broadly as "judging the authenticity, worth or accuracy of something, such as a piece of information, a claim or assertion, or sources of data."[10] Critical thinking focuses on a justification, or set of reasons to support a conclusion.[11] A justification is usually set forth in an argument. The emphasis in critical thinking, whether in building an argument or in criticizing the arguments of others, is usually on analyzing the way evidence is used to support a point of view.

Creative thinking, on the other hand, is "thinking guided—indeed driven by—the desire to seek the original."[12] Instead of following rules, creative thinkers break them. Creative thinking usually results in creative products or services, inventions, or new processes. Creative outcomes stretch or break boundaries, but they are also well suited and relevant.[13]

Dialogical thinking involves appreciating and being able to evaluate different points of view at the same time. Some issues can be "settled within one frame of reference and with a definite set of logical moves," and they usually have a "right" answer.[14] Other matters, however, are not so easily settled and depend upon some defensible choice among alternative frames of reference, so that not only the evidence but the whole way of looking at the issue must be tested. Such matters usually have more than one arguable answer, and to deal with alternatives, one needs to enter into a dialogue with another thinker. Through dialogical thinking—a kind of role play of the thinking of others—we are able to enter empathetically into opposing arguments and viewpoints, thereby examining our own thinking and recognizing its strengths and weaknesses.

Some writers stress that the sharp distinctions among critical, creative, and dialogical thinking are inappropriate. These are overlapping constructs, but they are used to identify a particular emphasis in what are highly complex thinking processes. Various forms of thinking are complementary.[15] As one writer put it, "When reason fails, imagination saves you! When intuition fails, reason saves you!"[16] Although thinking is often complex and does at times contain overlapping aspects, we have identified these three areas as our focus for thinking about thinking. Although different types of thinking exist, the central strategy for cultivating thinking is inquiry: asking questions that make students become aware of and improve their own thinking.

Origins of Learning Through Inquiry

Unlike some of the other ways of learning in this book that have relatively recent origins, inquiry is rooted in classical antiquity. One of the great contributions of philosophers has been their effort to clarify, each for their own age, what is meant by thinking. Thinking did not mean the same thing to Aristotle, Bacon, Descartes, Locke, or Russell. Philosophy, as a way of thinking about thinking, preceded science by almost two thousand years, and many of the things writers today have to say about thinking—the difference between inductive and deductive reasoning, the procedures for examining syllogisms, and the nature of dialogue—go back to the classical philosophy of Plato and Aristotle.

The modern history of thinking began in the early twentieth century with the work of Bertrand Russell and Alfred North Whitehead, based on earlier work in the nineteenth century by mathematician George Boole. Goodwin Watson and Edward Glaser developed early tests of critical thinking. Studies of creativity, on the other hand, emerged somewhat later. One of the early studies of the so-called "men of genius" was produced by Galton in 1869, but the turning point for research on creativity was the 1950s with the work of Joy Guilford on the factors of human intelligence related to creativity and the work of Paul Torrance in making tests of creativity. A strong case for teaching by asking questions is made by Neil Postman and Charles Weingartner in *Teaching as a Subversive Activity.*[17]

Many college teachers are familiar with the concept of the Socratic method, as it is commonly called. Originating from Socrates, many associate this method with the practice of a teacher asking questions and calling on students to provide answers. However, the true purpose of Socratic questioning is not the simple act of asking questions, especially recitation questions, jokingly referred to by Postman and Weingartner as "guess-what-I'm-thinking" questions.[18] Questions with one right answer do not promote thinking. True Socratic questioning uses questions to challenge and expose errors in reasoning. Similarly, questions that support learning through inquiry are designed to get students thinking about their thinking process as much as about the content of the question.

What We Know About Learning Through Inquiry

As with other ways of learning, inquiry requires a particular set of behaviors for teachers and a specific role for students. In some ways, learning through inquiry poses special problems in its use because it emphasizes behaviors that are exactly the opposite of those found in the dominant lecture paradigm. It is hard for teachers to give up telling and for students to get beyond listening. Unfortunately, many college teachers want their students to engage in critical, creative, and dialogical thinking, but class time is focused on a one-way exchange of information. What could be worse for actually cultivating thinking skills than having to listen to a presentation that offers no chance to speak, make arguments, generate and test ideas, or see what others think? For the teaching of thinking to be effective, students should be able to practice thinking under the guidance of a skilled facilitator. Sharing some of what is known about thinking along the way can be helpful, but this is not done by a lecture on thinking skills but by describing and labeling what is happening when students are actually thinking. The facilitator, therefore, needs to understand thinking, develop expertise with the process, and actively engage students in thinking.

How is this done? Primarily by asking the right kind of questions to produce productive inquiry. As Paul reminds us, "It is not possible to be a good thinker and a poor questioner. Thinking is not driven by answers but, rather, by questions."[19] By emphasizing asking as opposed to telling, the facilitator systematically assaults typically passive classroom behavior—what Paulo Freire has called the "culture of silence."[20] For the facilitator this is often a challenge, and resistance is sometimes stiff because habits are hard to break, and thinking is usually hard work.

Is it really possible to teach people to ask questions and to become good (or at least better) thinkers? Isn't thinking just a matter of intelligence? Well, yes and no. As Nickerson, Perkins, and Smith point out, "Intelligence relates more to the 'raw power' of one's mental equipment. Raw power of intelligence is one thing, the skilled use of it is something else!"[21] Researchers have come to see that thinking involves other important elements as well: knowledge (the subject one is thinking about), operations (the steps and processes used), and dispositions (attitudes or habits of mind about thinking).[22] Effective thinkers must become aware of their own thinking, consider how their thinking matches up to certain standards or more sophisticated ways of thinking, and actively take measures to improve their thinking. If thinking is something that can be done well or poorly, efficiently or inefficiently, then one can learn to do it better. This self-reflection is called *metacognition*. The role of the teacher in inquiry is to help students develop the awareness—the metacognition—to improve their own thinking.

Critical Thinking

What is critical thinking? How does it occur and how do people learn to do it? Notice in this example how critical thinking is cultivated.

> Among the desired outcomes Greg Reihman sets for students in his introductory philosophy courses at Lehigh University, taught online and in the classroom, are the ability to analyze and evaluate the arguments made by various philosophers. To do this, many aspects of thinking need to be developed. These include being able to identify arguments "in the wild," that is, in texts where such arguments might not be presented very carefully; to reconstruct such arguments in a way that more precisely reveals their logical form; to identify the difference between various types of argument (inductive and deductive) and the meaning of key terms (*premise*, *assumption*, *conclusion*, *validity*, etc.); and to apply these terms to arguments the students have reconstructed from the original text. The process of learning to analyze arguments takes place in various stages as the course progresses. "It begins on the first day when I explain the role argumentation plays in supporting one's own views and the importance of trying to

understand the reasoning behind views one finds difficult to understand," says Greg. In his courses, students are encouraged to "be philosophical" in all their reading and in their discussions. "By this I mean that they are encouraged to pay attention to claims made, whether by the philosophers we read, by me, or by their classmates. I also reinforce the idea that, while it's okay to notice whether one agrees or disagrees with claims others make, it is more important to think carefully about what sort of justification is offered to support those claims." These ideas are put into practice early in the course by directing students to approach texts with specific prompts in mind. At first, such prompts are basic questions such as, What is the author's conclusion? What sort of arguments are provided in support of that conclusion? At first glance, does this argument seem persuasive to you? Having identified these aspects, Greg begins to dig deeper. "Walking through several of these arguments, I typically shoulder the burden of reconstructing several arguments from the first texts we read, but I do so in a way that involves the students, for example, by showing them a poorly restated claim and asking if it accurately captures what the author said, or by leaving out steps and asking them to see where the logical leap took place. When we finally get the argument into good form, we move on to study its validity and soundness." In subsequent lessons, students are given a new text and asked to produce these reconstructions, or parts of them, on their own and then check their work by talking with a peer in a live class or through a discussion board in an online class. Greg facilitates and offers commentary on these discussions, looking for ways to recast the language, clarify the logic, or supply missing steps as needed. Finally, students demonstrate their ability to identify, reconstruct, analyze, and evaluate arguments by writing short papers. "In this way, as the course progresses, students gain the ability to think critically about arguments and come to appreciate the need for precision and care in such matters."[23]

Teachers of critical thinking can employ the following questions to analyze the content of an in-class or online discussion:

What assertion is being made? Someone says or writes something, and someone else says, "Is that so?" Raymond Nickerson, author of *Reflections on Reasoning*, provides this definition: "An assertion is a statement that asserts (states positively) something to be true. It is a claim about reality."[24] What are we to make of assertions?

Is this assertion an opinion or a belief? An example of an opinion is, "Pepsi tastes better than Coke." A skilled teacher notes immediately that this is an opinion, a matter of taste, and that nothing will settle this dispute. A *belief*, on the other hand (used here as philosophers, not theologians, use the term), is different from an opinion because evidence can be called on to support a belief. If we rephrase the statement about soft drinks to read, "More people in Ohio prefer Pepsi to Coke," we now have a belief, and it is possible to gather evidence to support the belief. For assertions to be beliefs they need to be clear and explicit, to have some relation to a reality that evidence can support, and to be capable of being believed or disbelieved, depending on the evidence.

Can the belief be supported? Warranted statements have evidence, something to back them up. When a belief has a lot of good evidence to back it up, we can call it a factual statement. When the statement corresponds to a state of affairs, and there is good evidence for it, we are more inclined to believe it. That is why we call it a belief—a statement that we are convinced is the truth.

What is the argument? Critical thinkers use the word *argument* quite differently than the everyday conception of a verbal disagreement. "An argument is a sequence of assertions, some of which are premises and one of which is called a conclusion."[25] More simply, an argument is a chain of statements designed to support a conclusion. Nickerson suggests some points we ought to remember about arguments: they have a purpose (to convince); they can be strong or weak; they have parts; they can be taken apart, changed, and put back together; they can have steps missing; they can be simple or complex; and they can be evaluated.[26] A skilled teacher listens to a discussion and asks what kind of argument is being built. What is this person trying to prove?

What is the conclusion? The first element to look for in an argument is the last one, the conclusion. What is it we are supposed to believe? Usually some words serve as clues to finding the conclusion, such as, *thus, proves, therefore,* or *We can conclude that . . .* Descriptive conclusions are statements about the situation as it currently exists; prescriptive conclusions are statements about how the situation ought to be. For example, in a business class, the argument "This company is in poor financial health" is a descriptive conclusion. The argument "This company ought to downsize by three hundred workers" is a prescriptive conclusion. A skilled facilitator listens for conclusions, the part of the argument the maker of the argument wants you to believe.

What are the premises? A premise is simply a statement that provides evidence.[27] Premises are warranting statements used to support conclusions, usually several. To support the conclusion "This company is in poor financial health," we would look for statements that seem to be providing evidence about financial health, such as sales, gross revenues, profits, market share, and productivity. Premises contain the facts and figures of the evidence. Note, however, that premises are debatable. They can be questioned, and because the evidence is being assembled to support a conclusion, some perfectly good evidence that might support a different conclusion can be left out. Arguments, we need to remember, are designed to support conclusions.

What are the assumptions? Assumptions are statements that people already believe and are obvious, or they are statements no one has questioned. They may be used as evidence, and often are, without having been examined carefully. Sometimes assumptions are identified and labeled, and the clue is usually the wording, such as, "For the purposes of our argument, let's assume that . . ." Or assumptions may not be identified, so we have to find them and label them. Or even worse, assumptions may be missing completely, not having been identified at all, and yet the conclusion depends heavily on them. Teachers watch for assumptions because they are dangerous; they often operate as evidence and go unchallenged or unidentified.

The elements of critical thinking discussed here are easier to spot in writing, as in an excerpted text or online threaded discussion, where it is possible to go back to review text and analyze the statements. In a face-to-face discussion these elements can fly by fairly fast, and sometimes it is hard to tell what is going on. A skilled teacher using inquiry knows how to listen for the structure of the argument: its conclusion, premises, and assumptions. While students are expressing their ideas, the facilitator is silently asking, What is being sold here? What are the reasons offered for buying it? What is being assumed? A teacher using inquiry helps students see the assertions and assumptions in their thinking.

Types of Arguments

Arguments can be inductive or deductive. They can use metaphors, or they can take the form of a legal argument. Skilled facilitators also help students discover what kinds of arguments they are making and how to make them well.

Inductive Arguments

Inductive arguments are the easiest to understand and are probably most widely used in higher education. An inductive argument uses several pieces of evidence and draws a conclusion from that evidence. Edward Corbett, author of *The Elements of Reasoning*, offers Thomas Huxley's example of green apples to illustrate induction.[28] If you pick up a hard green apple and find it sour when you bite it, you form a hypothesis: Maybe hard green apples are sour. If you find several hard green apples are sour (a way of testing your hypothesis), you are ready to make a generalization (conclude) that hard green apples are usually sour. If you try to find hard green apples that are sweet (to counter your hypothesis), but you don't find any, then you are ready to conclude that all hard green apples are sour. Inductive arguments are the very foundation of most scientific research in the sciences and social sciences. The evidence in inductive arguments can be strong or weak depending on how it was gathered, how much of it was gathered, how it was analyzed, and what efforts were made to test the hypothesis or alternative hypotheses. Inductive arguments tend to pile up evidence, and a skilled teacher listens to see what is being tossed in the evidence pile and how deep the pile is. Is there enough of the right kind of evidence to support this particular conclusion? Inductive arguments use evidence to lead up to a conclusion.

Deductive Arguments

Deductive arguments work the other way around. They start from an assertion and work backward. To use the green apple example again, we start with the statement about hard green apples (which serves as a premise now) and reason toward a conclusion.[29] All hard green apples are sour. The apple you are offering me is hard and green. Therefore, this apple is sour. The conclusion has been reasoned from the content and arrangement of the premises. I do not have to taste the apple to know it will be sour; it is a logical conclusion. Logicians have elaborated a whole system of rules for the arrangement of deductive arguments, and these are useful, but even Aristotle, the originator of the syllogism (the form of the green apple argument discussed previously) recognized that this is a somewhat artificial construction. As a teacher, it is unlikely that you will see students building arguments in a discussion by hurling syllogisms at each other, but you may see students using pieces of a syllogism in their arguments, what Aristotle called an enthymeme. An enthymeme employs just one premise and a conclusion, the other premise being implied. For example:

Maria must be a happy student because she's smiling all the time.

The full syllogism would be

A student who smiles all the time is happy.
Maria is a student who smiles all the time.
Therefore, Maria must be a happy student.

The skilled teacher learns to spot these fragments of deductive arguments and knows how to raise questions to get students to think them through.

Analogies

Analogies are comparisons, and an argument that uses analogies trades on the similarities of the items being compared. For example, one might hear people say that being a good manager is like being a good parent. The comparison being made is between managing and parenting, and it is about the manager that conclusions are being drawn. The evidence in this case grows out of the similar characteristics, such as wisdom, experience, deep concern, and ability to guide. The analogy works to the extent that illuminating similarities are found, but the analogy breaks down (as all analogies will eventually) over crucial differences. The hierarchy implied in parenting, with its potential for paternalism or maternalism, may be seen as a serious enough difference to begin to spoil the analogy. The skilled teacher learns to spot the analogy in the argument and to tease out the similarities (which make it a good analogy) and the differences (which make it a weak analogy). Above all, the teacher knows that "an analogy never really proves anything . . . and can only be persuasive, never conclusive."[30]

Legal Arguments

Legal arguments employ the form used in a legal case, often referred to as the Toulmin system.[31] Stephen Toulmin, a twentieth-century British philosopher, published a book in 1958 titled *The Uses of Argument* in which he laid out a system of argument that prevails in the legal profession. Every legal case has a claim. A datum is a fact or reason that supports the claim. The datum needs backing, the supporting evidence needed to warrant the claim. The claim is usually not absolute, and it is possible, therefore, that one can take exception to the claim in the form of a rebuttal. The Toulmin system is interesting in that it deals with degrees of proof. As Corbett notes in describing the system, "The logic of the courtroom is that often cases are decided not by proven facts but by argued probabilities."[32] A skilled teacher will note when an argument has taken on a courtroom tone.

Building Blocks of Critical Thinking

Teachers who employ inquiry also look for the four important building blocks of critical thinking: definitions, type of language used, categories, and relationships among ideas.

Definitions

When people think, they think about something, and they usually use concepts to describe what they are thinking about. Naturally, concepts are learned, and people bring with them their own understanding of them. For a concept like dog, people will have a high degree of shared similarity, but their concept of leadership may be quite different, depending on their understanding and experience. A teacher can help students become clearer about the concepts they are talking about by helping them make definitions. Making definitions involves agreeing on words that represent adequately the phenomenon being described.

Language

Sometimes language is used metaphorically, as a poet would use it, full of image and emotion. At other times language needs to be used in a precise way, with as much direct correspondence as possible between the words being used and the reality being described. Language is the carrier of ideas, the vehicle of concepts, and the conveyer of meaning. Unfortunately, language is also often the source of misunderstanding and muddy thinking. Language can be slippery. Consider this humorous example provided by Nickerson: "Nothing is better than eternal happiness. A ham sandwich is better than nothing. Therefore, a ham sandwich is better than eternal happiness."[33]

Note how the word *nothing* changes in meaning from the first to the second premise, thus leading to the ludicrous conclusion. Critical thinkers are careful about how they use language, and skilled teachers are alert to how problems in language usage can derail a discussion.

Categories

Clear thinkers often have to put ideas into larger bundles called categories. This involves sorting out and classifying ideas, the what-goes-with-what task. The names of categories are not always known in advance, and sometimes they emerge from a list of similar things. A skilled teacher recognizes when a group needs to use categories and provides help to students in establishing and naming categories and then getting the particulars into the right category.

Relationships

Clear thinking also involves gaining clarity about the relationship of one idea to another or one category of ideas to another. Does one set of variables cause another so that it makes sense to think of causes and effects? Or is one set of factors simply correlated with another without a causal relationship? Is the relationship temporal or spatial, linear, circular, or spiral? Can the ideas be put into a matrix or a web? Often the participants in a discussion are too close to the material to see how it needs to be organized. A skilled teacher can point out the importance of trying to describe the relationships among the ideas being expressed and may make some suggestions the class can test. Sometimes it is useful to make diagrams to illustrate the relationships of concepts.

Logical Fallacies

Critical thinking also involves certain hazards. Scholars who write about critical thinking call these hazards logical fallacies. An experienced teacher knows these logical fallacies very well and can spot them quickly, identify them for students, and talk about them. This list of fallacies is not exhaustive, nor is an extensive discussion of them provided, but these are some of the things to anticipate and avoid.

Fallacies Involving People

- Ad hominem—attacking the person, name-calling. The Latin phrase meaning "to the person" suggests an attack on the credibility or trustworthiness of the person who supports a particular position.
- Ad populum—appealing to the people. The argument is shaped in such a way to appeal to the fears, prejudices, or emotional needs of the people involved.
- Association—credit or discredit by association, or testimonials. The argument is strengthened by associating it with the views of close friends or famous people or weakened by associating it with someone disreputable.

Fallacies and Outside Support

- Appeal to authority—using an expert. Increases the strength of the argument by associating it with the name or words of an authority.
- Appeal to tradition—justifying the present by the past. A case is made for the status quo by arguing that things have always been done in a certain way.
- Appeal to numbers—mass support. An effort is made to show that large numbers of people approve of or disapprove of a particular idea or position.

Fallacies Involving Language

- Stereotyping—using labels. Labels are used to cover the need for deeper explanation, such as "She's uncooperative" or "He's having a midlife crisis."
- Glittering generalities—using showy terms, fancy jargon, or clever phrases. They may sound good but usually cloud understanding.
- Equivocation—changing the meaning. Sometimes the meaning of a term is changed as a discussion proceeds, as with the word *nothing* in the ham sandwich example on p. 117.
- Begging the question—restating the conclusion. Sometimes evidence is not really evidence; it is just a restatement of the conclusion. (Not to be confused with inviting a question.)
- Red herring—changing the subject. Sometimes another issue is thrown in that takes the discussion off track. The term derives from an old folk custom in which a fish is dragged across a trail to mislead the pursuing hounds.

Fallacies and Frameworks

- False dilemma—setting up only two alternatives when in fact there may be several.
- Simple explanation—failure to admit rival causes or multiple causes.
- Confusing *should* and *is*—mistaking normative and descriptive statements by confusing what ought to be with what is.

Fallacies and Evidence

- Biased information gathering—seeking only data that support a position rather than examining all the evidence in an unbiased way.
- Selective use of evidence—using only data that support a position while contrary evidence is ignored or dismissed.
- Irrelevant evidence—bringing in extraneous information that has nothing to do with the point being argued.

Fallacies and Conclusions

- Overgeneralizing—concluding too much from limited evidence.
- Hasty closure—jumping to conclusions. Lacking sufficient evidence, some conclusions may need to be regarded as tentative, serving best as hypotheses for further exploration.

- Seeking the perfect solution—rejecting partial solutions. Some solution may be better than no solution at all, even though it addresses only part of the issue or may work less than perfectly.
- Contrary conclusions—rejecting the conclusion of a poorly made case. Just because an argument is poorly made does not mean the conclusion is not true; it may just need better support.

Although critical thinking may appear to be somewhat complicated, the essence of the process is really quite simple. In plain language, critical thinking is the process used to determine what case is being made and how it is being supported. Students become better critical thinkers by becoming aware of and avoiding fallacies in their thinking. Critical thinking is learned by having opportunities to practice it under expert guidance.

Creative Thinking

What is creative thinking, and how does it fit within the larger concept of creativity? What does the following example tell us about the nature of creativity?

Marvin Bartel taught art at Goshen College for over thirty years, and one of his goals was to help students develop creative thinking habits. In one assignment he asked students to transform concepts from one abstract realm to another by representing nonvisual relationships with visual relationships. With the assurance they did not have to share anything personal, students were asked to analyze their family relationships and represent these relationships without using images or subject matter. Students could use shape, size, line, color, and texture to create a two-dimensional composition using any color media. Part of this process included student experimentation. "One way that artists come up with ideas is to try two or more preliminary ideas, compare them and try to improve the best one," says Marvin. To encourage creativity, students engage in comparisons or experiments by trying the same thing two or more times and comparing similar but different iterations of the same thing. Through these experiments students explore what effects they saw when they repeated a color or a line while changing its size, shape, intensity, or value (tone). The comparisons helped students find out which way works best to show what they are after. During this assignment, Marvin asked questions such as, How might you produce the simultaneous effects of harmony and dissonance in a design? What effects do you want viewers to notice about your composition? What aspects of your composition do you want to keep less apparent, but still present? When stuck, students would often ask to see an example, but Marvin intentionally avoided the use of examples. "I would explain that once you see an example it is like a song that is stuck in your head while you are trying to write a new song." An important creative teaching strategy is to avoid proposing any preconceived answer or hypothesis that might hinder student-initiated experiments and discoveries. "Students sometimes think they have to wait for inspiration. They do not realize that there are visual experiments and comparisons that will coach their subconscious creativity. I reassure them that in my experience, many ideas grow out of the working process itself."[34]

Theories of Creativity

Psychologist Mihaly Csikszentmihalyi, author of *Creativity: Flow and the Psychology of Discovery and Invention*, believes the word *creative* applies to people who express unusual thoughts, who are interesting or stimulating, who experience the world in novel and original ways, whose perceptions are fresh, whose judgments are insightful, and who may make important discoveries only they know about, individuals who, like Leonardo, Edison, Picasso, or Einstein, have changed our culture in some important respect.[35] The definition that grows out of Csikszentmihalyi's interview research is: "Creativity is any act, idea, or product that changes an existing domain, or that transforms an existing domain into a new one."[36]

Where does creativity come from, and how does it work? There are numerous theories about creativity, beginning with the ancient Hebrew belief in divine inspiration and the Greek concept of the Muses, goddesses of song, poetry, the arts, and the sciences.

The Genius Theory

Among the earliest studies of creativity are Galton's studies of "men of genius."[37] The idea of inherited genius dominated theories of creativity for almost a century, so much so that many people still think of creativity as a matter of genius, that is, having it or not. Robert Weisberg argues that "the genius view is in fact a myth," a perspective that assumes "that truly creative acts come about when great individuals, on their own and independently of what has been done before, produce some great achievement in a burst of inspiration." Individuals who produce creative works may not be just the same as ordinary individuals, "but the thinking processes are not different," argues Weisberg.[38] In other words, the opportunity to do creative thinking is initially open to all; what matters is how one builds on the past yet goes beyond it.

The Association Theory

Another theory stresses associations, putting together ideas in a systematic way, especially in ways that ordinarily might not occur. The associative theory of creativity is the basis of a test developed by Mednick called the Remote Associations Test. One section of the test provides three seemingly unrelated words and asks the respondent to find a fourth word related to all three. Thus, for *out, dog, cat,* an associated word would be *house.* According to this theory, creativity involves the way associations are made, the number of associations that can be made, the selection of appropriate associations, and the organization of these in an associative hierarchy.[39]

Divergent-Thinking Theory

J. P. Guilford was interested in testing for factors involved with creativity and differentiating them from the characteristics usually used to describe intelligence.[40] He named and described these factors as fluency (generation of large numbers of divergent ideas), flexibility (spontaneity in changing one's mental set), originality (uniqueness of an idea compared to typical responses of another), and elaboration (ability to flesh out the details). Guilford's categories were developed into a full-blown theory of creativity by E. Paul Torrence, who also produced a series of tests of creativity that have become a widely used measurement device for creativity.[41] Guilford's theory and Torrence's tests provide a standard list of the kinds of skills, abilities, and habits of mind associated with creative thinking.[42]

The Creative Process

The idea that the creative process involves certain steps can be traced to Wallas in 1945, who described them simply as preparation, incubation, illumination, and elaboration.[43] The research study by Csikszentmihalyi sets forth a five-stage process based on what the interview subjects described about their work: preparation, incubation, insight, evaluation, and elaboration.[44] Csikszentmihalyi's position supports the old adage "Creativity favors the well-prepared mind."

Cultivating Creative Thinking

As with critical thinking, the cultivation of creative thinking takes place best when people are given the opportunity to think creatively under guidance.

Although there is a growing belief that creativity can be developed, often too much is promised by brief exercises in so-called "out-of-the-box thinking." Creativity is a complex matter and not something that can be established in an ongoing way through a few creativity workshops or webinars.

Based on what is known about creativity, teachers should focus on the following:

- Preparation—spending more time on nurturing the prepared mind in the subject matter field where creativity is desired, recognizing that this nurturing process is an essential part of creativity
- Acquaintance—letting participants know about and experience the components of creative thinking, particularly fluency, flexibility, originality, and elaboration
- Concrete projects—having participants work on concrete projects potentially useful to an individual or organization

The key to cultivating creative thinking is the same as for critical thinking—asking questions. Although critical and creative thinking are quite different, employing different forms of inquiry, they are both learned by asking questions to help students become aware of their perceptions and insights and to help students ask their own questions.

Dialogical Thinking

Critical thinking requires carefully reasoned steps moving systematically toward a well-informed resolution. Creative thinking involves long preparation, bursts of insight, an ability to see things in a new way, and the persistence to elaborate. A third type of thinking, dialogical thinking, is necessary to reach a better understanding when people disagree.

People who care deeply about thinking are concerned that thinking skills can be misused. Critical thinking, in particular, can be used for selfish purposes by those who are good at it. In Plato's time in ancient Athens, the Sophists taught young citizens the social skill of how to get along in law courts and other public forums, that is, how to reason well and get the better of the argument. This use of critical thinking to achieve one's own purposes carries a name with ancient roots: sophistry.

Egocentric and Fair-Minded Thinkers

Richard Paul, one of the leaders of the critical thinking movement in the United States, over many years provided interesting descriptions of the human tendency toward egocentric thinking. "We all have a side of us willing to distort, falsify, twist and misrepresent." Paul suggests that "our egocentric side never ceases to catalogue experiences in accord with its common and idiosyncratic fears, desires, prejudices, stereotypes, hopes, dreams, and assorted irrational drives."[45] The corrective to this egocentric tendency is to make conscious efforts to understand how other people think.

Fair-minded thinkers, on the other hand, work hard to be intellectually humble while treating all viewpoints fairly. Fair-minded thinkers are dialogical thinkers. Dialogical thinking involves dialogue or extended exchange between different points of view or frames of reference. According to Paul, "Dialogue becomes dialectical when ideas or reasonings come into conflict with each other and we need to assess their various strengths and weaknesses."[46] Surely there is a need today to help students understand another's point of view.

Encouraging Dialogical Thinking

The essence of dialogical thinking is truly experiencing the inner logic of alternative viewpoints. At a minimum, this means being able to present sympathetically more than one side of an issue. This sympathetic presentation can be achieved by role-playing the thinking of another. What would he or she say? How would he or she make the argument? What issues would receive the highest priority? The challenge is to become willing to enter sympathetically into opposing points of view and to recognize weaknesses in one's own point of view. The goal is discovery, not victory. To do this, participants learn to argue for and against opposing views and to critique their own views as well as the viewpoints of others. Furthermore, it becomes important in dialogical thinking to let emotion resurface as an important component of, and perhaps a deterrent to, thinking and to analyze the role it is playing. Dialogical thinking is especially well suited to ethical issues, where matters of good or bad or right or wrong, are at stake. Ethical issues call for inner dialogue as well as dialogue with others. The purpose is to get students to think across points of view, whether based on culture, peer group, religion, discipline, points in time, or emotional state. Consider the following example:

> Laura Heymann teaches dialogical thinking in her first-year torts class at the College of William & Mary's Marshall-Wythe School of Law. Dialogical thinking is part of nearly all law instruction, as thinking like a lawyer often involves being able to see multiple sides of an argument. Laura

teaches using what is commonly called the *Socratic Method* but is careful about staying true to the essence of this method. "The Socratic method should not be about simply asking for factual answers. Rather, in its best form, it pushes students to construct arguments for a particular point of view and then pushes them to consider the implications of those arguments by considering their application to other fact patterns," says Laura. In one example, Laura and her students discuss a case in which an investigative news reporter posed as a patient to expose an eye clinic's practice of recommending unnecessary surgery. After the report aired, the clinic sued for trespass, claiming that it never would have let the reporter on the premises had it known of his true intent. Students are asked to analyze this case from both sides. What was the reporter's argument? What was the clinic's case? After discussing the court's conclusion that the reporter did not commit trespass, Laura then asks the students to apply this ruling to other scenarios. What would be the result for a restaurant critic who conceals his identity? An individual scoping out his competitor's business by pretending to be a customer? Predicting the results in these cases requires a sense of the principles that guided the court's decision in the original case and testing those intuitions against hypothetical situations. "The ultimate goal in all of these exercises is not simply to get the students to provide thoughtful answers, it's to get them to anticipate what the questions will be, such that they will become skilled in vetting potential solutions on their own." Laura uses various inquiry methods throughout her classes. In some instances, she asks students to play the role of counsel on each side of a case. She or another student takes the role of judge, probing each side with questions and pushing students to identify the weaknesses in the other side's arguments. "Above all, I try very hard to emphasize that the process is what's important, and that trying out arguments that ultimately don't stand up is perfectly okay. It's very important to me that students don't feel intimidated or embarrassed, and I think that a professor's response to misguided arguments must be careful and thoughtful. The goal of Socratic dialogue is to help students think through issues by modeling the kinds of questions that need to be asked, not by simply providing answers."[47]

What does the teacher do in a discussion where the goal is dialogical thinking? Perhaps the teacher has now met the most difficult challenge of all: to help students engage in a true Socratic dialogue not only with the teacher but with each other. Richard Paul suggests the teacher's role in this kind of Socratic inquiry is to keep raising "root questions and root ideas."[48] Noting four types of root questions that can be asked of all beliefs, Paul provides a useful framework, condensed as follows:

- *Origins.* How did you come to think this? Can you remember the circumstances in which you formed this belief?
- *Support.* Why do you believe this? Do you have any evidence for this? What are some of the reasons people believe this? In believing this, are you assuming that such and such is true? Do you think that is a sound assumption?
- *Conflicting thoughts.* Some people might object to your position by saying . . . How would you answer them? What do you think of this contrasting view? How would you answer the objection that . . . ?
- *Implications and consequences.* What are the practical consequences of believing this? What would we have to do to put it into action? What follows from the view that . . . ? Wouldn't we also have to believe . . . in order to be consistent? Are you implying that . . . ?[49]

Such discussions do not move forward in a linear way from question to question. Paul suggests more of a "criss-crossing, back-and-forth effect."[50] Another writer on dialogical thinking, Matthew Lipman, calls it thinking in community and likens it more to walking, "where you move forward by constantly throwing yourself off balance. When you walk, you never have both feet solidly on the ground at the same time. Each step forward makes a further step forward possible; in a dialogue, each argument evokes a counter argument that pushes itself beyond the other and pushes the other beyond itself."[51]

How the Teacher Facilitates Inquiry

As we have demonstrated, different kinds of thinking exist, and to teach thinking, what the teacher does will vary depending on what kind of thinking processes are desired. The teacher first needs to ask: What kind of thinking is this? What are the intended outcomes of this thinking process—critical analysis of assertions, creative new ideas, or better understanding of different points of view? Where is the thinking going, and what kinds of thinking skills are being cultivated through the activities being used? To facilitate learning through inquiry effectively, the teacher needs to do the following:

Understand the Thinking Process

The teacher needs to know about thinking processes—the elements, concepts, rules, and fallacies—and should be able to use that knowledge to guide inquiry. The teacher of inquiry is on the alert for problems in the discussion and keeps in mind as much as possible all the points where thinking gets off track and uses knowledge of the thinking process to craft the discussion. An effective teacher also models the thinking process for students.

Use Questions Strategically

Having clearly determined the type of thinking desired and the common components of that type of thinking, the teacher is best served by returning to the standard technique for any form of inquiry: asking the right questions and getting participants to do the same. But what are the right questions, and of all the questions that could be asked, how does the facilitator select the best ones? Drawing on the work of James Dillon, author of *The Practice of Questioning*, and Steven Brookfield and Steven Preskill, authors of *Discussion as a Way of Teaching*, we offer these guidelines[52]:

- *Avoid recitation.* Distinguish between inquiry and recitation. Recitation usually involves asking a question that has a right or wrong answer. Nothing will shut down genuine inquiry like recitation.

- *Choose questions carefully.* Focus on the goal of the question. What will people learn from the inquiry, and how will a particular question move them toward that understanding?

- *Anticipate answers.* Project likely answers and what to do with them. Reexamine questions. Ask how the question worked. Would another question have been better?

- *Look for assumptions.* What are the assumptions behind a question? Assumptions force certain kinds of responses.

- *Avoid dichotomous questions.* Questions that allow two alternatives, sometimes called either/or questions, will impede inquiry. These questions can be rephrased, for example, "Some people think X, but others think Y; what do you think?"

- *Use open questions.* Open questions provide for a wide range of responses.

- *Use narrative questions.* Some questions invite a narrative response as opposed to a direct response. For example, "Where were you last Thursday?" invites a direct response, as opposed to, "Can you tell us what happened last Thursday?"

- *Phrase questions carefully.* Questions will get different responses depending on the wording and ordering of terms.

Ask Meaningful Questions

Questions also have answers, but answers are not by definition something said in response to a question. Instead, it is better to think of responses to questions. Some questions get a nonresponse. Other questions get a nonanswer response. Therefore, in an inquiry it is best not to look for answers but to look for useful and honest responses that add to the discussion. What one hopes for are responses that enrich or elevate the dialogue, including producing additional questions. Teachers look for responses that provide valuable information, definitions and redefinitions, clarifications, ground rules for evidence, identified values, workable hypotheses, creative insights, other viewpoints, and tentative conclusions.

Effective teachers begin to collect basic questions that work in a particular subject or class. A repertoire of basic questions can be useful when a teacher is stumped about what to ask next and can be especially useful in taking an inquiry in a new direction. The following examples of basic questions by type are taken from Brookfield and Preskill.[53] These can get a teacher started and keep a discussion going.

- Questions that ask for more evidence—How do you know that? What does the author say that supports your argument?
- Questions that ask for clarification—Can you put that another way? What do you mean by that? What's an example of what you're talking about?
- Open questions—What does the author mean by this? Why do you think X is the case?
- Linking or extension questions—Is there any connection between what you just said and what X said a moment ago? Does your idea challenge or support what others are saying?
- Hypothetical questions—How might things have been different if X didn't happen?
- Cause-and-effect questions—What might be the likely effect of X?
- Summary and synthesis questions—What are one or two important ideas that emerged from this discussion? What remains unresolved about this topic? What do you understand better as a result of today's discussion?

Teachers also want students to generate their own questions. Students should be asked to practice generating good questions until they have developed the habit of doing so themselves.

Create a Safe Environment

The inquiry process depends not only on carefully constructed and well-formulated questions but also on a climate where students are encouraged and motivated to share their ideas. A safe environment must be created where participants can learn and practice the process of thinking without fear of appearing foolish or being judged for their comments. Especially for students who represent a historically marginalized population, international students, or those with a minority opinion in a class, a supportive class climate can overcome barriers to help students feel their ideas are respected and valued. There is nothing worse than mustering up the nerve to speak up in class or posting a brave viewpoint online only to have your question or thought ridiculed or belittled.

The attitude of the teacher and the presentation and tone of the way questions are expressed will greatly influence the way individuals respond. The teacher should strive to create an atmosphere where thinking can actually take place by listening to participants actively, appreciating different viewpoints, encouraging open discussion, promoting participation, accepting unusual ideas, permitting mistakes, allowing time for participants to think, building their confidence, and truly valuing what they have to say. Writing ideas on paper or talking in pairs are helpful ways for students to first work through their initial thoughts before sharing them with the class. For courses where sensitive topics will be discussed regularly, it is helpful to develop ground rules for discussion with the students, for example, strive to let all voices be heard equally, focus on understanding before responding, acknowledge that disagreement is healthy and part of learning, keep disagreements focused on ideas and not people, speak up when something feels offensive and use it as a teachable moment, and search for value in all ideas.

Should every student participate equally in the discussion, or is it acceptable to let those who are most willing and comfortable with sharing their ideas take the lead? There is value in hearing multiple perspectives in a discussion, and often the teacher can use techniques such as student response blogs, dyads, or small groups to allow all students to voice their opinions. When the whole class is involved, especially when the class is larger than fifteen students, it may not be necessary for all students to speak, and it is important to recognize that some students are simply uncomfortable with speaking up in class. Because the purpose of inquiry is to challenge each student's thinking, some level of discomfort may be natural and even necessary. Setting the right climate helps students know they will not be penalized or embarrassed for sharing their thoughts or for remaining silent. The goal is 100 percent engagement in thinking, not 100 percent speaking. Sometimes teachers may need to work with individual students to come up with appropriate and comfortable ways of showing their involvement.

Actively Manage and Facilitate the Discussion

In addition to setting the climate and selecting questions, the teacher must be an active manager of the discussion. The teacher paraphrases, reflects back an idea, asks for a clarification, seeks agreement or disagreement among the participants, asks for another viewpoint, suggests what people seem to be agreeing or disagreeing about, and above all raises more questions. In *Teaching as a Subversive Activity,* Postman and Weingartner suggest that teachers who manage a successful inquiry are reluctant to accept a single statement as an answer to a question; they encourage student-to-student interaction, they rarely summarize conclusions, and they usually let the lesson develop from the students' responses to a problem that has been posed.[54] The teacher, therefore, walks a fine line between directing the discussion and letting it flow. A good analogy for this comes from George Collison and colleagues, who compare discussion facilitation to the art of making popcorn: jump in too early and many kernels, or ideas, do not get their chance to emerge. But jump in too late and students might feel the frustration of being led down an unproductive path (and with the unpleasant smell of burned popcorn).[55]

Inquiry also depends on the flow and sequencing of questions in the discussion, that is, the pace at which questions are asked, the wait time for answers, and the time between questions. Teachers tend to move too quickly during inquiry and in their impatience do not provide enough time for participants to think. It is often recommended that teachers wait at least three to five seconds after asking a question before speaking again, longer if the question is complex and challenging. In fact, Brookfield argues that silence in the classroom should be welcome and is an important aspect of developing thinking. In that silence teachers can ask students to spend some time reflecting on the process and to write down their thoughts. If thinking is as complex and difficult as it has been described to be, it will surely take time, even under expert guidance, to do it. Effective teachers work hard at framing and pacing questions, listening to responses, and identifying and summarizing valuable comments to develop a discussion that has direction, momentum, and outcomes.

Because discussions in written form have a permanent record, and in a sense make the thinking process visible, teaching thinking through an online asynchronous medium has been the basis of much fruitful study of the process of inquiry. Over the past decade Canadian scholars have developed a model for critical thinking in online courses based on John Dewey's Practical Inquiry Model. Their Community of Inquiry model proposes four stages for the development of thinking skills: triggering events, exploration, integration, and resolution.[56] Others have described online discussions as having two main phases: sharpening the focus and deepening the dialogue.[57] Recognizing these phases, effective teachers focus first on setting up the right issues, texts, or triggering events. During the main phase of exploration, or sharpening the focus, the teacher asks questions that help students identify direction, sort ideas for relevance, and focus on key points. This is where much questioning takes place over the course of days or even weeks. The teacher also needs to deepen the dialogue by helping students question all aspects of the topic, make connections, and honor multiple perspectives in the hope of bringing about integration and a tentative resolution of the topic at hand. In this way, the online teacher actively manages and furthers the flow of discussion.

Whether online, in writing, or in person, teachers should take a neutral tone in their responses to student comments. Oddly enough, the positive reinforcement used in behavioral learning (discussed in chapter 4) can become disruptive with inquiry. As soon as the teacher says, "Yes, you're right," or "Great idea," that signals students that they do not need to think about the topic any further. Neutral facilitation responses and follow-up questions keep students thinking.

A good inquiry centers on debatable issues and goes somewhere. An effective facilitator knows what questions to use to launch the discussion, motivates all students to be involved, knows when and how to change course, and is comfortable traveling toward an undetermined destination.

Assessing Learning Through Inquiry

As with other ways of learning, it is fundamental that teachers articulate their goals as a basis for assessing learning. Is the goal to get better at evaluating the pros and cons of an issue, to argue a case from a different viewpoint, or simply to recognize various sources of bias? Each of these implies different aspects of thinking, and their articulation should help the instructor determine how to assess each student's progress.

Although the teacher may eventually want to evaluate the quality of thinking through a form of summative assessment, the focus of learning through inquiry is more often on the process, making formative assessment and participation the more important means of evaluation. Because thinking is best carried out in a safe atmosphere where trial and error is encouraged and making mistakes is accepted, grading based on the quality of what students say in a discussion can be counterproductive. How can students try out new ideas and play devil's advocate if they have to worry about how peers and the teacher judge what they say in class?[58] Assessing learning through inquiry, therefore, often takes the form of making inferences about the quality of participation—active listening, insightful questioning, and intelligent contributions to the discussion. In the classroom, this is usually easy to observe. In an online discussion, this is often measured through a number of thoughtful contributions posted during the current week's discussion.

Teachers will likely rely on formative assessment for gaining feedback on the process of inquiry. Classroom assessment techniques (CATs) can be extremely useful for monitoring the progress of student thinking. Angelo and Cross, the creators of an entire book of CATs, have listed a few techniques in particular that can be used to assess critical thinking skills: categorization grids, pro and con grids, content/form/function outlines, and analytic memos, among others.[59] Such methods can be used prior to and after discussions to let the teacher know how students are progressing in their thinking processes. Such feedback can help teachers assess their own progress, choose new or different materials, and redirect questioning patterns. CATs are also a means of self-evaluation for students, helping them to monitor and improve their own thinking.

Summative measures of critical, creative, and dialogical thinking often involve careful observations of students' thinking processes in discussions, but written assessments are also important, such as papers, presentations, or creative works. Although this chapter focuses on live discussions as the main method of inquiry, questions can also be used to structure written assignments. What better way to assess thinking than to define a controversial issue, ask provocative questions, and evaluate student responses? Students can also be asked to analyze their own thinking as presented in their responses. Rubrics can be very useful tools when the end product is a paper, presentation, debate, or creative work. Many examples of well-developed critical thinking rubrics can be found online.[60] Because thinking is based on development, grading drafts and revisions of assignments can help the instructor and the student see evidence of progress.

Useful Technologies for Learning Through Inquiry

Discussions driven by inquiry do not happen only in classrooms. Online courses, blended or hybrid courses, and even courses delivered primarily on campus may use online asynchronous discussions in which questions and comments are posted in a threaded format to indicate who is responding to whom. Students participate when they are available, allowing an inquiry to occur over the course of a week or few days rather than in one short portion of a class period. These types of discussions are becoming more common and are a natural fit for teaching thinking. In fact, some argue that written online asynchronous discussions are the ideal means for developing reflective and critical thought.[61] Scholars like Garrison and Vaughan are exploring what type of thinking is best suited for what type of discussion medium.[62] They point out that online discussions allow for reflecting before contributing, unlike a live or classroom discussion where all too often reflection happens after contributing to the group. Unlike a live classroom setting, students and instructors have all the time they need to think through a response, find supporting evidence, and properly articulate their thoughts before they speak up.

In an online discussion, teachers take on many of the same facilitation roles as in the classroom, but the tasks are slightly different. Online, the teacher posts triggering questions to start discussions, posts follow-up comments and questions, redirects thinking that gets off track, summarizes posts, calls attention to insightful student posts, chooses when and how to respond to individual student posts, keeps up with the pace set by the group, and wraps up the discussion. The teacher's role is to "clarify and extend the thinking of other people."[63] Teachers can adopt different voices and tones in their postings to elicit different types of responses and additional thinking among students. For example, the role of a nurturing reflective guide takes on a different purpose than that of a neutral mediator. But the essence goes back to questioning. According to Trisha Bender, "The instructor always needs to keep in mind that when facilitating online discussion, asking the right question is almost always more important than giving the right answer."[64]

Final Thoughts

Developing thinking skills takes time. Because the development of thinking is the creation of a habit of thinking, critical, creative, and dialogical thinking should be part of nearly every class in colleges and universities. Students need to be informed of the purpose of inquiry and learn to get better at thinking under expert guidance over time. Likewise, a teacher cannot just do inquiry once and expect it to be successful. It takes practice.

A teacher wants to facilitate a stimulating discussion each time this way of learning is used, but the longer-range goal is to model and teach habits of inquiry, gradually giving the teacher's job over to the students, who themselves get better and better at asking the right questions and providing insightful responses. Asking questions usually spreads once people learn how to do it effectively. One might say that college graduates who can truly ask questions can go on to learn anything they want or need to know in life.

For the teacher, facilitating inquiry may feel like making students do all the work, and some students feel the same. Students accustomed to taking a more passive role in the classroom sometimes feel shortchanged or frustrated by inquiry. Although learning through inquiry is a challenging and engaging way of learning for students and teachers alike, it can't be neglected or dismissed. What good, after all, is a college graduate who can't think? Inquiry can be unpredictable and may never go quite as planned, but the adventure of it can be tremendously rewarding. As Brookfield and Preskill state, they use discussions "because it's so enjoyable and exciting. Unpredictable and risky, it is the pedagogical and educational equivalent of scaling a mountain or shooting dangerous rapids."[65]

Points to Remember

Teachers who want to use learning through inquiry effectively should do the following:

- ✓ Know about the thinking process—the elements, rules, and fallacies—and use that knowledge to guide inquiry.
- ✓ Provide opportunities for students to actually do thinking.
- ✓ Create a safe environment to practice thinking, setting ground rules if necessary.
- ✓ Use questions strategically and avoid recitation.
- ✓ Allow students time to think during inquiry.
- ✓ Ask meaningful open-ended questions and anticipate possible responses.
- ✓ Actively manage and facilitate the discussion, keeping students on track while encouraging multiple perspectives.
- ✓ Use formative assessment methods to make student thinking visible and observable.
- ✓ When necessary, use summative assessment to measure reflective thinking in a way that does not interfere with experimentation and creativity.

Notes

1. Matthew Lipman, "Some Thoughts on the Foundations of Reflective Education," in *Teaching Thinking Skills: Theory and Practice*, ed. Joan Baron and Robert Sternberg (New York: W. H. Freeman, 1987), 153.

2. Richard Paul, "Dialogical Thinking: Critical Thoughts Essential to the Acquisition of Rational Knowledge and Passions," in *Teaching Thinking Skills: Theory and Practice*, ed. Joan Baron and Robert Sternberg (New York: W. H. Freeman, 1987), 139.

3. Richard Paul and Linda Elder, *Critical Thinking: Tools for Taking Charge of Your Learning and Your Life* (Upper Saddle River, NJ: Pearson Prentice Hall, 2006), xxii.

4. For examples of shallow learning in higher education, see R. F. Gunstone and R. T. White, "Understanding Gravity," *Science Education* 65 (1981): 291–99; R. T. White, "Implications of Recent Research on Learning for Curriculum and Assessment," *Journal of Curriculum Studies* 24 (1992): 153–64; J. Handelsman et al., "Scientific Teaching," *Science* 304 (2004): 521–22.

5. Paul Ramsden, *Learning to Teach in Higher Education* (London: Routledge, 1992), 92.

6. Michael Scriven and Richard Paul, "Defining Critical Thinking," The Critical Thinking Community, accessed April 24, 2010, http://www.criticalthinking.org/aboutCT/define_critical_thinking.cfm.

7. Virginia S. Lee, *Teaching and Learning Through Inquiry* (Sterling, VA: Stylus, 2004), 9.

8. Thanks to Mary Reda, PhD, Associate Professor of English at the College of Staten Island (City University of New York), for granting permission to use her example. E-mail message to author, January 26, 2012.

9. Robert Ennis, "A Taxonomy of Critical Thinking Dispositions and Abilities," in *Teaching Thinking Skills: Theory and Practice*, ed. Joan Baron and Robert Sternberg (New York: W. H. Freeman, 1987), 12–15.

10. Berry Beyer, *Practical Strategies for the Teaching of Thinking* (Hillsdale, NJ: Erlbaum, 1985), 19.

11. Joanne Kurfiss, *Critical Thinking* (Washington, DC: Association of the Study of Higher Education, 1988), 2.

12. Beyer, *Practical Strategies*, 33.

13. Ibid., 27.

14. Paul, "Dialogical Thinking," 128.

15. Robert J. Marzano et al., *Dimensions of Thinking* (Alexandria, VA: Association for Supervision and Curriculum Development, 1988), 17, 28.

16. Loren Crane, "Unlocking the Brain's Two Powerful Learning Systems," *Human Intelligence Newsletter* 4, no. 4 (1983): 7, quoted in Barry Beyer, *Practical Strategies*, 36.

17. Goodwin Watson and Edward M. Glaser, *Watson-Glaser Critical Thinking Appraisal Manual* (Psychological Corporation, 1964); Francis Galton, *Hereditary Genius* (London: Macmillan, 1892); Joy Paul Guilford, *Creative Talents* (Buffalo, NY: Bearly Limited, 1986); E. Paul Torrence, *Why Fly* (Norwood, NJ: Ablex, 1995);

Neil Postman and Charles Weingartner, *Teaching as a Subversive Activity* (New York: Delacorte Press, 1989).

18. Postman and Weingartner, *Teaching as a Subversive Activity*, 20.

19. Paul, "Dialogical Thinking," 118.

20. Paulo Freire, *Pedagogy of the Oppressed* (New York: Continuum, 1993), 12, 69, 87.

21. Raymond Nickerson, David Perkins, and Edward E. Smith, *The Teaching of Thinking* (Hillsdale, NJ: Erlbaum, 1985), 44.

22. Beyer, *Practical Strategies*, 20, 25.

23. Thanks to Greg Reihman, PhD, Adjunct Professor of Philosophy and Director of Faculty Development at Lehigh University, for granting permission to use his example. E-mail message to author, February 14, 2012.

24. Nickerson, *Reflections on Reasoning*, (Hillsdale, NJ: Earlbaum, 1986), 35.

25. Ibid., 68.

26. Ibid., 69.

27. Ibid., 36.

28. Edward Corbett, *The Elements of Reasoning* (New York: Macmillan, 1991), 11–46.

29. Ibid., 23–26.

30. Ibid., 23.

31. Ibid., 42–45.

32. Ibid., 45.

33. Nickerson, *Reflections on Reasoning*, 4.

34. Thanks to Marvin Bartel, PhD, Professor Emeritus of Art at Goshen College, for granting permission to use his example. E-mail message to author, January 24, 2012.

35. Mihaly Csikszentmihalyi, *Creativity: Flow and the Psychology of Discovery and Invention* (New York: HarperCollins, 1996), 25–26.

36. Csikszentmihalyi, *Creativity*, 26.

37. Robert Weisberg, *Creativity: Beyond the Myth of Genius* (New York: W. H. Freeman, 1993), 246.

38. Ibid.

39. John Baer, *Creativity and Divergent Thinking: A Task-Specific Approach* (Hillsdale, NJ: Erlbaum, 1993).

40. Guilford, *Creative Talents*, 41–50.

41. E. P. Torrence and J. Presbury, "The Criteria of Success Used in 242 Recent Experimental Studies of Creativity," *Creative Child and Adult Quarterly* 9, no. 4 (1984): 238–43.

42. Baer, *Creativity and Divergent Thinking*, 15–16.

43. Graham Wallas, *The Art of Thought* (London: Watts, 1945).

44. Csikszentmihalyi, chap. 4, "The Work of Creativity," in *Creativity*.

45. Richard Paul, *Critical Thinking: How to Prepare Students for a Rapidly Changing World* (Santa Rosa, CA: Foundation for Critical Thinking, 1995), 263–65.

46. Richard Paul, "Dialogical Thinking: Critical Thoughts Essential to the Acquisition of Rational Knowledge and Passions," in *Teaching Thinking Skills: Theory and Practice*, ed. Joan Baron and Robert Sternberg (New York: W. H. Freeman, 1987), 292.

47. Thanks to Laura Heymann, JD, Professor of Law at the College of William & Mary's Marshall-Wythe School of Law, for granting permission to use her example. E-mail message to author, March 8, 2012.

48. Paul, *Critical Thinking*, 297.

49. Ibid., 279–98.

50. Ibid., 299.

51. Matthew Lipman, *Thinking in Education* (Cambridge, UK: Cambridge University Press, 1991), 232–33.

52. James T. Dillon, *The Practice of Questioning* (London: Routledge, 1990), 14–15, 131–44; and Stephen D. Brookfield and Stephen Preskill, *Discussion as a Way of Teaching: Tools and Techniques for Democratic Classrooms* (San Francisco: Jossey-Bass, 2005), 85–89.

53. Brookfield and Preskill, *Discussion as a Way of Teaching*, 85–89.

54. Postman and Weingartner, *Teaching as a Subversive Activity*, 34–37.

55. George Collison et al., *Facilitating Online Learning: Effective Strategies for Moderators* (Madison, WI: Atwood, 2000).

56. "Community of Inquiry," accessed September 5, 2011, http://www.communityofinquiry.com.

57. Collison et al., *Facilitating Online Learning*, 129.

58. Mary Reda, *Between Speaking and Silence: A Study of Quiet Students* (New York: SUNY Press, 2009).

59. Thomas A. Angelo and K. Patricia Cross, *Classroom Assessment Techniques: A Handbook for College Teachers* (San Francisco: Jossey-Bass, 1993).

60. For example, see Richard Paul, "Critical Thinking Class: Grading Policies," Critical Thinking Community, accessed February 12, 2012, http://www.criticalthinking.org/pages/critical-thinking-class-grading-policies/442.

61. D. Randy Garrison and Norman D. Vaughan, *Blended Learning in Higher Education: Framework, Principles, and Guidelines* (San Francisco: Jossey-Bass, 2007).

62. Ibid.

63. Collison et al., *Facilitating Online Learning*, 104–5.

64. Trisha Bender, *Discussion-Based Online Teaching to Enhance Student Learning* (Sterling, VA: Stylus, 2003).

65. Brookfield and Preskill, *Discussion as a Way of Teaching*, 4.

7

CULTIVATING PROBLEM-SOLVING AND DECISION-MAKING ABILITIES

Learning With Mental Models

Intended Learning Outcomes	Way of Learning	Common Methods
What students learn	Origins and theory	What the teacher provides
Cultivating problem-solving and decision-making abilities	**Learning with mental models**	Problems
		Case studies
Mental strategies for finding	Gestalt psychology, problem	Labs
solutions and making choices	solving, and decision theory	Projects

Is this learning that involves solving problems or making decisions? Does it involve challenges for students to organize their knowledge into systematic strategies? Do students need to learn how to find and define problems, how to generate solutions, and how to evaluate and choose among solutions? Does this learning require students to deal with issues they need to make choices about, weigh the values of different options, and predict outcomes as probabilities? These are learning outcomes well served by learning with mental models.

A physics teacher uses a series of problems called overload to challenge students to calculate and design the wiring system for a new house. How many outlets and circuits are needed, and how can these be set up to minimize blowing the circuit breaker? How does the teacher guide students to solve the problem?

L ife is full of problems calling out for solutions. Some of these problems are real problems people face in their daily lives at home, in the community, or on the job. Organizational life today may be thought of as an ongoing process of problem finding, problem solving, and solution implementation activity. Problems can also be about opportunities, such as those related to research, inventing new products, or establishing new services. Some problems are of a more abstract and impractical nature, such as certain mathematical and logic problems used mainly to stretch the mind or even entertain. Classroom settings are often used to solve impractical and real-life problems, and most postsecondary teachers are eager to help their students expand and sharpen their problem-solving abilities.

How do students learn problem solving and decision making? They learn through sample problems, case studies, laboratory assignments, and projects. Case studies are short narrative descriptions of situations that contain one or more problems and usually call for a decision about a course of action. They are used in many different types of educational settings in which complex problems are posed by some aspect of a setting, a process, or an individual, and they are usually addressed through discussion by the whole class, established groups within a class, or online. Laboratory assignments often pose problems that require experimentation and systematic investigation. Laboratory work in the sciences increasingly uses problem-based learning. Projects are undertaken by individuals or groups independently outside class, in a class study group, or in a clinical setting. Projects also address some identified problem or important decision and usually include an elaboration of the problem, collection of background information, gathering of new data or observations, and a set of recommendations. This way of learning is used to teach students to solve problems and make decisions in effective and efficient ways. This is the main focus of this way of learning: problem solving and decision making.

Consider this example of how a physics teacher uses problems as a stimulus for learning.

> Barbara Duch used problems as the main teaching method in her physics courses when she taught at the University of Delaware. "I wanted to teach students to develop the ability to reason and solve problems like a physicist," says Barbara. "Problems engage them in making decisions based on knowledge and principles they are learning, and asks them to justify their reasoning." Problems have to be authentic to be motivating to students, centered on real-life issues rather than fill-in-the-blank worksheets. A favorite problem Barbara developed is called Overload, which is really a series

of problems with students working in groups to help design the circuitry for a friend's house.[1] The problem begins by describing the basic outline of a newly designed house with some comments from the friend: "Stan tells you that he doesn't know how many circuits his house needs in order to be safe. In fact, Stan isn't even sure he knows what a circuit is, or how a circuit breaker works." Students first need to address a series of questions asked by Stan that focus on electrical circuit concepts. Once students have given their responses to their instructor, they receive the second part of the problem, which contains more detail about the house and its use: "Sharon tells you that they will have many appliances in the kitchen. A microwave, refrigerator, blender, toaster oven. . . . Stan says that his computer and printer, and Sharon's ironing and sewing 'stuff' will be in the same bedroom." Now the students need to determine the minimum number of outlets for each room and sketch a wiring diagram. The instructor urges groups to check local housing ordinances for the number of outlets needed in rooms, what type of circuits are needed in kitchens, garages, and so forth. Student groups are encouraged to list questions they have or information they need to find to proceed with the problem. Sometimes the instructor will have groups report their progress to the rest of the class. Finally, after checking in with the instructor once more, students are asked to construct a wiring plan for the entire house, making sure no circuit breakers will trip during peak use. Barbara says, "This problem activity involves students identifying what assumptions they can make about the problem given the constraints, seeing what they know and what they don't know, and what methods are available to them to solve the problem. Using a problem of this complexity ensures that students are not just plugging numbers in an equation, but are indeed understanding the concepts of electric circuits."[2]

Problems and Decisions

A problem is a question proposed for solution or discussion, usually a matter involving doubt, uncertainty, or difficulty. Diane Halpern, a well-known scholar in the field of problem solving and critical thinking, cites the following classic example of a problem:

> Suppose you are driving alone at night on a long, dark stretch of freeway that is infrequently traveled when you suddenly hear the familiar "thump-thump" of a flat tire. You pull onto the shoulder of the road to begin the unpleasant task of changing a tire, illuminated only by the light of the moon and a small flashlight. Carefully, you remove the lug nuts and place

them in a hubcap by the roadside. A speeding motorist whizzes past you hitting the hubcap and scattering the lug nuts across the dark freeway and out of sight. Here you sit, spare tire in hand, a flat tire propped against the car, and no lug nuts, on a dark and lonely stretch of freeway. To make matters worse, a cold rain is beginning to fall. What would you do?[3]

The problem is classic in many respects. There is a desired outcome at the center of it: get the spare tire on the wheel. There is information given in the problem, some of it relevant, some not. The loss of the lug nuts makes the situation a problem that may have to be recast or worked on systematically to arrive at a solution. How can the problem be solved? What kind of problem is it? Have we seen any problems like this before?

Halpern reports that one of her students claims to have had this problem during the daytime, and residents from a nearby mental hospital helped him find a resolution. They suggested he attach the spare by removing one lug nut from each of the other tires. With only three lug nuts, each tire would hold securely for a short distance until he could reach a gas station.[4]

Decisions, on the other hand, are different from problems. People make decisions by making choices on the best course of action. Because decisions involve values and feelings, it is natural that people will disagree about them. Decisions arouse partisan feelings, and in fact that is usually a good test of whether something is a decision or problem. Once the solution to the lug nut problem has been offered, someone still has to decide whether that is the preferred solution and what probability it has of succeeding. Might it be better to call AAA on the cell phone? Problem solving is focused on generating solutions that will make a change for the better. Problem solvers make recommendations; they say how they think a particular problem can be addressed with a particular solution. Then it is up to decision makers to decide what to do.

Why Use Mental Models?

Most problem solving and decision making gets complicated. The greater the number of influences (variables) relevant to the situation, the more difficult it is to keep them all straight. Picture the juggler keeping all the tenpins in the air, or the circus performer spinning ten plates on ten sticks simultaneously. Such a sight boggles the mind, we say, and *boggle*, the dictionary tells us, is to overwhelm or to bewilder. So our mind must find some alternative to getting boggled. Psychologists call this boggling *cognitive overload*. Our mind needs some system for dealing with complexity. That is why we turn to mental models.

We operate with mental models all the time in our daily life. Usually these are fairly simple pictures of how things work. Thomas Ward, Ronald Finke, and Steven Smith described the concept well:

> We actively construct mental models to comprehend complex phenomena, and we use our general knowledge about the workings of the world to do so. We might want to understand the nature of the digestive process in humans, how a clutch or brake system operates, or why the sun, moon, and stars appear and disappear in a consistent sequence. The mental pictures we form of the component parts of these systems and how those parts interact are called mental models.[5]

When we use mental models, "they allow us to set up hypothetical situations, make predictions about outcomes, and mentally 'run' the model to test those predictions."[6] Most expert problem solvers use mental models to proceed systematically through the various steps involved in solving the problem. Decision makers use mental models to weigh the factors in a decision and to predict likely outcomes.

The first step in making a mental model is to generate some sort of mental image of the situation. Consider what is meant by making mental images. Which of the following dogs have ears that stick up above the head: German shepherd, beagle, cocker spaniel, or fox terrier? When people are asked how they think about that, they report that they try to picture the dogs and visualize the ears. People generally do not approach this question verbally because no one has ever had to memorize a list such as shepherd-up, beagle-down, and so on.[7] This simple process of making and manipulating images is the main focus of using mental models as a way of learning.

Mental models are sometimes referred to by other names. They may be called mental tactics, languages, programs, strategies, or even tools. Piaget and other educational psychologists use the term *schemas*. The important point is not what they are called but how they function as conceptual tools for problem solving and decision making.[8] Mental models are also referred to sometimes as heuristics or rules of thumb. From the Greek word *heuriskein*, meaning "to discover," heuristics are general rules, guidelines, or models that may be useful in discovering solutions to problems. No one can guarantee that using mental models will help people find the right solutions to problems, but at least the likelihood is increased. One might say that using mental models is better than having a boggled mind.

Origins of Learning With Mental Models

The use of mental models has a fascinating history. As with behavioral psychology, some of the early research was done with animals. The classic experiments by Wolfgang Köhler in 1925 were conducted with monkeys.[9] Köhler devised a series of ingenious experiments with a caged chimpanzee named Sultan. The experiments involved Sultan's solving the problem of reaching a banana tied high in his cage. Sometimes he was given sticks, sometimes boxes to be piled on top of each other, and sometimes he was given a combination of sticks and boxes. As Köhler observed the behavior closely, he noticed that after some period of puzzlement and frustration, the chimp appeared in a sense to be thinking it out. After some insight occurred, he piled up the boxes, climbed them, and used the sticks to reach the banana. After many observations of this behavior with Sultan and other chimps, Köhler concluded that problem solving, even in animals, involves some "mental manipulation of operations toward a goal solution," an insight that goes beyond trial and error.[10] Were Köhler's chimps using mental models?

The modern history of problem solving began with the work of Karl Duncker in 1945. Following the approach of Köhler and other Gestalt psychologists in Germany, Duncker asked his subjects to think aloud as they attempted to solve problems so he could trace their reasoning processes and cognitive states. Duncker discovered there was a close connection between the way subjects represented the problem to themselves and the accuracy of their solutions.[11] One of the classic treatises on problem solving, also from the 1940s, is the work of George Polya, titled *How to Solve It.*[12] Polya was a famous mathematician born in Hungary in 1887 who began teaching at Stanford University in 1940. He brought the term *heuristic* into common use.[13] Perhaps the most cited contribution to the theory of problem solving is Allen Newell and Herbert Simon's general model of problem solving, first published in 1972 in their book *Human Problem Solving.*[14] They coined the terms *goal state, initial state,* and *problem space,* now referred to in almost every text on problem solving.[15]

Decision making involves weighing choices and predicting outcomes, and it depends to some extent on probability theory. Decision making in the formal sense can be traced to philosopher and mathematician Blaise Pascal (1623–1662), who developed what some consider to be the first decision-analysis technique, which he used to weigh the consequences of living or not living the Christian life without knowing whether God exists.[16] Pascal's Wager, as it came to be known, involves probabilistic decision making in the face of uncertainty. The idea of decision worksheets for weighing the pros and cons of a decision comes from, as so many things do, Benjamin Franklin. Modern decision theory is complicated and often mathematical. A general theory of decision making, now known as expected utility theory, was developed by John von Neumann and Oskar Morgenstern in 1947.[17] Their theory set the basic directions for psychological research on decision making.

Teaching Problem Solving and Decision Making

As with critical, creative, and dialogical thinking, there is a growing awareness that the techniques needed for problem solving and decision making can be learned. Perhaps the first challenge is to convince students who think they are not good at problem solving to believe that help exists and that they can improve. Frustrated by years of struggling with homework problems, and because there was no school subject called problems in general, many students have come to hate problems and have developed the self-concept that they are not good at solving them. Without workable problem-solving strategies, which do in fact exist, they learn to avoid problems, which John Bransford and Barry Stein call the "let me out of here approach" to problem solving.[18] Teachers need to be able to identify the escape artists and make sure they experience incremental successes that will rebuild their confidence as problem solvers.

It is important to let students know how problem solving and decision making actually work, what the basic processes involve, what the steps are, what techniques exist, and which mental models are useful for which types of problems. It is also important for students to know that problem solving and decision making, like creative thinking, are improved through domain-specific knowledge, that is, by knowing one or more academic fields well. As with other ways of learning, it is best not to lecture on techniques but to provide students with learning settings where they can practice under expert guidance. As Alan Lesgold concludes, "Practice is necessary if learning is to occur. One should invest one's effort in problem solving and not just listening to a teacher talk about it. . . . The best instruction involves the student in actual problem solving, with the instructor making the process more efficient by preventing the student from pursuing wild goose chases and providing hints if no progress is being made. . . . To learn to solve problems, one has to solve some problems successfully."[19]

If this is so, the role of the teacher is to provide real-life problems or the next best thing—cases, labs, and projects—and to give students sustained opportunities to work on problems. Consider this example of a class project.

Anton Camarota teaches an Environmental Policy and Management course at University College at the University of Denver. In this course, students learn Environmental Management Systems (EMS) standards and requirements. "Because students in this program go on to work in EMS management, we want them to know how to use the standards and frameworks proactively and systematically," says Anton. "Students need to be able to identify aspects, impacts, and legal requirements applicable to a business, and translate those into a series of targets and programs that provide an effective foundation for systemic environmental management. They need to see the big picture and how everything is integrated." To achieve these goals, students complete a large project in which they develop a comprehensive EMS manual for a small- or medium-size company. "A complete EMS manual is more comprehensive than a business plan and takes a team and an entire academic term to develop." To solve their term-long problem, students use a template that acts as a framework or mental model for the project. They must make choices and choose from different procedures or documentation to use along the way. In the end all the small choices and options need to be integrated into one coherent plan that is practical and can be implemented. "Each piece is a practical step, but fitting them all together is a more abstract, complex process, and that's where the framework is useful." Students work in groups online using actual data to develop the manual together. One group develops a part of the manual one week and then passes it along to the other group. Anton provides comments and feedback, and the next week the other group addresses his comments and adds new material. This process goes on back and forth through the term but becomes more difficult as the project progresses because the groups need to integrate new material with the existing material. The class uses ongoing discussion threads to facilitate the development process and learn how the existing parts of the manual are related to the new content they learn each week. Anton grades the project based not only on the product but also on the process. "In the real world, the process aspect is the focus they need," he says. "Students really have to know how each element interacts with others, understand the overall framework, and be able to weave everything together into one integrated whole."[20]

Finding Problems

One of the first steps identified in most of the writing about problem solving is problem finding. This is important because our general orientation in life is toward avoiding problems, not finding them. Our parents told us to stay out of trouble, and part of the folk wisdom of our culture is, "Don't go looking for trouble; it will find you."[21] In academia students usually have to focus on getting the right answers to problems that someone else has created, but there is much to be learned from finding and defining problems. The case can be made that the first step in effective problem solving is to find the right problems to work on in the first place.

A Basic Problem-Solving Model

The classic study of problem solving is Newell and Simon's *Human Problem Solving*. They provide the theory and a general approach to problem solving now represented in various texts and outlined briefly here.[22]

- *Goal state.* Most problems call for a solution. In the flat tire problem, having the spare tire on the wheel is the goal state, or even more generally, driving the car again is the goal. It is possible to observe people engaged in a flurry of problem-solving activity without first having arrived at a clear concept of the goal state or some idea of what things will be like when the problem is solved.
- *Initial state.* The conditions that are given along with the statement of the problem describe the initial state. They are what the problem solver has to work with at first, that is, all the givens that people bring to the problem: conditions, boundaries, and information currently available.
- *Problem space.* The distance (gap) between the initial state and goal state is the problem space, which is the area where the problem can be worked out.
- *Solution paths.* Within the problem space, a number of options can be generated. Options are the potential solutions or steps in the process that might add up to a solution. Solution paths are the ideas people generate as possible solutions or steps toward a solution of the problem.
- *Operations.* Also in the problem space, certain operations must be performed to move from the initial state to the goal state. Mental models become very useful in performing operations, because usually the operations are quite challenging.
- *Barriers.* The problem space is filled with barriers. It is not so easy to move from the initial state to the goal state; if it were easy, there would not be a problem. If there are no barriers, these operations

might best be referred to as tasks, the algorithmic activities for which the solution methods are already known. If there are no barriers, there is no problem.[23]

This simple, but very useful mental model for thinking about a problem is diagrammed in the following figure.

Problem Space

Newell and Simon's general framework for thinking about problem solving provides a useful model that more specific mental models can fit into. They fit in the problem space, where they are used for performing operations to generate solution paths.

The following several rules, based on work by Wayne Wickelgren, can be applied in using the general model effectively:[24]

1. *Define the goals.* Problems seldom are stated clearly. Most problems require further definition, redefinition, and clarification of goals before seeking solutions.

2. *Decide whether the problem should be solved.* Ian Mitroff and Harold Linstone offer this good advice in *The Unbounded Mind: Breaking the Chains of Traditional Business Thinking*: "Question whether a problem is to be 'solved,' 'resolved' or 'dissolved.' To solve a problem means to produce an exact or optimal solution to it. To resolve a problem means to seek a solution that is 'good enough.' On the other hand, to dissolve a problem is to realize that there may be some other problem that is more important to focus one's attention on."[25] Is this problem worth solving?

3. *Identify the givens.* Givens are the facts and figures, whatever information is available, as well as the factors that define the problem and constrain solutions. What part of this information is valuable, and what is really just extra, useless, or maybe even misleading information?

4. *Manage the solution paths.* The object is not to generate large numbers of solution paths, but only the right and best ones.[26] When many

approaches come to mind, which solution paths have the most promise?

5. *Do not confuse problem solving and creativity.* Problem solving, contrary to popular ideas about it, does not involve pushing the envelope or out-of-the-box thinking. *Creative problem solving* is probably a misnomer, and brainstorming is probably not the best technique for it. Generating solution paths is not so much a matter of creativity as it is the skillful use of mental models to produce the most promising solution.

6. *Identify the type of problem.* A crossword puzzle provides challenges that are different from those of a jigsaw puzzle. Analytical problems contain the evidence needed within the problem; synthetic problems require reaching outside the problem to gather new information and possibilities.[27] Some problems involve rearrangement, as with anagrams, where the task is to take a series of letters, such as ISTSCTSITA, and arrange them into a word, STATISTICS. Other problems involve discovering a structure or relationship, as with analogy problems. Problems are classified as transformational when objects must be rearranged within a fixed set of rules, as in "move the coin to . . . without doing . . ."[28] Prohibitive problems have too many possible solutions, like the Rubik's Cube, and the challenge is to reduce the number of solution paths, hoping the correct one can be found. As Barry and Rudinow note, "Problems come in an extremely wide variety of shapes, sizes, and kinds. The specific strategies and skills one needs to be an effective problem solver are equally diverse."[29]

Using Mental Models to Generate Solutions

What happens within the problem space is crucial, of course, and this is where mental models come into play directly. This may be, in fact, the most important part of the process. Expert problem solvers monitor their thinking and use normative models, which provide the "best thinking for achieving the thinker's goals."[30] The following are some of the mental models that can be used to attack problems.

Random Search

Random search is sometimes called trial and error. An exhaustive search involves examining every possible option on the solution path. For example, in working with the anagram THA, there are only six possible solution paths for arranging these letters: THA, TAH, ATH, AHT, HTA, and HAT. The problem solver will arrive at HAT as the solution, eventually and inevitably, even if it is last, through trial and error. This mental model works well for problems with few options and where testing all alternatives is possible. When there are many potential solution paths, and the solution paths themselves are complex and branching, an exhaustive search becomes highly inefficient. When students try one idea and then another in rapid succession, testing an idea, withdrawing it, proposing another, they are learning primarily through trial and error. Köhler's chimp probably did better than this solving the banana problem. If random search is being used without success, the situation calls for something better.

Systematic Random Search

This mental model consists of classifying the random search efforts and noticing the degrees of effectiveness that certain options may have. If a large number of options are available, it may be possible to classify a whole group of similar options. Or it may be possible to systematically test the options of an experiment with computer software. Some of these efforts take the randomness out of random search and make it more systematic.

Hill Climbing

Picture yourself blindfolded on a hill. Your goal is to get to the top. You start out in some direction, and you get some feedback from your legs that this is downhill. You try again and move in the other direction. You start moving up. The steps are small, but you can tell that you are getting closer to the goal, even though you do not know exactly where the goal is.[31] Physicians sometimes use hill climbing in arriving at the right dose of medicine for a chronic patient. The drug can be increased in small doses until the unspecified goal has been reached. Unlike trial and error, there is feedback in this situation as the goal is approximated.

Means-Ends Analysis

If the goal is the end, and the means for getting there are not clear, it is sometimes useful to find subgoals and then devise the means for reaching these. One might say more simply that this is a way of dividing a problem into subproblems to work on the easier parts first. A frequently cited example known as the Tower of Hanoi Problem (shown in the following figure) illustrates means-ends analysis.[32] The object is to move three coins of one stack (quarter, nickel, penny, with the quarter on the bottom) from the first site and restack them in the same order at a third site by using only an intermediary second site and moving only one coin at a time.

In this problem the goal state looks exactly like the initial state, but the rule that one may move only one coin at a time makes it a problem. The idea of an intermediary site suggests that coins can be moved there for staging. The solution to the problem is not difficult if it is taken in steps. One step toward the solution, then, is to seek a subgoal. One subgoal is to get the quarter to the third site. Another subgoal is to get the nickel and penny off the quarter so it can be moved. That can be done by moving the penny to the third site, the nickel to the second site, and the penny back to the nickel. At this point, the third site is vacant and the quarter can be moved to it. The next subgoal is to get the nickel back on the quarter. This can be achieved by moving the penny temporarily back to the first site, thus freeing the nickel to move back on the quarter at the third site. Then the penny goes back on the nickel. The point, of course, is that the mental operations required for solving the problem can be managed better by working on subgoals one at a time.

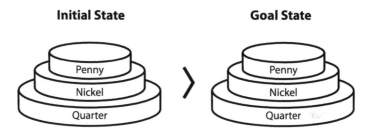

Working Backward

The natural question for all of us to ask is, What should I do first? With certain kinds of problems it may be best to ask, What should I do last? Next to last? And so on, back to the beginning. The paper-and-pencil mazes children enjoy working on are usually more easily solved by starting at the goal and working backward.[33] If you work forward, each turn in the maze is a decision point; but if you work backward, the decision points turn into inevitabilities. Once again, Diane Halpern provides a marvelous illustration:

> Water lilies on a certain lake double in area every twenty-four hours. From the time the first water lily appears until the lake is completely covered takes sixty days. On what day is the lake half covered?[34]

Try working backward. On the sixtieth day the lake is covered. What is it like on the fifty-ninth day? Well, if the growth doubles every day, it is half covered on the fifty-ninth day.

Split-Half Method

Halpern illustrates this mental model with a game she has invented. It is possible to guess the age of anyone under one hundred in seven guesses using this method. First, one asks the subject if he or she is under fifty. If the answer is yes, the next question is whether the person is older than twenty-five, and so on. The next question always splits the remaining amount in half until the answer is found.[35] This method is often used as a technique for locating a difficulty, such as a power outage, a cut cable, or a blocked drainpipe. To avoid tearing up the whole line, it is best to check out sections of it and by the process of elimination determine the spot that needs to be fixed. Some problems can best be solved through a narrowing-down process.

Simplification

Some problems are complicated, and simplifying them by temporarily suspending the rules or cutting down on the details may help. Consider, for example, what Wickelgren calls the reverse tenpin problem, shown in the following figure.[36]

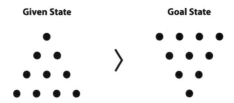

Assume Susie has a bowling set and she has set the pins backward at the end of the hall. The pins need to be rearranged from the (given) backward arrangement to the (goal) correct arrangement. Susie may have set them up wrong, but she knows how to fix it by moving only three pins.

Several actions can be taken to simplify this problem. First ask yourself if the pins have to remain in the exact same horizontal rows, or can the configuration move forward or back a row or two? If only a small number of pins need to be moved, then consider which will remain in place. Think about which pins will stay in place instead of which pins will move. Perhaps you can visualize a central core of pins that need not be moved. Consider what new arrangement will keep the maximum number of pins in place. Now the problem has been greatly simplified, and it may be possible to consider what pins to move. (If you still need a hint, try moving the left and right pins in the row of four back to the row of two. Then what?)

Using Actual Data

Many problems are hard to deal with in the abstract, but they sometimes become more manageable when actual numbers or objects are used.[37] For example, consider this abstract problem:

> Prove that all six-place numbers in the form of *abcabc* are evenly divisible by thirteen. It may be best first to try it with numbers: 416416 ÷ 13 = 32032

This example does not prove the relationship. Proof takes some factoring and algebra to show that the relationship will always hold, but using numbers shows that it works at least in some instances. A good approach to be taken with many problems is to use actual data to see if and how the proposed solution works.

Contradiction

For some problems it is easy to get overwhelmed by the number of solution paths, and it may be necessary to eliminate some of them.[38] One way to do this is to see if the potential solutions are contradictory to the givens in the initial state or incompatible with what might be reasonably expected in the goal state. In some cases an eyeball comparison or an estimate will generate the comment, "It *couldn't* be that!" Some of the potential solutions can then be rejected, and one's mental efforts can be focused on more promising solution paths. The method of contradiction, therefore, is very much like estimating and is used to sort out impossible or absurd solutions from plausible ones. Unfortunately, research shows that not everyone is good at estimating.[39] One of the best questions we can ask about a potential solution is, Could this possibly be the answer, or should it be discarded?

Graphs, Diagrams, Visualization Methods

No rule says that all problem solving has to take place exclusively in our heads. Although we may enhance problem solving through the use of mental models, we might also enhance the use of the mental models by putting information into visual form. Sometimes there is too much information—

the mind will be boggled—and the creation of a diagram or chart would be useful. Putting things on paper takes the mental model out of the head. Today, many problems can also be visualized through computer software projections and other data visualization programs.

Analogy

Perhaps the problem at hand is analogous to another. This does not mean the two problems are similar necessarily; in fact, they can be quite remote from each other, but something can be learned from one problem that might be applied to another. In a series of clever experiments, psychologists Gick and Holyoak tested students to see whether an analogous situation in a story would provide a model that might suggest possible solutions not otherwise generated.[40] They used Karl Duncker's famous radiation problem involving a doctor faced with treating an inoperable stomach cancer with radiation. They then provided an analogous military problem of a general who needs to find the best route to capture a fort. The results of the analogy experiments showed that 75 percent of the participants come up with new solutions when exposed to the analogy, but only 10 percent of the students not exposed to the analogy did so. The trick, of course, is to generate good analogies (they will not always be provided) and to have the ability to learn from them and apply them to the problem.

Selecting the Right Mental Model

Effective problem solvers think carefully about what kinds of problems they are dealing with and what models apply. It is helpful to be able to say, "Oh, this is like the Tower of Hanoi problem, and we need to work on subproblems" or "This is one of those maze problems where we need to work backward" or "This is just the radiation problem in a different form." In any discipline, certain types of problems will occur frequently, and effective problem solvers learn from previously solved problems which mental models work best. Effective problem solvers become good at spotting the similarities and differences among problems and knowing which mental models to select.

Being able to solve a new problem based on the way a previous problem was solved is called *transfer*. Transfer is one of the most valued aspects of learning; after all, isn't it the main purpose for college students to learn from their studies so they are better able to go out and solve real-life problems when they graduate? However, transfer does not occur as easily or as often as we would hope. When trying to transfer problem solving from one problem to another, it is easy to get caught up in the surface-level elements of a problem rather than the more important deeper structures.[41] For example, when faced with math word problems, transfer is easier if the problems have the same surface-level elements—word problems using money seem related to other word problems about money. However, when a new problem (not about money) but with a similar structure is suddenly cast as a problem about time, students have trouble finding and relating to the deeper structure of similarities between the two problems.

How can transfer be enhanced? It is helpful if teachers identify similarities and differences in problems and focus on deep knowledge structures. Teachers can help students to identify these structures by asking such questions as, "What if we changed this one aspect of the problem? What if we changed another aspect? Is it the same problem or a different problem now? Is it more similar to this problem now or not?" This can help students determine the fundamental nature of the problem and identify the essential models to use. In addition, teaching problems in multiple contexts can help students see that the underlying structures are applicable to other situations.

Sometimes the selected mental model just isn't working, and it may be time to switch to another model. Wayne Wickelgren notes in *How to Solve Problems*, "You may repeatedly think of the inadequate methods for solving the problem and get the feeling that you are going around in circles . . . thinking of the same inadequate ideas over and over again. . . . An excellent first step in getting out of a loop and doing something different is to analyze what you have been doing . . . rather than think about the problem itself."[42]

At a certain stage it may be important, as Wickelgren suggests, to back away from the problem itself to engage in some careful reexamination of the mental model being used, to reassess the effectiveness of a particular mental model, and to consciously select another. Effective problem solvers monitor their selections and uses of mental models—the term for such monitoring is *metacognition* (discussed in chapter 6, p. 111)—and individuals displaying metacognition as problem solvers know how to switch effectively from one model to another.

Avoiding Pitfalls

Certain common pitfalls, things to watch out for and avoid, are associated with problem solving.

Lack of Sufficient Background Knowledge

It is tempting for teachers and students to want to take on challenging problems. But students need a sufficient level of knowledge to solve a problem. The entire experience can be an exercise in frustration without this important component. On the other hand, students need to begin to practice solving problems even though sometimes they may not be completely ready.

Misunderstanding the Problem

Rushing to find solution paths can lead to confusion about the goal state or an inadequate reading of the initial state. Two things happen with initial-state information: when one rushes the search for solution paths, good information gets ignored or irrelevant information is mistakenly regarded as valuable. The following example, the sock problem, illustrates how important it is to be clear about the goal state and to sort out the essential from the irrelevant information in the initial state.

> If you have black socks and brown socks in your drawer mixed in a ratio of four to five, how many socks will you have to take out to make sure of having a pair of the same color?[43]

Participants do all kinds of interesting things with this simple little problem. For some reason they have trouble seeing that the goal is to select one pair of socks of the same color with the fewest picks. They think they need two pairs or that the goal is to get the owner to reorganize the sock drawer so this problem will not exist. They bring up all kinds of worries (Are the socks the same size?) and rules (Do I have to put each sock back in after I have taken it out?). They want to know if they can look, and then they sheepishly recognize that if they can, it will not be a problem anymore. They tend to ignore the most important piece of information in the initial state (that there are only two colors), and they tend to focus on the irrelevant and misleading information (that the ratio of black to brown is four to five). The solution comes fairly quickly once the problem is understood: with some luck (and without looking into the drawer) one may draw two socks of the same color in two picks, but to be sure, one needs to make only one more pick, for surely then two socks of the same color will have been drawn. Problem-solving efforts are doomed when the problem is misunderstood.

Unrecognized Presuppositions

Presuppositions are the constraints imported to the problem from general knowledge (or lack thereof), usually without the individuals' being aware of them. Presuppositions cause problem solvers to frame the problem in a certain way and narrow down the number of options within the problem space. Recognizing and discarding presuppositions allows more potential solutions to flow into the problem space.

Functional Fixedness

The tendency to employ the labels we have learned for the use of certain objects or concepts in such a rigid way that we cannot think of using them for anything else is called functional fixedness. A screwdriver is for twisting in screws, and it is hard to think of using a screwdriver for anything else because that is what it is for. But if we stop thinking of it as a screwdriver and call it a gadget or doohickey, that rethinking opens up many more possible functions for it. "When the name of a thing is left open, the possibilities for using the device seem also to remain open."[44] The same is true for abstract concepts, such as accounting or leadership.

Expert and Novice Problem Solvers

Many studies have been conducted to better understand how experts solve problems. deGroot's famous studies from the 1960s compared expert and novice chess players by asking them to think aloud as they decided on the next move to take in games of chess.[45] His studies showed that experts and novices think very differently. Experts may not think through more options than novices, as was his first hypothesis, but rather experts think of more strategic options. Their choices are based on familiar patterns, common strategies, and relationships between the chess pieces that come only from hours and hours spent playing the game. Expert chess players are different in the way they structure knowledge.[46]

   In another study that demonstrates this rather clearly, undergraduates who had taken one physics course were compared with graduate students and professors of physics.[47] Both groups were asked to sort physics problems into categories. The novice group of undergraduates sorted the problems based on the surface-level context of the problem: problems using incline planes, problems using springs, and so forth. The expert group sorted the problems based on the underlying principles behind the problems: problems that focused on energy conservation were grouped together regardless of whether the problem used incline planes or springs. Experts understand the principles and strategies behind problems in a coherent and connected way, whereas novices tend to form only superficial connections.

Here is what we know from these and other studies conducted to compare expert and novice problem solvers.

- Problem-solving ability, like creativity, presupposes a high level of domain-specific knowledge. As John Bransford and Barry Stein note, "Problem-solving abilities often depend on specialized knowledge in a discipline. Our ability to solve problems is not simply equivalent to a set of problem-solving skills."[48] We have finite capacity in our working knowledge, which is one of the limiting factors of thinking through a problem. Experts have a high level of background knowledge that allows them to chunk information and thus have more capacity in their working knowledge.
- Experts have developed sophisticated knowledge structures to hold domain-specific knowledge; they tend to construct physical models or diagrams to represent the problem, and through these representations they use complete, coherent, and specific schemas to think through the problems.[49]
- Experts are good at determining what information is relevant or irrelevant to a problem. They are able to pull out the essential information and, even when they are incorrect, make better informed choices.
- Expert problem solvers are good at figuring out what kinds of problems they are dealing with. They have a repertoire of mental models in their head, and they can represent and classify problems correctly even when they have only one-fifth of the problem, long before they have enough data to actually formulate a solution.[50]
- Expert problem solvers become very proficient at using metacognition to monitor their problem-solving efforts. They focus on solving the problem, and they monitor their own efforts as they do so.[51]

Expert problem solvers have more background in the subject at hand, but they also handle their mental resources better than novices.

From Problem Solving to Decision Making

College graduates in every discipline are called upon frequently to participate in making decisions about such matters as hiring new personnel, planning a new program, or managing an emergency. Whereas problem solving requires moving through various solution paths to get to the desired goal state, decision making involves weighing various pros and cons and selecting the best (or lesser of the evils) option, often among many alternatives. Decision making differs from traditional problem solving in that there is usually no one correct decision; there are usually several options, and the task is to select the best. Furthermore, in problem solving the choice is usually known to be good or bad at the time as a result of the logic that relates the givens to the solutions, but in decision making usually some time must pass to tell whether the decision was a good one.

What problem solving and decision making have in common is that they both use up cognitive capacity, the ability to juggle all the mental activities needed to solve a problem well or make a good decision. Most decisions involve many different variables and require multidimensional comparison.[52] The central challenge in decision making, therefore, is to assess which and how many dimensions are going to be taken into consideration and how to weigh them. This decision-making process is where mental models again become advantageous, and this is why decision making and problem solving are considered together in this chapter: both can boggle the mind and both can be made easier by using mental models.

Decisions can be made without the use of mental models, of course, but usually they are improved when a model is used. As John Mullen and Byron Roth note in *Decision Making: Its Logic and Practice:* "Sometimes when you make a decision in a slipshod way, with little thought or analysis, it turns out well. That's when you thank your lucky stars. More often than not, decisions that are made badly produce bad results. This points up the fact that there is a difference between the *process* of making a decision and whether or not the decision produces favorable *outcomes.* When we say of a decision that it was smart, or reasonable, or rational, we should be referring to the thinking that went into the decision, not to its favorable outcomes."[53]

Good decisions that result from a poor process might be called guesswork. When we make decisions, many other people are often the beneficiaries (or victims) of our choices, and we are acting as trustees as we make decisions.[54] Therefore, it is important to follow a decision-making model and to evaluate regularly the results that model is producing.

Basic Decision-Making Model

The mental model for decision making has ten key steps.[55] Throughout the explanation of the ten steps, an example is provided, a personnel choice, such as hiring a faculty member or dean.

1. *Determine values.* Values are well-reasoned statements of what is desirable or has utility.[56] In decision theory, reasoned values have to

do with what individuals or decision bodies in the organization believe are desirable, meaning more desirable than something else, and these values drive the decision process. Some decision models use the term *utility*. What utility will this decision have? In a hiring decision, one asks, What values of the organization are most important to consider in filling this position?

2. *Determine outcomes.* The important part of this step is to establish outcomes that fulfill values. In a hiring decision one asks, What specific outcomes will result from having this person on the staff? The goal is to "select the choice that leads to the outcome with the greatest value."[57]

3. *Weigh the outcomes.* If several outcomes are possible, they may not all be equally desirable. Some outcomes may be assigned greater weight than others. Outcomes can be ranked, or they can be assigned numerical weights.[58] The weighting process establishes the relative importance of different outcomes. In a hiring decision, one asks, Of the many outcomes that could result, which are of the highest priority for the new hire to produce?

4. *Generate options.* Decisions involve choices among options. Options can be plans, programs, or people. In a hiring situation, the options are the candidates. Decision making is enhanced by having a large number of suitable options.

5. *Identify attributes of options.* Options always have attributes. In a hiring decision these are the characteristics and qualities of the candidates. Some of these attributes may be viewed as compensatory, which means that a weakness in one area can be made up for with strengths in another.[59]

6. *Match attributes to outcomes.* What attributes appear to be most closely related to producing the desired outcomes? In a personnel decision, the attributes of the candidates (options) are matched to the weighted characteristics of expected outcomes. What characteristics of which candidates are most likely to produce the most desired outcomes?

7. *Make a choice.* Consider carefully the attributes of various options and how they will produce desired outcomes. In a personnel decision, this means selecting the candidate who has the characteristics most likely to bring about the highly rated outcomes that fulfill organizational values. Make a choice and frame the choice as a recommendation for action.

8. *Cast the choice as a probability and consider the consequences.* No one knows for sure how a decision will work out. Even a very carefully considered personnel decision still carries the risk of being a bad choice. That is why prediction is part of decision making, and choices are usually cast as probabilities. Defend the decision in terms of probable outcomes and consequences. Because outcomes are uncertain, one must ask how uncertain they are and then consider the consequences. Decision theorists call this expected utility theory. How much usefulness (or potential disaster) is there in the consequence?

9. *Predict the likelihood of outcomes.* Probability has been described as a "willingness to bet."[60] If you are willing to bet, is the bet a sure thing or is there some risk? If there is risk, how much? In a personnel decision, several variables (the attributes of the selected candidate) combine to produce likely outcomes. These are the things you bet on. Someone has to predict the most probable outcomes of a decision and base those predictions on something.

10. *Align the steps.* Check the alignment of values, outcomes, options, the attributes of options, and actual choices. The tendency in using the model is to focus too much on one aspect of the process, such as identifying outcomes or generating options. In a personnel decision this can involve spending too much time fussing over the job description (outcomes) or amassing a large pool of candidates (options). For the model to work, all the steps need to be brought into play and kept well aligned.

More Pitfalls

As with problem solving, decision making has its pitfalls.

Wishful Thinking

Sometimes known as the Pollyanna Principle, wishful thinking is the tendency to overestimate the chances of being successful, to see the wonderful things that could happen from a particular decision, and to minimize or deny the risks.[61] Expert decision makers evaluate risk realistically, and they ask what the consequences will be if the decision proves to be wrong.[62] It is possible to be wrong, of course, in choosing a certain option, but it is also possible to be wrong in not choosing it. Risks show up as missed opportunities as well as blunders. In terms of the general decision-making model, wishful thinkers tend to overvalue the attributes of particular options, exaggerate the way the options will attain outcomes and fulfill values, or overproject the utility and probability of a particular option.

Entrapment

Most decisions exist in the context of other decisions, and one decision, especially a bad decision, can affect another.[63] Sometimes previous decisions that have turned out badly have already cost a great deal in time, money, and effort. If a person, or the people in an organization, has already made a big investment, he or she constantly becomes trapped in previous decisions so that a free, fresh, rational choice becomes difficult for the decision at hand. The best way to avoid this pitfall, of course, is to separate decisions and view each on its own terms.

Trade-Offs

Trade-offs occur when decision makers are willing to give up one outcome for another or to forget about a weak or missing attribute because it is compensated by another.[64] The questions to be asked include these: What is being given up and how important is it? Is the trade-off truly compensating? In business terms, a trade-off often contains opportunity costs, real and measurable costs for not pursuing a particular course of action. Once one trade-off has been made, there is a tendency to engage in others. Sometimes known as the slippery slope tendency, engaging in a series of compromising trade-offs can eventually lead to a collection of bad decisions. The slippery slope tendency can be countered with guidelines that set limits to what is nonnegotiable.

Aversion to Loss

Aversion to loss refers not to the prospect of losing but to the loss we suffer when we have to give up something we already have. Consider the following example: Mr. Smith buys a case of wine for $5 a bottle. Several years later he is offered $100 a bottle for the same wine. Although he never buys wine for more than $35 a bottle, he refuses to sell.[65] Why? Mr. Smith would have to give up his wine. Even though this is a terrific opportunity and would no doubt pass through any decision-making model with flying colors, aversion to loss gets in the way.

Gambler's Fallacy

In so-called "wheel of fortune games," people tend to think that if number seven has come up twice already, it is unlikely to come up again, or if number seven hasn't come up lately, it is about time for it. In a truly random situation, however, every number on the wheel has a chance of coming up on every spin because the wheel has no memory. Over a very large number of spins, the random distribution will play itself out, but in any limited period, there is no memory for what has or has not been played. This irrational tendency to impute memory in situations involving chance has been called Gambler's Fallacy. Probable outcomes are not likely to be random, as with spinning a wheel, but people may still think in terms of Gambler's Fallacy.[66] Watch out for symptoms of irrational decision making in phrases such as "I'm due," or "It's our turn."

Misinterpreting Trends

Another pitfall associated with predicting outcomes relates to understanding trends. Trends are true only if all the factors producing them stay the same. Sometimes, however, trends are shaky to begin with because they are based on a limited data pool.[67] For example, a trend toward 60 percent female births would not be unusual in a small rural hospital because the number of births is too small to average out as they would in a large metropolitan hospital. Projecting probable outcomes of a decision includes careful use of trend data.

How Teachers Facilitate Learning With Mental Models

There is no better way to learn problem solving than solving problems and no better way to learn decision making than having to make decisions. Although people have opportunities to solve problems and make decisions all the time, they may not get any better at it, or at avoiding common pitfalls, because they don't understand the processes and have no guidance. This is where teaching with mental models comes in by providing the opportunity to develop problem-solving and decision-making abilities under expert guidance through cases, labs, and projects. Consider how this business professor uses cases.

> Grandon Gill teaches at the University of South Florida. In his capstone Enterprise Information Systems course, he uses case studies to help students develop the ability to make decisions about implementing information technology. "Students need to realize that the effective use of information technology depends heavily on the organizational and managerial context in which it is to be used," says Grandon, "and these are complex decisions." In these weekly case studies, students are expected to spend two to

three hours preparing the case, reading it in detail, taking notes, trying to decide what information is relevant and what is unimportant, and preparing a summary of key points. Although Grandon does not provide precase study questions—he wants to replicate the real world where individuals have to determine relevant information for themselves—he does provide a case preparation worksheet that helps students organize the decision-making process. This worksheet provides students with a mental model for making information technology decisions. It typically involves identifying the environment and stakeholder units of analysis and determining the positive or negative impacts of each, conducting a SWOT (strengths, weaknesses, opportunities, threats) analysis for the context facing the protagonist of the case, and listing and analyzing all possible alternatives with their accompanying impacts and responses. During class, following a written precase question, the case method begins with a short discussion reviewing the important aspects of the case. Grandon cold calls on students to introduce the case and make initial recommendations, a tactic that also gives students the incentive to come to class prepared. The discussion that follows is the meat of the case method. "I often take a less-directed role in facilitating the discussion, somewhat like an 'effectual facilitator,' whose role is primarily to ask questions and pull out the nuances of the case itself." Grandon always provides time for summary and synthesis at the end, reflecting on the discussion, the decision-making process, and "helping students better understand the types of situations to which the lessons of the case might apply."[68]

Cases

The idea of using cases for educational purposes, though common in the Jewish Talmudic tradition, dates to the 1880s, when Christopher Langdell introduced cases at Harvard Law School, and to Harvard President Lawrence Lowell, who advocated the use of cases when he founded Harvard's Graduate School of Business in 1909.[69] Lowell made this amazing observation about how to teach business: "The case method of business training is deemed the best preparation for business life, because the discussion of questions by the banker, the manufacturer, the merchant or the transporter consists in discerning the essential elements in a situation and applying to them the principles of organization and trade. His most important work consists of solving problems, and for this he must have the faculty of rapid analysis and synthesis."[70]

Harvard appears to have been the place of origin of the case method for learning about problem solving and decision making in organizations, and to this day Harvard faculty are leaders in teaching through the case method and in producing cases.

The case method is an "active, discussion-oriented learning mode, disciplined by case problems drawn from the complexity of real life."[71] Consider the definition provided by Michiel Leenders and James Erskine in *Case Research: The Case Writing Process*: "The case method refers to the use of cases as educational vehicles to give students an opportunity to put themselves in the decision maker's or problem solver's shoes. Through repeated personal analysis, discussion with others, definition of problem, identification of alternatives, statement of objectives and decision criteria, choice of action and plan for implementation, the student gains an opportunity to develop analytical and planning skills in a laboratory setting. In medical analogy, the case provides the corpse for the student to practice on."[72]

The essence of the case method is problem solving and decision making. The reason for this focus is that cases require the learner to specify solutions and courses of action, which is why the case method involves discussion, analysis, and a case report.[73]

Although teachers may at times turn to prepared (off the shelf) cases, the more real and relevant the case material, the more likely significant learning will occur. Although Harvard is arguably the leader in creating prepared cases, many Harvard cases are designed for top-level executives. Students who will not attain those types of positions soon after graduating might be better served by more relevant case situations. In Grandon Gill's example in the preceding section, he uses small- and medium-size local companies as the basis of his cases. Many other sources for case material can be found through simple Internet searches.

Teachers may draw from several types of cases:

- Traditional case—The traditional case provides a detailed sum of background and current information, includes descriptions of key decision makers, poses problems or asks for recommendations, and may unfold through time over several stages. In a traditional case, participants are expected to read the case ahead of time, be prepared to analyze and discuss it, and eventually report recommendations.
- Live case—Another type of case, originated by Walter B. Murphy at the Wharton School of Finance and Commerce at the University of Pennsylvania, is known as the live case and involves a brief written statement and a live presentation by an actual representative of the

organization, someone who has lived through the case.[74] Participants provide reports on the case, which the live presenter reviews before returning for another visit to tell students how the case actually turned out.

- Key incident case—This case, known as the Pigors, involves the presentation of a key incident that stimulates questions the discussion leader (the person with the facts) answers in some detail, thus providing the factual basis for the case.[75] Participants are asked to focus on the key elements and diagram the issues, present reasoned opinions, and then reflect on the case as a whole, coming back to it to reconsider certain aspects.

- Clinical case—Sometimes a case is more specific to a diagnostic decision, as is common in social work, psychology, and the medical or nursing fields. In these cases, a specific scenario, often involving one person, is presented along with relevant and sometimes irrelevant information. Some of the information might not initially be offered, as part of the learning process involves the student's deciding what questions to ask or what information to gather. The purpose is usually to select the right model or way of framing the problem to make a diagnosis or plan a course of action.

Because some cases are quite long and require much preparation time, teachers sometimes may need to use abbreviated cases, single-problem cases, and critical incidents. Comparing cases can also be useful. In one study, students who were specifically asked to analyze two contrasting cases showed more learning transfer than those who studied the cases individually.[76] This process asks them to deliberately seek and identify elements of the cases that are important to the larger structure of the model being taught.

Managing and facilitating cases is a challenging process many instructors learn through trial and error, which can be avoided by seeking guidance from experienced case facilitators. Skilled facilitators may make it appear a discussion is driven spontaneously by the students, when in fact the teacher is guiding the discussion through the main topics and important aspects of the case quite deliberately.[77] They structure the case discussion around key decisions.

Labs and Problems

Science labs present good opportunities for students to learn problem solving through experimentation. By conducting experiments students can see for themselves how different aspects of a problem influence the overall outcome or how adjusting one variable will create different results. Sometimes science labs end up as formulaic recipe exercises in which students complete an experiment by following specific instructions yet have little idea what the results mean or why the entire exercise was important. In the 1970s Marshall Herron developed the Herron Scale as a means of determining the amount of structure involved in a particular lab. The scale has four levels: confirmation, structured, guided, or open, based on whether the teacher supplied the problem or the procedure and whether the solution is already known. All levels may be appropriate in some courses because students need a knowledge base to use mental models effectively, but the guided and open labs where students actually come up with the problem to be explored or the procedures to use to solve it are where the expert use of mental models truly develops. The effective lab teacher keeps the focus of the lab on the why aspect of the activity—why the model is being developed—as well as on the relevance of the findings, and how they relate to other problems in the course.

Those who teach the sciences are no doubt familiar with *problem-based learning* (PBL), a teaching method based on problems and popularized in medicine but now used in many disciplines. The origins of this model date from the 1970s with reforms at the medical school of McMaster University in Canada, and its use has been widespread since then. In medical education, labs and clinics are fundamental to learning. PBL transforms teaching into conceptual exploration taught in the context of clinical cases. Small groups of students are typically assigned a clinical case, and to make a diagnosis they must decide for themselves what is already known, what needs to be known, and what methods they must use to find the needed information. The outcome is not just to create a diagnosis but in the process to learn the basic science of medicine and techniques of problem solving. Unlike cases and projects in which students are often given the mental model first, the focus of PBL is to have students grapple with selecting or developing the appropriate mental model to use.

PBL has spread to many other disciplines, and using problems in different contexts has become an effective way to teach mental models. End-of-chapter textbook problems are often written as well-defined problems with one answer. This type of problem eliminates the need for the students to try to define the problem and make a decision about which steps to take to solve it.[78] The method students end up using is simply to find a similar-looking problem in the chapter and plug in the formula or algorithm. Instead, a problem that teaches how to use mental models focuses on the process of making decisions about what procedure to follow or what formula to use. Textbook problems can be rewritten into open-ended, real-life, ill-defined problems, or teachers can write their own problems based on real-life applications. Such problems should be difficult enough to be challenging but not so difficult that students end up frustrated.[79] Many such problems are designed in stages so the focus remains on the process and steps involved, not just the solution.

Projects

A project may begin like a case or lab with a description of a problem, an incident, or an issue to be decided. Students may work individually but often work together in teams, going out to gather data, seeking input from key people, generating and testing solutions, and reconvening from time to time to check progress. Authentic projects usually involve a real problem or preparation for a real decision, and the task takes on added seriousness because the results matter. Some projects may take several weeks to complete. Usually project teams designed for problem solving and decision making will have a project leader, a fixed schedule of deadlines, a deliverable, and the opportunity for regular consultation with the teacher.

The Teacher's Role

What is the role of the teacher with cases, labs, and projects? As planner, the teacher selects the case, lab activity, or project; makes its purpose clear; provides additional factual information as needed; and models the communication process of questioning, summarizing, and reflecting. The teacher is not only the manager of the activity but also the consultant, mentor, and technical adviser.[80] The teacher must juggle all these roles, playing them well and at the right time. As the behind-the-scenes expert on problem solving and decision making, the teacher is continually urging students to be systematic as opposed to being random in their quest for problem solutions. The teacher sees the activity's potential as a vehicle for learning about problem solving and decision making. Above all, the teacher asks students patiently and persistently what mental model they are using and how they are using it. Consider this example.

> Manju Bhat teaches physiology and life sciences at Winston-Salem State University. In courses such as Anatomy and Physiology, students are divided into groups and given real-life problems to solve as a means to conduct lab work. "In addition to gaining a detailed understanding of the

anatomical and physiological aspects of the human body, we want students in this course to use the scientific method to develop a deep understanding of the physiological interactions and compensatory mechanisms used by the body's organ systems in maintaining homeostasis," says Manju. "The lab sections are not seen as a separate entity; rather, students experience an integration of required text material with the laboratory experience through the use of basic dissection techniques, histological studies, and associated physiological phenomena of representative vertebrates." In a typical problem-based learning experience, Manju begins with a short presentation, and then student-led groups of two or three study models to identify anatomical structures. Next, Manju presents a problem. Students are encouraged to use all the information they have learned in class, and the resources they have at their disposal (lab manual, online tools, etc.), to come up with a solution or answer to the problem. The problems are usually phrased as real-life situations. "I find that when a real life example is used, students tend to express more interest not only in learning, but also participate more in group discussion, often relating the problem to examples of their own," Manju says. "They get to see how the body structure and functions they learn about apply to a real situation." For example, when studying the integumentary system, students need to study the overall structure of skin, its layers, types of cells, and their function. They explore how dead cells at the surface layer fall away and are replaced with new cells. A problem scenario is presented to students in which Timothy Jones, whose skin color is light, spends the entire spring break lying on the beach in Florida. When he returns, his skin color has turned dark. It takes about six weeks before his skin returns to its original color. Students are asked to explain this: How did Jones's skin turn dark, what is the mechanism, why does it take six weeks for the color to return, and so forth. The exploration also addresses further problems related to the impact of sunscreen and why dark-skinned people might be less susceptible to skin cancer. "Some students find it difficult to make the connection between the facts and concepts they learn and their functional significance, in this case the structural components of skin. But that's exactly what these problems are designed to do: allow students to explore this connection and see how the facts relate to each other."[81]

Assessing Learning With Mental Models

The teacher who advocates the use of mental models is asking students to consider and reconsider the underlying knowledge structures they use to solve problems and make decisions. Essentially, students are being asked to be systematic. Assessing this way of learning, therefore, focuses on helping students to make visible the thinking patterns they are using and the way they are organizing the information they are using. Assessment procedures that ask students to show their work and explain their thinking are effective methods for this way of learning.

Formative assessment methods that support the development of mental models can help teachers see how students organize their knowledge. Some popular classroom assessment techniques (CATs) that make thinking visible can be adapted by asking students to sort types of problems or aspects of a problem into categories, identify the type of problem represented in sample problems, create a concept map of the important variables, or categorize problems according to the presence or absence of certain features.[82]

When summative measures are needed, problem-based tests can be used to assess conceptual understanding as long as the thinking process is made visible for assessment. Asking students to describe their use of models or to explain how they solved a problem either verbally or in writing can shed light on the processes they used. In addition, it can be effective to set due dates for some things at intermediate points in the process of creating a project or completing an experiment, or to have groups give their reports at various points during a case discussion, and to provide feedback and clarification along the way. Naturally the final product is important, but a brilliant solution could be arrived at accidentally. Work submitted for grades should always contain not only the conclusions reached but the methods used for arriving at them.

Grading group cases or projects, especially when the product is a written work, can be a problem because writing is difficult to complete collaboratively. Typically, one or a few students tend to do most of the writing. Similarly, when faced with project presentations students can take a divide and conquer approach with each student doing one part, and in the end each student learns less than the group as a whole. Instead, the goal is to allow all students to understand the entire process and be able to explain how solutions were formed or decisions were made. When using groups in mental models, some individual work might need to be graded or at least reviewed, and many of the same lessons of grading group and teamwork in chapter 8 are applicable.

Michaelsen, Knight, and Fink have put forth a method for a specific type of group learning that addresses these concerns and is applicable for using mental models.[83] They suggest assigning complex cases or problems that contain difficult concepts but that provide choices that can be represented in a simple form, such as asking, "Would you choose option A, B, or C?" By providing clear choices to be defended, the focus shifts from the final product to the process of arriving at that choice, that is, on comparing and contrasting the various rationales, thinking patterns, and consequences of the different choices. Whenever possible, assessment should mirror the fact that when using mental models, the learning is more in the process than in the product.

Useful Technologies for Mental Models

As with other ways of learning, many technologies can support teaching through the use of mental models. Concept mapping software, spreadsheets, charts and diagrams, and a myriad of software programs can help students create visual displays of relevant data. Similarly, computer models can help students explore how separate components interact with each other and otherwise support the models being used to assist with problem solving and decision making. As information processing tools, computers can assist the boggled mind.

Many problems and cases are available online. For example, Harvard Business School Publishing, the most well-known source for case studies, has over thirteen thousand cases available to teachers in a variety of disciplines.[84] Many of its multimedia cases include audio and video segments along with interactive charts or data sets for students to work with. The University of Delaware, which has been a leader in PBL for over a decade, maintains a collection of peer-reviewed problems.[85] Its clearinghouse, along with the Multimedia Educational Resource for Learning and Online Teaching (MERLOT) and other websites, contains collections of cases, projects, and problems created by teachers and available for free use by other teachers.[86]

In addition, some technologies are available to help teachers get a sense of a student's thinking process. Being able to see a recorded history for a group project wiki allows some insight not only into who has contributed but into the changes, revisions, and development of the project. Smart pens, which record audio while a student is writing, or other audio tools, can be used for problem assignments. Students can talk through solving the problem, allowing instructors to analyze the problem-solving method as well as the solution.

Finally, vast amounts of easily accessed information can provide students with the background data they need in considering problems and decisions.

However, it should be noted that large amounts of information do not necessarily assist students when working with mental models and can in fact divert them from the challenging mental operations required. The teacher as content expert can help students discern the differences between relevant and irrelevant information and identify the most valuable sources of information. Most teachers are search experts in their fields of expertise and can model this expertise for their students. When enough information has been gathered, teachers will recognize they need to nudge students back to the hard work of solving problems and making decisions through mental models.

Final Thoughts

The use of mental models is part of what separates a novice from an expert in nearly any discipline. Beyond just gaining knowledge or practicing skills, developing mental models allows someone to organize vast amounts of information into meaningful structures that can be acted upon. With practice, students can learn the appropriate models to use in their fields that allow them to transfer knowledge to solve problems and make decisions.

Points to Remember

Teachers who want to use learning with mental models effectively should do the following:

- ✓ Realize that the best way to learn problem solving is by solving problems, and the best way to learn decision making is by making decisions.
- ✓ Convince students that problem-solving and decision-making techniques can be learned.
- ✓ Find or develop appropriate, relevant materials for students to practice with (problems, case studies, lab activities, and projects).
- ✓ Identify the steps or stages involved in solving a problem.
- ✓ Make sure students have the appropriate background knowledge to be able to solve the problem.
- ✓ Share useful theories on problem solving and decision making, and help students select the right mental model for the problem.
- ✓ Model the effective use of mental models to students.
- ✓ Help students sort relevant from irrelevant information.

✓ Draw on computer technologies to find and display information.
✓ Keep the focus on the process and steps rather than the final solution or decision.
✓ Revisit common pitfalls if things are not going as planned.
✓ Use formative as well as summative assessment measures to help students demonstrate their thinking processes and use of mental models.

Notes

1. Barbara Duch, "Problems: A Key Factor in PBL," Physics Level 3: Overload, last modified February 20, 1997, http://www.udel.edu/pbl/cte/spr96-phys.html.

2. Thanks to Barbara Duch, PhD, former Associate Director of the Math and Science Education Resource Center, with faculty appointments in Physics and Education at the University of Delaware, for granting permission to use her example. E-mail message to author, February 6, 2012.

3. Diane Halpern, *Thought and Knowledge: An Introduction to Critical Thinking* (Hillsdale, NJ: Erlbaum, 1984), 160.

4. Ibid., 160.

5. Thomas Ward, Ronald Finke, and Steven Smith, *Creativity and the Mind: Discovering the Genius Within* (New York: Plenum Press, 1995), 53.

6. Ibid., 55.

7. Sam Glucksberg, "Language and Thought," in *The Psychology of Human Thought*, ed. Robert Sternberg and Edward Smith (New York: Cambridge University Press, 1988), based on Stephen M. Kosslyn, *Ghosts in the Mind's Machine* (New York: Norton, 1983).

8. James Adams, *Conceptual Blockbusting* (New York: Norton, 1979), 76.

9. Wolfgang Köhler, *The Mentality of Apes* (New York: Harcourt Brace Jovanovich, 1925).

10. John Dworetzky, *Psychology*, 2nd ed. (New York: West Publishing, 1985), 237–38.

11. Denise Dellarosa, "A History of Thinking," in *The Psychology of Human Thought*, ed. Robert Sternberg and Edward Smith (New York: Cambridge University Press, 1988), 9–10.

12. George Polya, *How to Solve It*, 2nd ed. (Princeton, NJ: Princeton University Press, 1957).

13. Raymond Nickerson, David Perkins, and Edward Smith, *The Teaching of Thinking* (Hillsdale, NJ: Erlbaum, 1985), 74.

14. Allen Newell and Herbert A. Simon, *Human Problem Solving* (Englewood Cliffs, NJ: Prentice Hall, 1972).

15. Ibid.

16. Ibid., 315–16.

17. Scott Plous, *The Psychology of Judgment and Decision Making* (New York: McGraw-Hill, 1993), 80.

18. John Bransford and Barry Stein, *The Ideal Problem Solver: A Guide for Improving Thinking, Learning, and Creativity* (New York: W. H. Freeman, 1993), 8–9.

19. Alan Lesgold, "Problem Solving," in *The Psychology of Human Thought*, ed. Robert Sternberg and Edward Smith (New York: Cambridge University Press, 1988), 207–8.

20. Thanks to Anton Camarota, PhD, Managing Director of Tellari LLC and Adjunct Faculty at University College, University of Denver, for granting permission to use his teaching example. In discussion with the author, February 20, 2012.

21. Vincent Barry and Joel Rudinow, *Invitation to Critical Thinking*, 2nd ed. (Fort Worth, TX: Holt, Rinehart and Winston, 1990), 366.

22. Newell and Simon, *Human Problem Solving*, 53–63, 787–91.

23. Norbert Jausovec, *Flexible Thinking: An Explanation for Individual Differences in Ability* (Cresskill, NJ: Hampton Press, 1994), 10. The author refers to the distinction between problems and tasks made by the well-known German psychologist Dietrich Doerner.

24. Wayne Wickelgren, *How to Solve Problems: Elements of a Theory of Problems and Problem Solving* (San Francisco: W. H. Freeman, 1974), 10–17.

25. Ian Mitroff and Harold Linstone, *The Unbounded Mind: Breaking the Chains of Traditional Business Thinking* (New York: Oxford University Press, 1993), 49–50.

26. Kathy Yohalen, *Thinking Out of the Box* (New York: Wiley, 1997), 5.

27. Wickelgren, *How to Solve Problems*, 63.

28. Jausovec, *Flexible Thinking*, 10–11.

29. Barry and Rudinow, *Invitation to Critical Thinking*, 363.

30. Jonathan Baron, *Thinking and Deciding* (New York: Cambridge University Press, 2000), 17.

31. Ibid., 68.

32. Halpern, *Thought and Knowledge*, 182–84.

33. Ibid., 184–85.

34. Ibid., 185.

35. Ibid., 192–93.

36. Wickelgren, *How to Solve Problems*, 124–26.

37. Ibid., 26.

38. Ibid., 109–10.

39. Marilyn Burns, "Teaching 'What to Do' in Arithmetic Versus Teaching 'What to Do and Why,'" *Educational Leadership* 43, no. 7 (1986): 34–38.

40. Keith J. Holyoak and Richard Nisbett, "Induction," in *The Psychology of Human Thought*, ed. Robert Sternberg and Edward Smith (New York: Cambridge University Press, 1988), 82–83. The experiments are reported in M. L. Gick and Keith J. Holyoak, "Analogical Problem Solving," *Cognitive Psychology* 12 (1980): 306–55.

41. Daniel T. Willingham, *Why Don't Students Like School? A Cognitive Scientist Answers Questions about How the Mind Works and What It Means for the Classroom* (San Francisco: Jossey-Bass, 2009).

42. Wickelgren, *How to Solve Problems*, 63.

43. Halpern, *Thought and Knowledge*, 199–201.

44. Glucksberg, "Language and Thought," 225.

45. Adriann D. deGroot, *Thought and Choice in Chess* (The Hague, Netherlands: Mouton, 1965). See also deGroot, *Methodology: Foundation of Inference and Research in the Behavioral Sciences* (New York: Mouton, 1969).

46. National Research Council, *How People Learn: Brain, Mind, Experience, and School* (Washington, DC: National Academy Press, 2000).

47. M. T. H. Chi, P. J. Feltovich, and R. Glaser, "Categorization and Representation of Physics Problems by Experts and Novices," *Cognitive Science* 5, no. 2 (1981): 121–52.

48. Bransford and Stein, *The Ideal Problem Solver*, 4.

49. John Feldhusen, "A Conception of Creative Thinking and Creative Training," in *Nurturing and Developing Creativity*, ed. S. G. Isaksen, M. C. Murdock, R. F. Firestein, and D. J. Treffinger (Norwood, NJ: Ablex, 1993), 45.

50. Anthony J. Sanford, *Cognition and Cognitive Psychology* (New York: Basic Books, 1958), 309.

51. Nickerson et al., *The Teaching of Thinking*, 69.

52. Halpern, *Thought and Knowledge*, 225–26.

53. John Mullen and Byron Roth, *Decision Making: Its Logic and Practice* (Savage, MD: Rowman & Littlefield, 1991), 5.

54. Ibid., 11.

55. Ibid., 1–5. The ten steps presented here are adapted and elaborated on from Mullen and Roth's four-step process.

56. Ibid., 57.

57. Ibid., 55.

58. Ibid., 63–66.

59. Ibid., 62.

60. Ibid., 196.

61. Halpern, *Thought and Knowledge*, 221–22.

62. Raymond Nickerson, *Reflections on Reasoning* (Hillsdale, NJ: Erlbaum, 1986), 32.

63. Halpern, *Thought and Knowledge*, 222–23.

64. Baron, *Thinking and Deciding*, 346–49.

65. Ibid., 382–84.

66. Halpern, *Thought and Knowledge*, 136–37.

67. Baron, *Thinking and Deciding*, 230–32.

68. Thanks to T. Grandon Gill, Professor, PhD, College of Business, University of South Florida, for granting permission to use his example. E-mail message to author, January 25, 2012.

69. Paul Pigors and Faith Pigors, "Case Method," in *Training and Development Handbook: A Guide to Human Resource Development*, 3rd ed., ed. Robert L. Craig (New York: McGraw-Hill, 1987), 415.

70. Louis Barnes, C. Roland Christensen, and Abby Hansen, *Teaching and the Case Method* (Boston: Harvard Business School Press, 1994), 41.

71. Ibid., 34.

72. Michiel Leenders and James Erskine, *Case Research: The Case Writing Process* (London, Ontario, Canada: University of Western Ontario, 1973), 11.

73. Pigors and Pigors, "Case Method," 415.

74. Ibid.

75. Ibid., 418–19.

76. J. Lowenstein, L. Thompson, and D. Gentner, "Analogical Learning in Negotiated Terms: Comparing Cases Promotes Learning and Transfer," *Academy of Management Learning and Education* 2, no. 2 (2003): 119–27.

77. T. Grandon Gill, *Informing with the Case Method: A Guide to Case Method Research, Writing, & Facilitation* (Santa Rosa, CA: Informing Science Press, 2011).

78. Edward J. Mastascusa, William J. Snyder, and Brian S. Hoyt, *Effective Instruction for STEM Disciplines: From Learning Theory to College Teaching* (San Francisco: Jossey-Bass, 2011).

79. Barbara J. Duch, Susan E. Groh, and Deborah E. Allen, *The Power of Problem-Based Learning: A Practical "How To" for Teaching Undergraduate Courses in Any Discipline* (Sterling, VA: Stylus, 2001).

80. Pigors and Pigors, "Case Method," 422–23. We have used the basic categories as lead words, but we have greatly modified the descriptors; we want to give credit to the Pigorses for the good list.

81. Thanks to Manjunatha B. Bhat, PhD, Assistant Professor of Physiology in the Department of Life Sciences and Project Strengthen, Winston-Salem State University, for granting permission to use his example. E-mail message to author, February 16, 2012.

82. Thomas Angelo and Patricia Cross, *Classroom Assessment Techniques: A Handbook for College Teachers* (San Francisco: Jossey-Bass, 1993).

83. Larry K. Michaelsen, Arletta B. Knight, and L. Dee Fink, *Team-Based Learning: A Transformative Use of Small Groups in College Teaching* (Sterling, VA: Stylus, 2004), 46.

84. See Harvard Business Publishing for Educators, accessed March 15, 2012, http://hbsp.harvard.edu/product/cases.

85. "Problem-Based Learning at University of Delaware," accessed March 15, 2012, https://primus.nss.udel.edu/Pbl/.

86. "Welcome to MERLOT," accessed March 15, 2012, http://www.merlot.org/merlot/index.htm.

8

EXPLORING ATTITUDES, FEELINGS, AND PERSPECTIVES

Learning Through Groups and Teams

Intended Learning Outcomes	Way of Learning	Common Methods
What students learn	Origins and theory	What the teacher provides
Exploring attitudes, feelings, and perspectives	**Learning through groups and teams**	Group activities
Awareness of attitudes, biases, and other perspectives; ability to collaborate	Human communication theory, group counseling theory	Team projects

Is this learning that involves changing opinions, attitudes, and beliefs? Does it involve creating understanding from an awareness of multiple perspectives? Does it deal with feelings? Does it cultivate empathy? Is teamwork or collaboration being addressed here? These are learning outcomes that are well served by learning through groups and teams.

A political science teacher uses groups to explore controversial issues in her American government class. Brief scenarios are used to set in motion discussions, exchange of viewpoints, and further research to back up opinions. How does the teacher manage these groups and ensure civil discourse when strongly held opinions are involved?

Significant human accomplishments are often the result of teamwork. Making films, playing symphonies, designing skyscrapers, building bridges, performing heart transplants, conducting space flights, and finding the causes of exotic diseases all involve collaborative teams. Groups are commonly used for therapy in the work of treatment facilities, but groups are also used in organizational settings to explore attitudes and feelings, explore multiple perspectives, and develop what has come to be known as *emotional intelligence* for the purpose of better work relationships. Most organizations now rely on some type of group process or team collaboration to achieve their goals.

In fact, being able to work effectively with peers and contribute productively to groups and teams are basic expectations of college graduates. Hardly any careers today involve individuals' working exclusively alone. Work environments are also increasingly diverse and global, and it is very common for individuals who are different and come from different locations, even different continents, to collaborate virtually on shared projects. Unfortunately, collaboration does not always come naturally to *Homo sapiens*. Although studies of bees, ants, and geese have found they work together instinctively, humans often need to be taught to collaborate. Groups provide an effective means of exploring and altering opinions, attitudes, and perspectives, and teams are useful for teaching human collaboration. These are the two main reasons for using this way of learning.

Many teaching methods that involve students working together in groups are quite different from what we mean by learning from groups and teams. For example, asking students to talk to their neighbor for a few minutes during a lecture supports goals such as information processing and comprehension. Asking students to participate in a buzz group before embarking on a case study supports problem solving and decision making. Although both are useful tactics, we would not consider such activities to be what we refer to as learning through groups and teams. Because there are so many team-based approaches to instruction that come up in conversations about teaching today, we want to identify and describe the most prominent of these before presenting the unique kinds of learning we believe grow out of the properties of groups and teams themselves.

Cooperative learning. This name describes a method long employed and studied in K–12 education and made popular in higher education beginning in the 1980s through the work of many scholars, but most notably two brothers, Roger and David Johnson.[1] Cooperative learning involves the frequent use of structured activities throughout a semester in which students learn in pairs or small groups of three to four. In this format students work together to find the correct or best solutions to a given set of problems, while the teacher keeps them on track by providing just-in-time instruction. Through many years of study, Johnson and Johnson have identified many learning benefits of this approach and have defined five elements essential for successful cooperative learning teams, which they term *positive interdependence, promotive interaction, individual and group accountability, development of teamwork skills,* and *group processing.*[2] In cooperative learning, a strong emphasis is placed on students' helping other students to learn.

Collaborative learning. This term is also used for college classroom group work, but there are distinct differences between this approach and cooperative learning. Whereas cooperative learning is about working together in harmony to find the correct answer, collaborative learning often encourages dissent and disagreement.[3] Collaborative learning is based on learning in pairs or small groups of two to six students who work together, but the groups are often loosely structured and based on open-ended goals with no right answers, and the teacher is part of the learning community rather than the authority figure.[4]

Team-based learning. Proponents of team-based learning argue that it goes beyond cooperative and collaborative learning by using teams to change the nature and structure of a course.[5] Team-based learning is used to develop content knowledge as well as application of content and team skills. Classes are broken into groups of five to eight students that stay together for the entire semester. Teamwork is alternated with individual efforts through a sequence of in-class and out-of-class activities, with in-class group activity focused on application and problem solving. The instructor gives ongoing individual and group feedback, but unlike cooperative and collaborative learning, hardly any time is spent on group process skills. Instead, to avoid group process issues, activities are presented as make-a-specific-choice assignments. These assignments are based on sophisticated problems involving complex choices that need to be discussed and justified by the group, but the choices are represented in a simple form, such as choose option A, B, or C. In this way, group outcomes are easy to identify, and immediate feedback is easy to give.

Problem-based learning teams. Originally developed for use in medical schools, problem-based learning involves breaking students into groups of nine to ten students to work through clinical cases. This approach looks much like cooperative learning in structuring and running the groups, although tutors are used to assist them. Problem-based learning involves unstructured problems where the focus is on using groups to get students to identify what is important in the material. Problem solving, as a way of learning, is discussed in chapter 7.

The focus of learning through groups and teams can be confused with other ways of learning because nearly any teaching method can be carried out by students' working together. Just because students are arranged in groups does not necessarily mean that the way of learning we call learning through groups and teams is being employed. The focus of our use of learning through groups and teams is on the inherent benefits that occur when individuals explore attitudes, opinions, beliefs, viewpoints, perspectives, and feelings together. By doing so, students can see how their way of viewing the world is different from someone else's, can begin to appreciate these differences, and can reach a new level of understanding and awareness. Higher education is a very cerebral enterprise, and many teachers, including those who regularly use groups, may not agree that they should be addressing feelings in learning. But in fact, feelings are the main subject of groups. Groups and teams are best used for instruction when the intrinsic properties and strengths of groups are used to explore multiple opinions, attitudes, and perspectives and to build teamwork and collaborative skills. Consider the following example.

> Leticia Sara teaches political science at Red Rocks Community College, where she routinely uses groups for students to explore controversial issues. In her American Government course, she uses a group assignment to teach students about the Supreme Court. She says, "Beyond basic knowledge of how the Supreme Court operates, I want them to develop an understanding of civil liberties and rights, and the complexities of determining civil liberties." Her students work in groups to create presentations about a particular civil liberty issue, such as a controversial art exhibit or freedom of religion for a charity accepting public money. For example, one group is assigned the following scenario about public speech.
>
>> During the U.S. war in Afghanistan, some Middle Eastern students reserve a table in a busy section of the campus where they give out literature critical of the war. They put up a large banner that reads: U.S. Troops Out of Afghanistan! A crowd of angry students gathers and tries to rip down the banner. Some pushing takes place. Campus police arrive on the scene. The crowd demands that the banner be taken down. The students at the table demand that the police remove the crowd. What should the campus police do?
>
> Students meet in and out of class to grapple with the issue, find resources to back up the various viewpoints, and create the presentation. The students usually find and present actual court cases that have either been in

favor of or against the decisions made in their scenarios. During the class meeting, Leticia visits each group to provide guidance and feedback. "Normally the students choose a side to defend that they agree with, but a great way of avoiding argument is to encourage students to represent the side they don't necessarily agree with," says Leticia. This also enables them to understand the challenges social scientists face when conducting value-free research. "Our goal with this assignment is to explore all aspects of the issue; not to win or lose," says Leticia. "This allows the students to be more open and comfortable because they are supporting their opinions. I have also noticed that they respect each other's opinions more once they have examined actual cases and conducted research. The discussions are civil but lively."[6]

The Dynamics of Groups

What are the intrinsic properties of groups that make them useful vehicles for learning? Do predictable patterns of behavior occur when people are placed in groups? Why are groups used in organizational settings and for learning? The five main reasons for using groups are the following:

1. Groups are used when individual effort is insufficient. Some work requires only the sum of the outputs of each individual. In tasks where the total output is greater than the sum of individual efforts, there is an assembly effect. The assembly effect bonus is productivity that exceeds the potential of the most capable member and also exceeds the sum of the efforts of the group members working separately.[7] Groups consistently outperform individual efforts; thus, groups are used to accomplish work that requires collaboration.[8]

2. Groups are used to generate ideas. Research has established that groups produce more ideas than individuals working alone. Not only do people pool their ideas, but there is something about the process of the group that generates more ideas. In an early review of studies of group problem solving, it was found that ideation is 60 to 90 percent higher for groups than for individuals. Individuals tend to present far fewer options (they close down on a single solution), and their solutions are far less imaginative than when the same individuals discuss the options in a group. There is no guarantee that groups will come up with the best ideas, but they will usually generate more ideas.

3. Groups are used to bring about change in outlook. People hold opinions, attitudes, and beliefs that are in harmony with their group memberships and identifications. Ideas are often rooted in group affiliations, and may not be so much the result of individual thinking as we might believe. It is not surprising to learn, therefore, that opinions, attitudes, and beliefs are not easily changed through rational argument or persuasion, that is, by appeal to intellect. When opinions, attitudes, and beliefs do change, it is usually through the influence of a new reference group or affiliation.[9] Groups are used to help people overcome fears, work through their reservations, reconsider long-standing beliefs, address biases, and develop more positive attitudes. Groups, therefore, are especially useful for examining matters of the heart, what psychologists refer to as *affective learning*.

4. Groups are used to broaden participation and cultivate belonging. The early work of Kurt Lewin demonstrated there is a higher acceptance of outcomes when they are arrived at through a group process.[10] Members are more likely to accept an outcome (even if they don't agree with it fully) if they have had the opportunity to discuss it in a group. An outpouring of literature on management, leadership, and organizational change has stressed the importance of involvement (participation and inclusion) in bringing about acceptance of new ideas and change. Groups produce a sense of ownership over outcomes and a sense of belonging.

5. Groups are used to deepen understanding of subject content by acknowledging different perspectives. Exploring how others think and feel about issues can help students see their ideas in a new light while developing a deeper appreciation for the attitudes of others. In this way individuals acknowledge their own viewpoints, biases, and blind spots and come to appreciate alternatives as they learn informally from each other.[11]

Groups have become a favorite of teachers for the affective learning associated with exploring feelings and perspectives. When was this way of learning discovered and developed? What is it about groups that gives them this potential for bringing about learning? Clever group activities may be fun, but what should a teacher know about using groups and teams so participants actually learn from those activities?

Origins of Learning in Groups and Teams

For centuries human beings have assembled themselves into groups for a variety of purposes and have given their groups special designations, such as guilds, councils, tribunes, communes, congregations, troupes, teams, and companies. Groups have also been used for educational purposes, from the small bands that followed wandering scholars such as Confucius or Plato to the medieval guilds. In modern times groups have been used in more explicit ways for educational purposes. When did the formal study of groups begin, and who were the key leaders in exploring, identifying, and leveraging the educational potential that resides in group processes?

The conscious use of groups for educational and therapeutic purposes has its origin in employment settings. A classic set of research studies conducted by Elton Mayo and his colleagues at the Western Electric Company in the 1930s revealed the importance of human factors in the productivity of workers.[12] Although the factors being studied had to do with better working conditions, such as lighting, it turned out that the personal attention given to the workers *as a group* by the researchers proved to be the most important consideration. This discovery gave birth to the human relations movement.

The movement was advanced somewhat by accident in 1946 when Kurt Lewin and his associates were conducting group training for community leaders. Lewin, a professor at Massachusetts Institute of Technology and already well known for his work in group dynamics, was joined by his colleagues each evening to discuss the processes that were taking place in the groups that day. Some of the workshop participants began attending these meetings in which their own behavior and its effect on the group was discussed and analyzed openly.[13] Lewin and his associates discovered that when group members were confronted objectively with interpretations of their behavior and were encouraged to think about these interpretations in a nondefensive way, meaningful learning could occur. The staff began to theorize about what they were observing and planned ways that group experiences could be structured to heighten this kind of learning.

In the summer of 1947, shortly after Lewin's death, his associates met in Bethel, Maine, to sponsor the first formal group training programs in which trainers assisted the group in discussing its behavior.[14] This kind of group became known as a T-group or basic skill training group. In 1949 Lewin's former associates formed the National Training Laboratory under the auspices of the National Education Association.

Another important historical source for understanding the learning that takes place in groups and teams is the work of Carl Rogers. In 1946 and 1947, the same years Lewin and his associates were working in the East, Rogers and his associates at the Counseling Center at the University of Chicago were training personal counselors at the Veteran's Administration to become effective in working with GIs returning from World War II. In Rogers's own words, "Our staff felt that no amount of cognitive training would prepare them, so we experimented with an intensive group experience in which the trainees met for several hours each day in order to understand themselves better, to become aware of attitudes which might be self-defeating in the counseling relationship, and to relate to each other in ways that would be helpful and could carry over into the counseling work."[15] The Chicago groups led by Rogers focused explicitly on personal growth and differed somewhat from the training groups developed by Lewin and the National Training Laboratory. Eventually Rogers moved to California and became involved with the encounter group movement there. In California another strand of the group movement developed under the banner of humanistic psychology, drawing on the work of Maslow, Reich, Jung, and various Eastern religious traditions. In the 1960s an independent training center, the Esalen Institute, was established in Northern California, where the encounter group reached its fullest expression.

Another historical source for understanding this way of learning is group therapy. Although the idea of therapy conducted in groups dates from Freud and his followers, and although the term *group therapy* seems to have been coined by J. L. Moreno in 1920, the widespread use of groups for explicitly therapeutic purposes is also a post–World War II phenomenon.[16] Confronted with numbers of disruptive patients at a veterans hospital and inadequate resources to treat each of these patients, a group of psychiatrists and psychologists led by W. R. Bion developed a theory for treating patients in groups. Bion's work at the Tavistock Institute in London became the basis for modern group therapy techniques.

As groups began to be used widely in the 1960s and 1970s, they also came to be studied more seriously, and a vast literature on group processes eventually emerged.[17] Groups have been studied from many vantage points, but most of the literature that is valuable to teachers—insights about the underlying theory that supports learning through groups and teams—comes from the field of human communication studies.

What We Know About Groups and Teams

Years of studying group processes has yielded general principles and theories about the dynamics of groups. Here is what is known:

Groups Have Definable Characteristics

Because it is difficult to arrive at one definition of groups that is acceptable to all, it may be best to think of criteria instead. A collection of people is likely to be a group when it has a conscious and definable membership, a sense of shared purposes and goals, regular interactions and mutual influences, and the ability to act as a unit.

A Team Is a Group With a Mission

All teams are groups, but not all groups are teams. When people get together on a Friday night for salsa dancing, we would call them a group not a team. We would call a group that has the responsibility for achieving or producing something, such as a heart transplant, a team. Carl Larson and Frank LaFasto in their provocative book *Teamwork* define teams as follows: "A team has two or more people; it has a specific performance objective or recognizable goal to be attained; and coordination of activity among the members of the team is required for the attainment of the team goal or objective."[18] The salsa dance group becomes a team when its members decide to develop a shared purpose and work together to win a competition.

Groups and Teams Go Through Various Phases or Stages

It takes a while for a group to become a group, to develop an identity and become productive. Bruce Tuckman's classic formulation of these stages uses four catchy rhyming words.

- Forming—testing and member independence with emphasis on defining the task.
- Storming—intragroup conflict and emotional expression.
- Norming—development of group cohesion and establishing the rules.
- Performing—functional role relatedness and emergence of solutions.[19]

A fifth stage, called adjourning, has been added to acknowledge that groups often complete their tasks and dissolve.[20] Groups do not always become productive on day one. They take time to form and need time to develop a level of group maturity that allows them to be effective. Most groups go through some stages, and when old members leave and new members join, the group has to adjust.

Group Communication Focuses on Task and Process Needs

Put people in groups and they will interact. What do they talk about? Who talks most? What mediums do they use to communicate? How often do they communicate? Who responds mostly to whom? Many scholars who have studied groups have noted that communication seems to take place at two levels, often simultaneously.[21] At one level members are communicating about the *task* to be completed; at another level they are dealing with the *process* needs (sometimes referred to as social or maintenance needs) of the group members.

The task is the activity a group is required to perform. The task is what people do, what they work on, or what they produce in and through groups.[22] When people participate in groups, they bring with them their individual needs for recognition, identity, status, power, visibility, competition, and inclusion. All these factors can influence the social and emotional climate of the group and the group process.[23] These factors also affect the way the task is undertaken and completed. It is natural and expected that participants will not be focusing their attention exclusively on the task.

Groups Develop Cohesion

When the process needs of the group are being met in satisfactory ways, the group becomes cohesive. Cohesiveness refers to the ability of the group members to get along, their loyalty, pride, and commitment to the group. Or more simply, cohesiveness is the degree of liking that members have for each other. When there is a high level of bickering in a group, when members express boredom, search for excuses to avoid group meetings, or do not respond to each other, the group usually lacks cohesiveness. Something is going wrong at the process level. Sometimes challenging experiences not related to the task are used to accelerate building cohesion. As might be expected, cohesive groups are more productive but only up to a point. As cohesiveness increases, productivity increases until cohesiveness reaches such a high level that productivity might actually fall off. Why? When group members become too fond of each other, they spend too much time socializing and too little time on the task.[24]

Groups Have Structure

As groups mature, passing through various stages, they eventually develop a structure.[25] The group's structure is not always immediately obvious. Because some people have more to contribute they have more initial status, or because they have a strong personality they take a more central place in the group's structure, while others end up on the periphery. The composition of the group and its patterns of communication help determine group structure.

Group Participants Play Roles

In groups, roles are the "set of expectations which group members share concerning the behavior of a person who occupies a given position in the group."[26] Group members can assume many different roles. The classic delineation of these roles was worked out by Kenneth Benne and Paul Sheets during the initial National Training Laboratory meetings in 1947.[27] We have reclassified, paraphrased, and eliminated some items on the classic list in compiling the following roles.

Positive Task Roles

- Initiator/contributor—suggests new ideas or procedures
- Information seeker—asks for clarification of ideas, facts, or evidence
- Opinion seeker—asks for agreement or disagreement by other group members
- Information giver—gives facts or relates own experience
- Elaborator—clarifies and explains further
- Coordinator—shows relationships among ideas and pulls things together
- Orientor—defines where the group is, summarizes, keeps things on track, evaluates progress
- Energizer—prods the group to a decision or action
- Recorder—writes down suggestions, takes minutes

Positive Process Roles

- Encourager—agrees with, praises, or accepts the ideas of others
- Harmonizer—resolves conflicts, mediates differences, and reduces tensions, often with humor

- Gatekeeper—keeps channels of communication open, encourages others to participate and be heard
- Standard setter—expresses standards for the group to reach
- Group observer—evaluates the mood of the group
- Follower—goes along with the group trend, accepts the ideas of others, serves as audience

Negative Individual Roles

- Aggressor—attacks others, or the group, in various ways to promote own status
- Blocker—opposes others' ideas beyond reason and refuses to cooperate
- Recognition seeker—calls attention to self by boasting, acting in unusual ways
- Self-confessor—engages in irrelevant discussion, uses the group audience for expressing personal problems
- Pest—displays lack of involvement in the group through humor, cynicism, or horseplay
- Dominator—monopolizes the group for personal ends by asserting authority, interrupting, giving directions
- Help seeker—calls forth sympathy from the group through unreasonable expressions of insecurity or inadequacy
- Special interest pleader—presents a cause to the group

Not all groups contain members who play all these roles, but this list of task, process, and individual roles can be used as a valuable checklist of what to look for in analyzing group structure.

Groups Establish Rules

Eventually, when the roles people play in a group become well established and when the structure of the group becomes set, the group can be said to have established group *norms*.[28] As certain behavior patterns are repeated, they become endowed with normalcy.

In a classroom it becomes expected that a certain member will come into the room, take the same seat, play the same role, and participate in the same way each time. Similarly, an online group might usually wait for one particular member who always initiates the group discussion. Norms will differ, of course, from group to group, and what may appear to be a bold and abrasive confrontation in one group may be viewed simply as open and direct self-disclosure in another. Eventually, however, the behavior is established as a rule for that group, and individual members will internalize these norms and play by the group's rules. The skillful facilitator of a group learns how to assist group members in establishing and following productive roles and useful rules.

Groups Rely on Active Listening

Teachers who use groups become effective observers of the communication processes in the groups. They become good observers of what group members say and do, particularly of communication that involves personal self-disclosure and feedback from the group. Self-disclosure occurs when a person lets someone else know something about himself or herself the listener wouldn't ordinarily know.[29] This disclosure need not be a deep, dark secret (though it may be) but can refer to any idea or feeling a person is expressing. Feedback occurs when someone else, or several members of the group, makes a response in return.

For this transaction of self-disclosure and feedback to take place in an effective way, *active listening* must take place. Active listening is sometimes further differentiated into deliberate listening and empathic listening.[30] The deliberate listener is actively engaged in trying to understand ideas, standing ready to agree or disagree, criticize, summarize, or conclude. The empathic listener is focusing on feelings, trying to understand the speaker's emotions from the speaker's point of view. When active listening is taking place, the feedback is likely to be more appropriate and useful than when the quality of listening is poor. Poor listening occurs when the listener becomes prematurely involved emotionally (losing objectivity); is busy mentally preparing answers (before fully understanding the disclosure); is distracted, set off by emotionally laden words; or allows personal prejudices to interfere with understanding. Good listeners try to concentrate on listening, avoid interrupting the speaker if possible, demonstrate interest and alertness, seek areas of agreement, search for meanings, avoid getting stuck on specific words, and demonstrate patience. These factors can occur in person or virtually. Good listeners also try to provide clear and unambiguous feedback and repress the tendency to respond emotionally to what is said; they ask questions and withhold evaluation of the message until it is time to do so.[31] Usually teachers need to model such behavior intentionally and assist group members in becoming more skilled as active listeners.

Groups Use Nonverbal Communication

Nonverbal communication occurs in a variety of ways in groups, and sophisticated group watchers will look for the following:

- Proxemics—the way group members arrange themselves in space (through seating arrangements, physical distance, and general body orientation)
- Appearance—overall physical appearance or body language that may reveal attitude or mood
- Kinesics—body movement; postures; gestures; and movements of the head, limbs, hands, and feet
- Facial expressions—facial features, movement of the eyes and mouth[32]

Nonverbal communication is especially important in activities that require group members to get out of their seats and do something. Much can be learned about people by watching what they do as well as listening to what they say.

How does nonverbal communication relate to verbal communication? Sometimes directly by repeating or elaborating a verbal message, for example, by using a gesture to emphasize an important point. At other times, however, a nonverbal message may contradict the verbal message—for example, an arms-folded, tense denial of anger—sending a visible clue throughout the group that what is being said is not what is being felt. In some activities, the nonverbal message is the only communication. In a sense, then, group members are always communicating whether they speak or not, through gestures, facial expressions, or the place they take in the group.

Many groups exist entirely online and miss out on nonverbal cues. Such groups must work more diligently to obtain clear and open communication such as creating identified norms and defined roles. Virtual groups can exist without nonverbal cues, but more purposeful and deliberate action should be taken to support development of an online social presence.[33] Group norms are perhaps better set during synchronous live sessions. Holding at least one initial live session to develop social connections and a few occasional face-to-face or live online meetings to establish relationships can help develop the social cohesion important in groups.

Using Groups to Explore Attitudes and Feelings

Groups are often used for exploring issues that reasonable people may openly and honestly disagree with. As previously noted, groups are useful for bringing about changes in opinions, attitudes, and beliefs. The topics can range over a host of issues, such as immigration policy, abortion, civil rights, balancing the budget, tax policy, the right to privacy, gun laws, child welfare, global warming, modern art, religious beliefs, human evolution, cohabitation before marriage, and death and dying. Hardly any of these issues stand alone as an intellectual issue without a significant affective component, and groups are especially useful for bringing out feelings, identifying biases, and discovering blind spots. Even many science subjects considered to be value-free contain underlying assumptions and associated feelings. More specifically, the group allows students to state their viewpoints (opinions), discover the feelings associated with their viewpoints (attitudes), and understand the origins of these attitudes in previous experience (beliefs).

The process of launching a group discussion is quite simple but requires careful planning. When the groups have been composed, students are given an activity that sets the group in motion, usually a carefully selected quotation that frames an issue or takes a stand, accompanied by a set of questions to consider or instructions to follow. If the activity is well designed, a lively discussion ensues quite naturally.

Consider once again how Leticia Sara sets her groups in motion with brief scenarios embedded with controversial issues (see pp. 180–81). One can imagine the initial reactions of her students to the antiwar protest scenario. Opinions flow freely. Students begin to take sides. Attitudes about this war and war in general begin to surface. Soon the students are discussing the right to peaceful assembly, free speech, and the situation of the students who unwittingly set off this storm. The significant learning that comes from this scenario is when the individuals who discuss the issue in their groups begin to share their personal opinions, honestly explore their attitudes, and discuss where their beliefs may have originated. Thus, the issues examined go beyond the safe intellectual level to include the potentially riskier level of feelings. They do this in the supportive atmosphere of small groups that encourage an honest examination of feelings.

Sometimes learning in groups goes into deeper, sensitive, and more personal issues. Although teachers need to keep their work focused on learning, not therapy, the lines between the two are not always clear. Very few teachers would think of themselves as leading anything similar to what were once called encounter groups, but knowing something about the methods and processes of these and other therapy groups can be valuable to teachers who guide deeper learning through groups and teams.

As noted earlier, the principles that guide this way of learning have their roots in T-groups, encounter groups, training laboratories, and group therapy. Although these terms may have an odd ring today, and for those who lived through the late 1960s and early 1970s they may bring to mind some of the excesses of these experiments, much was learned through these groups about how people change and develop new attitudes about themselves and others. T-groups were designed to provide a setting in which "participants work together in a small group over an extended period of time, learning through analysis of their own experiences, including feelings, reactions, perceptions and behavior."[34] It was discovered that groups such as these could provide a laboratory for learning that is often denied in the real world. What are the outcomes of learning in the classic encounter group? Outcomes will surely vary, depending on the purposes and composition of the group, but consider the words of one of the founders, Carl Rogers: "In such a group the individual comes to know himself and each of the others more completely than is possible in the usual social or working relationships. He becomes deeply acquainted with the other members and with his own inner self, the self that otherwise tends to be hidden behind his facade. Hence he relates better to others, both in the group and later in the everyday life situation."[35]

How does this occur? Although therapy groups tend to emphasize mental health—the word *therapy* comes from the Greek *therapeia*, meaning healing—the processes employed in group therapy can be modified and used for the more modest goal of delving a little deeper into feelings. Irvin D. Yalom, author of a definitive text on group therapy, *The Theory and Practice of Group Psychotherapy*, lists eleven therapeutic factors that make therapy in groups effective.[36] The factors and brief paraphrased descriptors are as follows:

1. Instillation of hope—People who share a problem come to believe there is hope for resolving it.
2. Universality—Participants realize that they are not alone and that others have a similar problem.
3. Imparting information—Members of the group share information about how they have dealt with the problem.

4. Altruism—People discover they can be helpful to others.
5. Recapitulation of the family—Groups become like families, and members rediscover how they have acted as family members.
6. Development of social skills—Members become aware they are perceived as shy, regal, tactless, or aggressive and learn new interpersonal skills.
7. Imitative behavior—Participants imitate the positive behaviors of the facilitator and of other group members.
8. Interpersonal learning—By reviewing critical incidents in their lives, members can have a corrective emotional experience in which they relearn something about relationships.
9. Group cohesiveness—A sense of good feeling among group members provides the therapeutic setting for acceptance and an honest sharing of feelings.
10. Catharsis—The group becomes a place where members can get things off their chest, and this in itself can be therapeutic.
11. Existential factors—Participants get a new sense of what life is all about and learn to live their lives more honestly.

Some common applications today include creating a *circle of voices* in which each individual perspective in a group is heard equally. Something about the formation of a circle simulates a gathering of equals and encourages participation by all.[37]

Although many groups are not led by a teacher, sometimes when the topic and nature of the group invites deeper discussion, the teacher may wish to be present as the facilitator. What does a teacher do with groups that explore deeper feelings? A teacher does three important things:

1. *Deepens communication.* The teacher sets guidelines to establish desirable norms for deeper communication, such as active involvement, nonjudgmental acceptance of others, extensive self-disclosure, desire for understanding, and motivation for change. The teacher may give explicit instructions, comment on something that has taken place, provide an instrument or activity, raise questions, or reward members with praise for positive behavior, all with an eye toward deepening the level of communication. The teacher may also model the behavior that is appropriate to the norms through nonjudgmental acceptance, interpersonal honesty, and spontaneity.

2. *Deals with the here and now.* One of the most important parts of the teacher's role is to encourage students to talk about and deal with the here

and now. Students can be expected to deal with the real problems of their lives but, perhaps even more important, with real communication events taking place in the group at the particular moment. As the group experience develops, the group members will realize that their task is to focus on the here and now. How are ideas linked to feelings, and how are feelings being communicated at the present moment when ideas are being discussed?

3. *Comments on the group's behavior.* The teacher also monitors the process that is ongoing in the group and illuminates for the group what is taking place through process commentary. The commentary focuses on recurring themes, deeper meanings, and the relationship between outside problems members may be having and the problems they are discussing at the moment within the group. Without being judgmental, the teacher points out how a member's behavior makes others feel, how the behavior brings about reactions from others, and how in the end the behavior influences that member's own self-esteem. Sometimes the teacher will give a group process commentary, that is, feedback to the group as a whole about its behavior.

Especially when feelings and topics of a sensitive nature are explored, it is helpful to develop some guidelines, ground rules, and boundaries for the group, and revisit them periodically. Not every college teacher will feel comfortable about this hard-to-navigate realm of feelings, but separating ideas from attitudes and feelings is probably neither possible nor wise; and at some point, like it or not, discussions will go deeper. It is good to be prepared. In some subjects this *is* the subject. Consider the teacher's role in getting the group to dig deeper in the following example.

Damon Freeman teaches a social work course called Critical Race Theory at the University of Pennsylvania. Along with other goals, Damon wants his students to examine the workings of contemporary racism and investigate the theoretical relationships between race, class, gender, sexuality, and nation. He uses group discussions to explore personal opinions, attitudes, and biases about what are often sensitive topics. "I usually begin each class with something that occurred the previous week in the news that directly or sometimes indirectly deals with race, for example, a campaign commercial," he says. Damon might start the discussion with two or three questions of his own. Or he might use some of the questions the students have raised themselves in their weekly reflection essays. For example, one reading his class explores is Patricia Hill Collins's *Black Feminist Thought.*[38] Collins argues that historically there are three versions of Black motherhood based on one-dimensional stereotypes. She argues that Black women experience a continuum of reactions to motherhood, ranging from a self-actualization process that can lead to hope for the future to seeing motherhood as a burden that stifles and exploits Black women. Collins offers a complex definition of what Black motherhood means that differs from historical stereotypes. "For many students who read Collins, this is the first time they have been exposed to this kind of thinking, even if they have come from a women's studies background. I ask them to dig a little deeper, with what does this mean to you types of questions," says Damon. "Since many of the students are doing field placements in social work, they find themselves citing numerous examples of seeing motherhood as a burden. So I then ask them about the other side of Collins's coin, namely her point that the self-actualization process might exist side by side within the same individual. While many students think that's possible upon reflection, they almost always have failed to see it in their practice until then." The discussion usually becomes broader, rethinking social work practice itself in regard to motherhood and political activism. Damon sees his role in these discussions as a facilitator rather than someone who tries to guide the discussion in one direction or who mandates that certain ideas be discussed. Group discussions allow students to see that other students are thinking the same thing as they are, which can create a certain kind of excitement. Or it might result in disagreement, which is a different kind of excitement. "Sometimes I will let the disagreeing students discuss it with themselves, but at other times I will act as a devil's advocate for both sides," he said. Because the discussion is theoretical but also based in social work practice, students begin to ask questions of themselves and each other that encourage them to think critically and reflect on their ideas of motherhood. "The issue of motherhood intrigues the students and they soon begin asking their own questions with very little assistance from me."[39]

Using Teams to Teach Teamwork

As noted earlier, teams are slightly different from groups in that they have an identified mission. Teams require a high level of collaboration, and sometimes team members need to learn teamwork. After studying many types of teams in a variety of work settings, Carl Larson and Frank LaFasto developed the following list of characteristics of high-performance teams:

- Clear and elevating goal
- Results-driven structure
- Competent members
- Unified commitment

- Collaborative climate
- Standards of excellence
- External support and recognition
- Principled leadership[40]

They also noticed from their study of teams that not all teams have the same type of purposes nor do they function in the same way.[41] All teams need a results-driven structure, but the purposes and, therefore, the structure can be quite different. They identified three types of teams: problem-solving, creative, and tactical teams. Sometimes team activities are designed expressly to help members build collaboration, and often the collaboration must be of the particular type needed for the work of that team. For example, there is little place for creativity on a heart transplant team, which needs to practice the routines and procedures that make it the perfect tactical team. Consider the following example of how teams are used in an engineering course.

John Nolfi teaches a mechanical engineering capstone course at Purdue University where students work in problem-based teams to create a new product. "This is a course in which graduating engineers bring all of their previous courses to bear in designing, engineering, building and testing a product that generally does not exist in the world today," explains John. About a third of the projects are sponsored by a company to solve a specific problem. For example, the team named Team Roadster has a mission to increase tractor-trailer gas mileage with aerodynamic enhancements. The other projects are initiated by the students, such as Team Solar Stroller, which has a mission of creating a solar-powered motorized stroller. Teams typically consist of four to six engineering students working on projects that are either approved before the capstone class begins or are formed during the first week of the class. "Because these are high-performance teams, students feel the pressure to find other individuals who are known to work well in team environments," he says. John uses a program management team model to help the students practice and develop collaboration and communication abilities, and he acts as a program manager, overseeing multiple teams. "I treat the students as team members from the beginning. This essentially means that students are organized, directed and communicated with in a manner as if they were a team member, team leader, or project engineer, emulating an industry product team," he says. Each team has specific deliverables throughout the course, such as creating a name, logo, mission statement, performance and design criteria, concept sketches and design reviews with oral and written presentations, safety checks and testing of the product, and finally product demonstrations and a display competition. Through these deliverables John assesses the individuals and the team. "All deliverables with the exception of the final project demonstration are pass/fail," he says. "Some deliverables are team, and some are individual, but all deliverables are sequential, following the engineering process. If either an individual or team deliverable does not pass, it must be done over until it does pass before the team can go on." The final project must essentially operate as stated in its mission, and the final team grade is established in accordance with the degree to which the final product meets the performance criteria. The individual grades, accounting for 20 percent, are established by peer review and the instructor's judgment. "In the increasingly global and multicultural world of engineering, it is essential that mechanical engineers be able to work in teams, to be able to be engineers in a multidisciplinary system."[42]

Making Groups and Teams Work

Teachers need to do a number of things to make groups and teams work: determine the size of the group, compose the group, orient the group, provide the task, monitor progress, manage arrangements, and interpret the learning. (We use the term *group* to include teams here and in the following sections.) Most of this activity takes place behind the scenes, and it is a very different role from what many instructors might be used to.

Determining the Size

Once the purpose of using groups and teams is clear and determined to be the best choice, teachers need to decide on the size of groups. When is a group too small or too big? Can the interaction of two people, commonly referred to as a dyad, be considered a group? Although dyads are widely used and are generally treated as groups, the interaction of two people has some characteristics that are different from the interaction of three or more people.[43] When two people interact, there is only one channel to connect the two; when a third party is present, there are multiple channels, creating an opportunity for a network or system and, most important, the opportunity for the third party to observe and comment on the communication of the other two. A group, therefore, can be as small as two or three people but is usually larger.

The upper limit on size depends once again on the purpose of the group. Although some magic numbers have been proposed (the recommended group size is five to six for team-based learning, three to four for cooperative learning, two to six for collaborative learning, and nine to ten for problem-based learning), the upward limit actually depends on the scope and difficulty of the task to be accomplished. Depending on the purpose, adding to the group size can make an important contribution. Some activities require a specific number of people. One useful rule for size is: "A group needs to contain a number of people sufficiently small for each to be aware of and have some relation to the other."[44] Groups should also be small enough for everyone to fully participate in the task but big enough to include a diversity of opinions and viewpoints and availability of resources to complete the task.[45] If some members have no opportunity to interact because the group is too large, their contribution to the goal will be minimal or insignificant.

Composing the Group

One way to decide how to compose the group is not to decide but rather to use random assignment, such as counting off by number, or self-selection, such as letting participants drift to whatever group they wish. Occasionally this works if the composition of the groups is not important, but usually the teacher will want to have a method and some criteria for assigning participants to groups. For virtual teams, teachers may need to thoughtfully compose the groups early because of time constraints. The criteria arise naturally out of the purposes of the group. What does the group need to achieve, and who could best help the group achieve it? If the group needs some particular skill or background information, at least some of the members need to have it. Groups are usually arranged to achieve diversity, often in the area of ability and skill with the task at hand. Some instructors obtain students' GPAs as a quick measure of academic ability and arrange the groups to have a similar mean GPA score across the groups. If the task is going to generate conflict, maybe the group needs at least one person to keep the peace. If some people are more experienced than others, perhaps the group needs a good mix of experts and novices. In addition, it is often best for the teacher to compose the groups to limit problems that can arise when members of a group have prior relationships. Best friends and couples often do not make the best teammates. Groups work best when they are composed of the right people to do the work and who are not brought down by unrelated distractions.

In addition, roles may be assigned to group members either by the instructor or by the group members themselves. Sometimes roles should be set throughout the task, but at other times it makes sense for students to rotate the roles among themselves. Common group roles, in addition to those listed on pp. 187–88, include discussion leader, facilitator, recorder, reporter, timekeeper, and accuracy coach.

Orienting the Group

Sometimes teachers need to explain why groups or teams are being used. Teaching with groups and teams, although becoming more common, contrasts significantly with the traditional paradigm of lecture and discussion. Some students believe they should be taught by a teacher, not their peers. Many students have memories of bad experiences where groups were not used for the right purposes or were not managed effectively. It may be necessary at the beginning of the task, therefore, to explain to students the value of using groups for this particular task and to orient them to how groups work.

It is also often recommended that teams, especially those lasting an entire term, develop some sort of team charter or team contract. The instructor can offer guidance on creating the contract, but contracts are most effective when they are created by the teams themselves. Team contracts should address such questions as: How will the group communicate? What are the expectations for responding to each other? What roles will each person take? Who is responsible for what? What behavior is helpful when working in groups? What behavior is unacceptable? How will inappropriate behavior be addressed? Often the members of the team sign the contract and send it to the instructor as a first team assignment.[46]

Providing the Task

Usually it is best if the task is well conceived, preestablished by the teacher, and spelled out in writing. The task given to the group members, sometimes called an instrument, may call for discussion or activity. The task always contains instructions but also provides a strong stimulus for teamwork or for exploring attitudes and feelings—perhaps an interesting quotation, an activity, a news clip, or a simple problem—to get the group talking, moving, or doing something. Along with the stimulus comes some specific instruction: discuss, react to, build, share, solve, create, criticize, or compare your views. A good activity usually provides an excuse for the members of the group to talk about or do something they ordinarily would not do. When teamwork is the goal, the task should promote collaboration by establishing a shared mission, role guidelines, and criteria for completion. Most teachers create and collect good activities over time, but the key to using activities is tying them to the desired learning outcomes. Too often instruments are chosen because they are clever or fun, and although fun is one of the by-products of group activity, the main purpose of this way of learning is *learning*. Therefore, teachers need to begin with a purpose and find, adapt, or invent an instrument that serves that purpose. There is nothing worse—and most students recognize it—than an activity in search of a purpose.

Monitoring Progress

Most of the time, groups will manage themselves and may not need a facilitator. Groups that function on their own are called leaderless groups, although that is something of a misnomer because most groups, even after a brief time together, will generate someone who plays the role of leader. A large class of sixty students can be broken into ten groups of six students each for independent, leaderless group discussions. With leaderless groups, the teacher usually visits the groups to see how they are progressing, to check whether they are clear about their tasks, to see how they are performing the activity, or to ask if they have questions. Sometimes this wandering teacher will bring a new piece of information or provide a clue that helps groups get out of a situation if they are running into problems. By passing from group to group, or observing group interactions online, the teacher can see if the activity is working and can tell how much time or what additional resources the group may need to complete the task. The observant teacher will monitor the groups' task and process behavior, note what roles people are playing, ask for status updates, and watch for problems. Teachers may have to help set boundaries on too much or too little student participation and fair taking of turns. This can be done by setting time limits or requiring participation. For example, give students four "admission tickets" to the discussion and see who uses up all their tickets quickly and who at the end still has all their tickets. Teachers set their groups in motion, but they also watch carefully what happens.

Most of the time teachers need not be a member of the group. After all, the learning comes from sharing feelings with other students, not the teacher. However, in groups that are used to explore and rework strong feelings, where deep sensitivities are involved, or where there is high potential for serious controversy, the teacher may want to lead the group or have a trained assistant or appointed facilitator manage the group dynamics. When teachers serve as group leaders, they stick to their role of effective facilitator and, above all, avoid lecturing the group.

Managing the Arrangements

The total population of students may be broken into small groups, then reassembled to share thoughts and observations. A class can also be divided into participants and observers, with one group (the outer circle) watching the group behavior of the participants (the inner circle), often called a *fishbowl* technique. This can also happen online by making certain group activities public or private in the class. Sometimes one group is set against another in a competitive race for the best solution. At other times, the group tasks are not competitive, but the nature of comparing one group's solution to others' inspires students to do their best work. Groups can be asked to cooperate with other groups by sending a messenger to share their ideas. Teachers devise many creative ways to manage groups and the relations among groups.

Interpreting the Learning

Perhaps the most important aspect of the teacher's role is to interpret for the group at the end of the activity what learning occurred. Usually people have had fun, but they often miss the point. Some debriefing to drive home the learning or get feedback from the group is usually necessary. Because this way of learning involves attitudes, feelings, and perspectives, students may want to continue talking about a group experience long after it is over and may discover new meaning in the activity days later. But no teacher should terminate a group activity without the participants having a fairly clear idea about what they learned. Sometimes it is important to debrief the group not only on the learning that happens but on the process of working in a group or team as well. Consider how teams work in an online course in the following example.

> Debra Beck teaches a course called Nonprofit Management and Leadership through the University of Wyoming's Outreach School. During the course, students create a website about nonprofit management for executive directors and senior staff of rural nonprofits. Debra breaks the class into small teams that are each tasked with creating one section of the website. The teams use a wiki—a website that everyone can contribute to and edit—to collaborate and create their final product. Debra tries to get them collaborating in the wiki from the very beginning, telling them, "If you work from this starting point, you will be where you need to be, interacting with whom you need to be interacting with, and you will get off to a good start as a team. You will also be jointly accountable, since everyone knows exactly where the work will be done." Because the class is offered completely online to students across the country, the teams need to manage all

their interactions online. Debra takes many steps to keep everyone on board and increase the potential for a high-quality final project. At the outset she creates a video tour of the wiki, walking them through the space, showing where and how they will be interacting, and reinforcing her expectations for participation and the finished product. She also sets up benchmarks throughout the course to keep the projects moving along, which include an initial check-in, a rough outline of the group's plan, individual assignment of duties, group and individual status reports, peer feedback of other groups' projects, final reviews, and finally, making the wiki public. She makes it clear that she will be looking for their individual presence at each of those benchmarks. Because this is a team project, there is a significant team grade. She awards points to the team for the finished product, and also awards points for individual participation, assessed at the benchmarks. "Mostly students know that I expect them to be active participants and they rise to the occasion. The individual participation grade is more of a comfort to the group rather than a reward or punishment for individual students."[47]

Problems in Groups and Teams

Teachers who use groups and teams also know how to look for, spot, and deal with four common problems of group dynamics: conflict, apathy, groupthink, and social loafing.

Conflict

Some conflict in groups is normal and even necessary. Tension at a low level can be a productive force that holds the group together. But when tension exceeds an acceptable threshold and open conflict breaks out, tension can pull the group apart. Signs of group conflict include

- expressing impatience with each other,
- attacking ideas before they are completely expressed,
- taking sides and refusing to compromise, and
- making comments or suggestions with a great deal of vehemence and attacking one another on a personal level in subtle ways.[48]

Teachers also look beyond individuals for the sources of conflict. Sometimes conflict arises because the group does not have enough resources or time, lacks a well-defined task, or is being influenced by outside interests. In other words, conflict can be generated by structural problems.[49] If there are structural problems in the group, if the task is ambiguous, or if the resources or time allotted are too little, then these issues should be resolved. If group members can easily divide the tasks individually, then the task itself might not be a good fit for groups. If the conflict is growing out of genuine individual differences of opinion, standard procedures for resolving the conflict include taking a vote, compromising, mediating, arbitrating, or making determined efforts to reach a consensus. The key to the successful resolution of conflict in a group is to face it, identify what type of problem is occurring, and meet it head-on. Usually teachers ask students to try to mediate conflicts on their own first. If this is not working, the teacher may need to provide the students with resources to solve the problem themselves. As a last resort, intervention by the instructor might be necessary. Understandably, this may take some courage, but in the end, hopefully, the group that fights unites.[50]

Apathy

In some groups the members do not appear to care enough about the group to get excited about anything. Some of the members may do what they are told, but they have little commitment to the group's activity. Apathy can be expressed through lack of participation, low level of participation, dragging conversation, restlessness, hastily made decisions, failure to follow through on decisions, and reluctance to assume any further responsibility.[51] Apathetic groups can be made up of apathetic individuals, but more likely apathy is the result of structural problems in the group. Often the task the group is working on is perceived as unimportant or not as important as something else the members could be working on. In other instances, the task may appear to be important, but the group is afraid to take it on because it may seem overwhelming, requiring too much effort or risk. Sometimes the group does not know how to go about the task, sensing that the members lack essential knowledge, skills, resources, or leadership. Some members may believe they don't have the knowledge to contribute, or conversely may feel overqualified and bored by the task. At other times the group may feel that its efforts will not be appreciated and that the task is merely a sham exercise. A prolonged fight or unresolved conflict may cause a group to become so discouraged that individual members withdraw. All of these conditions, alone or together, can produce apathy. Almost always, some major restructuring of the group, the way the group is held accountable, or some new definition of the task and the conditions for achieving it must be undertaken to counter apathy.

Groupthink

Groupthink is a term coined in 1972 by social psychologist Irvin Janis that applies to "a mode of thinking that people engage in when they are deeply involved in a cohesive group, when the members' striving for unanimity overrides their motivation to realistically appraise alternative courses of action."[52] Groups sometimes reach premature closure without considering alternatives because no one wants to disagree. Teachers may need to be on the lookout for tight-knit groups that strive for harmony above all else. Sometimes students need permission and encouragement to disagree with each other. The teacher may ask each group to have certain members take on different perspectives, to play the role of devil's advocate, or to confer with individuals outside the group as a means of avoiding groupthink. An astute teacher can spot groupthink and challenge the group to go further, reconsider, or generate better alternatives.

Social Loafing

Sometimes group members do not do their part or carry their own weight. Some old experiments with tug-of-war games showed that two do not pull twice as hard as one, and three do not pull three times as hard, and so forth. Social psychologists call this *social loafing*, and it usually occurs when it is difficult to distinguish individual contributions.[53] Social loafing problems are often associated with the assignment or the task itself. Some assignments are too easy or involve too much writing, both of which lend themselves to some individuals' taking on more work than others.[54] Accountability perceived as fair to all should be built into the assignments. Group members collectively also tend to let the group take on risk that most people at the individual level would avoid.[55] Sometimes when everyone is responsible, no one is, and the entire group loafs. What works is to make students individually accountable for prework and group work—talking, contributing, and listening—and then grading for overall group performance. In some groups, the facilitator and other group members need to confront loafing members who do not contribute what they should.

> Managing teams is always an adventure. Returning to Debra Beck's Nonprofit Management and Leadership course, like many instructors who use teams she strives to find a balance between providing structure and guidance to the teams, but also allowing them to learn through the process. "I set up the wiki and the basic structures to get them started, but they own what they create there. I do monitor and offer feedback, but I don't go

into the wiki space and interrupt their creative flow," she said. When problems occur, she will advise the students on how to handle wayward members. "If there is a specific reason that I need to get involved, I am willing to do so. But I usually encourage them to work it out themselves. Virtually all of the issues that come to my attention are the types that they need to resolve together," she said. Debra monitors the groups' progress, and when the need arises she might even create a quick video that addresses a common issue the teams are encountering. But again, she strives to find a balance in her support. "It is impossible to give students too much information about a group project. No matter how much detail I give, they always want more, but that is not always appropriate. A critical part of the learning process for these assignments is to keep students exploring and figuring out the task themselves."[56]

Assessing Learning With Groups and Teams

Assessing learning in groups can be tricky because not only are individual and group elements at play but also task objectives and process objectives. Group and team assessment policies need to encourage students to be accountable to the group and the product of the group effort, and to avoid dividing up the task and completing it individually. As with any assessment strategy, it is best to start with the purposes of using groups and teams and the overall objectives for learning. What changes in attitudes or teamwork skills are desired? How important are task objectives relative to process objectives? In some groups students might only be graded for participation. In other cases, such as team projects or ongoing teamwork assignments, grading multiple aspects of task and process is necessary. The assessment methods used and the weight given to each type should match the desired goals.

Grading the work of teams is typically based on three things: individual performance, team performance, and individual contributions to the team.[57] Because teamwork is not a common means of learning in higher education, students need some incentive to fully participate in group tasks. A fair and well-balanced assessment plan helps alleviate problems such as social loafing. It is often recommended that grades be based at least to some extent on individual members' performance, because grades based solely on a single group product often involve uneven levels of participation and result in feelings of perceived unfairness.[58] In some team assignments this is done by weighting the assignments, products, or test scores, and assigning an overall grade of some combination, such as two-thirds of the individual grade and one-third of the group grade. In cooperative learning teams, members might receive two scores: their own and the average test score of the group. In other teams, group members are given credit only when there is successful completion of the group task or project.

Group and team grades often include some process aspect of individual contributions to the success of the team. Because instructors cannot be part of all groups or teams, instructors may ask students to individually write or talk about what they contributed to the group. Peer evaluations are also a common means of collecting information about individual contributions. Peers are well suited to evaluate the process aspect of their teammates because they have a front-row seat, but asking students to rate each other's level of contribution to the group may put them in an awkward spot. Precautions should be put in place to prevent abuse of peer evaluations if they are used. Written surveys and sample evaluations for assessment of group processes based on criteria for effective team contributions are available online.[59] Often peer evaluations are combined with instructor and even self-evaluation information. In this regard, feedback, as distinct from grading, may be very valuable to students in their continuing improvement on some of the more subtle aspects of this way of learning. Surely it is possible to tell students their listening is improving, their contributions are more insightful, or their awareness of biases and blind spots is noticeable and welcome. Just because these conclusions are more inferential does not mean they cannot be shared. In addition, formative assessment can play an important role in gathering information on how well the group process is going. Overall, grading groups and teams is seen as more objective and fair if it is transparent, meaningful, and ongoing.

Useful Technologies for Groups and Teams

Learning with groups and teams can happen in the classroom, but academic teamwork increasingly happens online and virtually, as students are asked to collaborate outside the classroom. In fact, in online classes almost all of what is accomplished could be considered an online group, although it is really only when a small group of students are working together on a shared project that they are considered a virtual team.

Much of the literature about virtual teams comes from the business world, where teams that never meet face-to-face are increasingly common.

According to Jessica Lipnack and Jeffrey Stamps, in their book *Virtual Teams*, some of the biggest difficulties in creating virtual teams involve developing trust and norms.[60] As with a face-to-face team, virtual team members need to develop norms about how to communicate and interact, but they might also need to be more deliberate about creating these norms. Virtual teams tend to have a harder time getting started, take longer to develop, and are more complex because of their dispersion across time and distance. Because of these challenges, virtual teams often need to accelerate group processes through face-to-face or live online meetings, especially in the beginning of a task, and usually need to be more intentional about developing group norms and relationships during these times. In addition, virtual teams need to develop a sense of public and private space online. They need to create virtual product and process spaces in which the team can operate.

Whether the groups or teams take place in face-to-face, online, or hybrid courses, many collaborative online workspaces support learning in groups and teams with group process and product spaces. Most learning management systems (LMSs) have tools built in for group work, including synchronous and asynchronous communication areas that are only accessible to group members and the instructor, as well as areas to share and collaborate on documents. Software programs outside an LMS can perform similar tasks, and there are numerous free online tools that allow students to collaborate virtually. Wikis are an easily available and promising technological application for groups and teams in which group members can collaborate in one online space as well as create online websites and documents. The software keeps a history of changes so the instructor has a record of who has contributed what and when to that space.

Even with all the options available, when individuals of various technical abilities and infrastructure work together, it is often best to use the simplest technology available to do the task. Sophisticated but unproven technologies can be unnecessarily distracting. Sometimes more can be accomplished with simple audio conferences or e-mail than with the distractions of robust but complicated and unreliable software. In fact, many instructors allow group members to use whatever tools they choose to use to collaborate and communicate. Some groups may be more comfortable communicating via e-mail, whereas others may prefer phone, texting, live meetings, or social media. Technical difficulties can and do occur, and it is wise to create backup plans and deal with any difficulties swiftly so that group collaboration is not discouraged.[61]

Final Thoughts

Students often complain about group work in college. Some students groan outright when the teacher announces, "Let's break into groups!" Why is this? Certainly learning is harder and messier in groups. Group work takes time and often involves difficult conversations with other students. Sometimes groups are used for the wrong reasons, and students can sense this. If a group project is easy for students to break up and divide and conquer individually, then the task is probably not the best use of groups. If a project is process-oriented and students need to become competent in each piece of the process, then it might not be the best use of groups. Groups are best used when there is some need to explore multiple attitudes, feelings, and perspectives on a topic, or when a team outcome needs to be greater then the sum of individual efforts. Group activities done well and for the right reasons can be incredibly productive and powerful learning experiences.

Points to Remember

Teachers who want to use groups and teams effectively should do the following:

✓ Use groups for the purpose of exploring attitudes, feelings, and perspectives.
✓ Recognize the various characteristics and stages of groups.
✓ Determine the appropriate size of a group.
✓ Compose the groups usually to maximize diversity of opinions, perspectives, or skills.
✓ Provide an activity or task that produces disagreement or encourages collaboration.
✓ Orient students to the process of working in a group.
✓ Help the groups set expectations, norms, and guidelines.
✓ Ensure adequate physical or virtual space for the groups to operate.
✓ Monitor the progress of the groups, keeping watch on communication patterns, roles, norms, and rules.
✓ Identify and help students address common group problems: conflict, apathy, social loafing, and groupthink.
✓ Use assessment methods that encourage individual accountability and group collaboration.
✓ Use assessment methods that address product and process objectives.
✓ Help students interpret the learning that has occurred.

Notes

1. For more about Roger and David Johnson, visit the Cooperative Learning Institute website, accessed March 15, 2002, http://www.co-operation.org/.

2. David W. Johnson, Roger Johnson, and Mary Beth Stanne, "Cooperative Learning Methods: A Meta-Analysis," accessed March 15, 2012, http://www.table learning.com/uploads/File/EXHIBIT-B.pdf; Johnson and Johnson, *Learning Together and Alone: Cooperative, Competitive, and Individualistic Learning* (Boston: Allyn & Bacon, 1999).

3. Kenneth A. Bruffee, "Sharing Our Toys: Cooperative Learning versus Collaborative Learning," *Change* 27, no. 1 (1995): 12–18.

4. Elizabeth F. Barkley, K. Patricia Cross, and Claire H. Major, *Collaborative Learning Techniques* (San Francisco: Jossey-Bass, 2005).

5. Larry K. Michaelsen, Arletta B. Knight, and L. Dee Fink, *Team-Based Learning: A Transformative Use of Small Groups in College Teaching* (Sterling, VA: Stylus, 2004).

6. Thanks to Leticia Sara, Instructor of Political Science at Red Rocks Community College, for granting permission to use her example. E-mail message to author, February 4, 2012.

7. Barry E. Collins and Harold Guetzkow, *A Social Psychology of Group Processes for Decision Making* (New York: Wiley, 1964), 58.

8. Michaelsen et al., *Team-Based Learning*, 46.

9. Bernard Berelson and Gary Steiner, *Human Behaviour: An Inventory of Scientific Findings* (New York: Harcourt, Brace & World, 1964), 557–60.

10. Kurt Lewin, "Forces Behind Food Habits and Methods of Change," *Bulletin of the National Research Council* 108 (1943): 35–65.

11. Michaelsen et al., *Team-Based Learning*, 61.

12. A. Paul Hare, *Handbook of Small Group Research*, 2nd ed. (New York: Free Press, 1976), 388, 392.

13. Robert T. Golembiewski and Arthur Blumberg, eds., *Sensitivity Training and the Laboratory Approach* (Itasca, IL: Peacock, 1970), 4.

14. Alvin Goldberg and Carl Larson, *Group Communication* (Englewood Cliffs, NJ: Prentice Hall, 1975), 163.

15. Carl Rogers, *Carl Rogers on Encounter Groups* (New York: Harper & Row, 1970), 3–4.

16. Thomas R. Verny, *Inside Groups* (New York: McGraw-Hill, 1974).

17. For an overview of the research on group processes, see Goldberg and Larson, *Group Communication*. One of the early classics in the field is James H. McBurney and Kenneth G. Hance, *Discussion in Human Affairs* (New York: Harper, 1939). A well-known study of groups from a sociological viewpoint is George C. Homans, *The Human Group* (New York: Harcourt, Brace & World, 1950).

18. Carl Larson and Frank LaFasto, *Teamwork: What Must Go Right, What Can Go Wrong* (Newbury Park, CA: Sage, 1989), 19.

19. Bruce W. Tuckman, "Development Sequence in Small Groups," *Psychological Bulletin* 63, no. 6 (1965): 384–99.

20. Bruce Tuckman and M. Jensen, "Stages of Small Group Development," *Groups and Organizational Studies* 2, no. 4 (1977): 419–27.

21. Goldberg and Larson, *Group Communication*, 46. The distinction between task and process goes back to some of the earlier work of George C. Homans. See also B. Aubrey Fisher, *Small Group Decision Making: Communication and the Group Process* (New York: McGraw-Hill, 1980).

22. Larry L. Barker et al., *Groups in Process: An Introduction to Small Group Communication*, 3rd ed. (Englewood Cliffs, NJ: Prentice Hall, 1987), 37.

23. Michael Burgoon, Judee K. Heston, and James McCroskey, *Small Group Communication: A Functional Approach* (New York: Holt, Rinehart and Winston, 1974), 10.

24. Fisher, *Small Group Decision Making*, 42.

25. Barker et al., *Groups in Process*, 53–62, provides a good discussion of group structure that we have drawn from extensively.

26. Hare, *Handbook of Small Group Research*, 131.

27. Kenneth D. Benne and Paul Sheets, "Functional Roles of Group Members," *Journal of Social Issues* (Spring 1948): 4, 41–49.

28. Fisher, *Small Group Decision Making*, 183–84, contains a good discussion of group norms.

29. Ibid., 29.

30. Charles M. Kelly, "Empathetic Listening," in *Small Group Communication: A Reader*, ed. Robert S. Cathcart and Larry A. Samovar (Dubuque, IA: Brown, 1970), 350–51.

31. Barker et al., *Groups in Process*, 83.

32. John E. Baird Jr. and Sanford Weinberg, "Elements of Group Communication," in *Small Group Communication: A Reader*, ed. Robert S. Cathcart and Larry A. Samovar (Dubuque, IA: Brown, 1970), 296. The list is shortened, adapted, and paraphrased.

33. E. Randy Garrison and Norman D. Vaughan, *Blended Learning in Higher Education: Framework, Principles, and Guidelines* (San Francisco: Jossey-Bass, 2008).

34. Charles Seashore, "What Is Sensitivity Training?" in *Sensitivity Training and the Laboratory Approach*, ed. Robert T. Golembiewski and Arthur Blumberg (Itasca, IL: Peacock, 1970), 14.

35. Rogers, *Carl Rogers on Encounter Groups*, 9.

36. Irvin D. Yalom, *The Theory and Practice of Group Psychotherapy*, 3rd ed. (New York: Basic Books, 1985), 3–69. The listing of therapeutic factors and their paraphrased descriptions is drawn from chapters 1–3. Each factor corresponds to a section heading in those chapters except for the discussion on catharsis, which is found on pp. 84–85, and the discussion of existential factors, found on 92–101.

37. Christina Baldwin and Ann Linnea, *The Circle Way: A Leader in Every Chair* (San Francisco: Berrett-Koehler, 2010).

38. Patricia Hill Collins, *Black Feminist Thought: Knowledge, Consciousness, and the Politics of Empowerment* (London: Routledge, 2000).

39. Thanks to Damon Freeman, PhD, Assistant Professor in the School of Social Policy and Practice, University of Pennsylvania, for granting permission to use his example. E-mail message to author, February 19, 2012.

40. Larson and LaFasto, *Teamwork*, 26.

41. Ibid., 42–55.

42. Thanks to John Nolfi, Continuing Lecturer of Mechanical Engineering, Purdue University College of Engineering, for granting permission to use his example. E-mail message to author, February 11, 2012.

43. See Fisher, *Small Group Decision Making*, 24–26, for information on group size.

44. John K. Brilhart, *Effective Group Discussion* (Dubuque, IA: Brown, 1967), 20–21.

45. Barkley et al., *Collaborative Learning Techniques*.

46. Rena Palloff and Keith Pratt, *Collaborating Online: Learning Together in Community* (San Francisco: Jossey-Bass, 2005), 27–28.

47. Thanks to Debra Beck, PhD, Adjunct Faculty at the University of Wyoming's Outreach School in Public Administration, for granting permission to use her example. E-mail message to author, November 14, 2011.

48. Leland Bradford, Dorothy Stock, and Murray Horowitz, "How to Diagnose Group Problems," in *Sensitivity Training and the Laboratory Approach*, ed. Robert T. Golembiewski and Arthur Blumberg (Itasca, IL: Peacock, 1970), 142.

49. Ibid., 142–43.

50. Fisher, *Small Group Decision Making*, 57–59.

51. Bradford et al., "How to Diagnose Group Problems," 145.

52. Irvin Janis, *Victims of Groupthink: A Psychological Study of Foreign-Policy Decisions and Fiascos* (Boston: Houghton Mifflin, 1972), 8–9.

53. Charles Pavitt and Ellen Curtis, *Small Group Discussion* (Scottsdale, AZ: Gorsuch Scarisbrick, 1990), 38–40.

54. Michaelsen et al., *Team-Based Learning*.

55. Fisher, *Small Group Decision Making*, 61.

56. Beck, e-mail message to author, November 14, 2011.

57. Michaelsen et al., *Team-Based Learning*, 41.

58. Robert Slavin, Eric Hurley, and Anne Chamberlain, "Cooperative Learning and Assessment: Theory and Research," in *Handbook of Psychology*, vol. 7, ed. W. M. Reynolds and G. E. Miller (New York: Wiley, 2003), 177–98.

59. For example, see "CATME Team-Maker," accessed March 15, 2012, https://engineering.purdue.edu/CATME. This instrument, funded by the National Science Foundation, gathers peer and self-evaluation data about how effectively each team member is contributing to the team and provides feedback to the instructor and the team members.

60. Jessica Lipnack and Jeffrey Stamps, *Virtual Teams: People Working across Boundaries with Technology* (New York: Wiley, 2000). See also Deborah L. Duarte and Nancy T. Snyder, *Mastering Virtual Teams: Strategies, Tools, and Techniques That Succeed* (San Francisco: Jossey-Bass, 2006).

61. Palloff and Pratt, *Collaborating Online*.

9

PRACTICING PROFESSIONAL JUDGMENT

Learning Through Virtual Realities

Intended Learning Outcomes What students learn	Way of Learning Origins and theory	Common Methods What the teacher provides
Practicing professional judgment Sound judgment and appropriate professional action in complex, context-dependent situations	**Learning through virtual realities** Psychodrama, sociodrama, gaming theory	Role playing Simulations Dramatic scenarios Games

Is this a kind of learning that involves developing professional judgment in a variety of different contexts? Does the development of judgment need to be practiced in a safe environment? Does this learning involve activities that could cause damage, expense, or even loss of life? Will students feel more confident and be more competent if they have been able to work first in a simulated environment before going into the real world? These are learning outcomes that are well served by learning through virtual realities.

Students at a law enforcement training academy practice making arrests in a class titled Arrest Control. Students engage in role playing the arrest procedure in pairs. They actually act out the standard control procedures. So far so good, but what happens if the people being arrested try to pull away or refuse to remove their hands from their pockets?

S ome professional roles need to be learned and practiced outside the
actual setting where they will be performed, because making big mistakes can be costly or even life threatening. Results from mistakes can
include physical harm, as in the case of mental health workers dealing with
out-of-control patients; environmental harm, as in working with nuclear or
other hazardous materials; or economic harm, such as investing and managing large sums of money. For some professions, such as medical, mistakes are
truly life-or-death matters. One hopes never to use emergency preparedness
training in a real-life situation, but a diverse range of professionals neverthe-
less must learn to use their best professional judgment while working in the
midst of disasters. Much learning comes from failure, and learning through
virtual realities allows students to see if they can use what they know and,
more importantly, see the consequences of failure in a safe learning environment rather than in a real-life setting with much at stake. For practicing
professional judgment, virtual realities provide a valuable way of learning.

Although *virtual reality* as a technical term is fairly recent, the concept
is old. Novelists create a type of virtual reality, a world of words constructed
from experience and imagination, and they invite interactions with that
world through the reader's own mental pictures. When we look in the mirror
we see what the field of optics has long called a virtual image—a flat surface,
seemingly three-dimensional and backward but lifelike. Films now enhanced
by computer imaging and 3D can create the frightening virtual reality of a
disaster at sea or battles in outer space. The newer and more technical use of
the term *virtual reality* refers to the ability to combine visual images and
computer programming capabilities to make it possible for people to experience a lifelike, created reality and to interact with it. The word *virtual*, then,
means existing in essence or effect but not in fact. A virtual reality is the next
best thing to reality, and for learning it is sometimes even better than reality.

This way of learning works best for practicing role-related behaviors
where professional judgment needs to be used in what are often very complicated situations in new environments. Students need to display systemic
thinking and procedural logic as they develop their understanding of how
multiple variables are at work in complex systems. Such learning is the ultimate form of application, "bridging the gap between the academics of a
profession and the practice of a profession."[1]

When virtual realities are used to facilitate learning, the activities can
include simple role play, more complex dramatic scenarios, and simulations
and games. Their common goal is to create a virtual reality learning environment that is like the world where actual professional roles will be performed.

The main focus of this way of learning is on using virtual reality learning environments for practicing professional judgment.

The correspondence between the virtual and actual setting can be low or high, and the use of technology can range from nil to very sophisticated, but the goal in each case is to provide a safe setting where students can learn and practice their roles comfortably and with increasing levels of proficiency. In the following examples, some form of virtual reality is used as a way of learning.

- Students in a research methods class conduct mock interviews with each other so they can practice their interviewing skills and gain feedback from other student observers.
- Information technology students set up a private computer network and enact a virus attack on the system. Multiple players are involved as this dramatic scenario plays out, testing what happens and how to respond to a computer virus.
- Undergraduate biology students use a software application that contains photographs of a body in forty different stages of dissection. The software allows students who would otherwise not have access to a human cadaver to experience a realistic lab setting and practice the process of dissection.[2]
- Graduate foreign relations students use an online role-play software called Peacemaker in which they take the role of either the Israeli prime minister or the Palestinian president and practice various forms of diplomatic and foreign relations skills as they try to find a peaceful resolution to the Israeli-Palestinian conflict. Students make decisions, enter into negotiations, engage in war, and deal with the consequences, based on real news footage.[3]

Bridging Realities

Role play, dramatic scenarios, and simulations and games are the most common techniques used for bridging the real world of performance and the virtual world created for practice. The first step in the use of all of these techniques is to select precisely those elements of the real situation that are most important based on the learning outcomes. Exactly which aspects of the real-life situation are necessary to evoke the desired learning? How will these elements be re-created in the simulated situation? What will students actually do, and how will they learn through what they are doing? Looking back on how they performed, how will they develop a better understanding of their professional role, display the abilities actually needed to perform their roles in context, and gain insights about themselves as players of a role?

The primary goal in learning through virtual realities is to bridge the gap as much as possible between the setting for learning and the real world. The enormous advantage of this way of learning is that it bridges this gap safely and often inexpensively. In this respect, learning through the use of virtual realities is far ahead of just telling students what they are supposed to do when a crisis arises. For students, there are great advantages to having practiced in a virtual setting.

Origins of the Virtual Reality Strategy

Viewed in one way, the idea of learning through virtual realities is general, deep, and old, dating as far back as primitive efforts in every society to simulate reality. It has been found that human beings in all societies have made what have come to be called folk models of how their environment works. Folk models have included, among other things, various types of games and activities designed to help participants discover and adapt to a culture's view of the world. Thus, puzzles have been created to explore the relationship of humankind and nature, as well as games of chance to cope with randomness, games of strategy to act out relations with others, and various crafts and ceremonies to express the social and aesthetic values of a group. Serious games played by adults have existed in every culture for centuries, using the low technology of bits of wood, stones, feathers, and lines drawn in the dirt.[4]

Efforts to simulate the real world are also found widely in children's play. By the midtwentieth century, scholars had recognized that play is children's work and that it involves the serious business of socialization, learning how to fit into the adult world. Through more formalized games, children learn to internalize rules, develop their self-image, try out or learn new roles, explore potential or future realities, have fun, and socialize.[5] In addition to the more general origins of folk models and children's play, the roots of this way of learning are found in the work of Jacob L. Moreno with role play, psychodrama, and sociodrama, as well as with the experiments in the military with simulations and war games.

Moreno was an eccentric doctor born in Romania in the late 1800s who struggled for at least part of his life with a messiah complex.[6] He knew at an early age that he would do something important, and he did. He is the indisputable father of *psychodrama* and *sociodrama*, the improvised acting out of personal problems or social interactions for therapeutic purposes. Moreno had the insight to see in children's play the seeds of a fruitful educational and therapeutic device. As a medical student in Vienna, where he grew up, Moreno often spent his lunch hours in the public gardens where children would gather around him at the foot of a tree to listen to his dramatic telling of fairy tales. Sometimes he moved up into the tree, taking on the role of director, giving the children roles, and urging them to take on new names or invent new characters. The children were captivated by his radical little dramas, but soon he was in trouble with teachers, parents, and the police, and he realized it was time to go work with adults. He started therapy groups for prostitutes, worked with refugees, and developed ingenious techniques for dramatizing the daily news. Along the way, he began to theorize and write about how dramatization could be used for learning and for therapeutic purposes.

Was it Moreno's fate that he would become the founder of psychodrama? In his own words he describes an early experience, which in retrospect appears to have many of the elements of the actual psychodramas he would later conduct.

> When I was four and a half years old my parents lived in a house near the river Danube. They had left the house on a Sunday to pay a visit, leaving me alone in the basement of the house with neighbors' children. It was empty except for a huge oak table in the middle. The children said: "Let's play." One child asked me: "What?" "I know," I said, "let's play God and his angels." The children inquired, "But who is God?" I replied, "I am God and you are my angels." The children agreed. They all declared, "We must build the heavens first." We dragged all the chairs from every room in the house to the basement, put them on the big table and began to build one heaven after another by tying several chairs together on one level and putting more chairs above them until we reached the ceiling. Then all the children helped me to climb up until I reached the top chair and sat on it. There I sat pretty. The children began to circle around the table, using their arms as wings, and singing. Suddenly I heard a child asking me, "Why don't you fly?" I stretched my arms, trying it. A second later I fell and found myself on the floor, my right arm broken. This was, as far as I can recall, the first "private" psychodramatic session I have ever conducted. I was the director and the subject in one.[7]

Another historical source of learning through virtual realities is the use of simulations and games in the military services. The first use of simulations is usually attributed to the Prussian army of the nineteenth century, not only for planning battlefield strategies but also for recruiting soldiers. The paper-and-pencil tests used for screening recruits were not producing the officers the army wanted, so army staff devised simulations to test how potential soldiers would actually cope with realistic command situations. The idea was taken up by the British army to test for different types of roles—officer, agent, and engineer. Some simulations placed the candidates in situations where they had to act alone, but others involved interactions in teams. Soon the simulations were used in training soldiers as well as in the selection process. Simulations were used in US business and industry originally for recruitment but then more generally for training, eventually evolving into complex management simulations.

The other military source is war games.[8] The original war games, played on boards, were developed by the Prussians; the first war game introduced at Schleswig in 1798 was called Kriegspiel. The boards were expanded to maps with grids and pieces that could be moved to represent and work out real military situations.[9] Before the game could be developed, the nature of the conflict had to be analyzed, and the antagonists and their material resources had to be defined. Real-world constraints were agreed to, and chance elements, such as weather or surprise attacks, were taken into account. With crude sand tables to simulate the terrain, alternative war plans could be tested at low cost.

During World War II at the Japanese Naval War College, a war game was developed to simulate the time period from mid-1941 to mid-1943 to try out Japan's military intentions. Sophisticated war gaming was used by the Allies to cope with packs of German submarines. Today, war games are simulated on computers or carried out through live military practice maneuvers.

After World War II, what was learned about games in simulated war was adapted for the foreign policy environment. Foreign policy games were developed to simulate diplomatic negotiations about world events in a controlled setting. Lincoln Bloomfield at Massachusetts Institute of Technology and Harold Gutzekow at Northwestern University were leaders in this effort, along with the Rand Corporation.[10]

War games today are considered part of the serious games movement, which is the development of games for educational or training purposes. The term *serious games* has been used since 1970 but became more popular after a public sector initiative in 2002 focused development on serious games for health care, management, social change, and other educational topics.[11] Defense has always been a focus, as some of the most popular serious games were commissioned by the US Army and released to the public for recruitment purposes. The military still has considerable influence in the serious games movement because of the continual military need to train individuals in highly complex scenarios.

The first business game is usually credited to Frank Ricciardi of the American Management Association, who applied what he had learned about gaming at the Naval War College to the development of a business game.[12] After a year of development it was released by the American Management Association in 1957 under the name Top Management Decision Simulation. Interactive team play was made possible in this game with rival managers competing for market share based on their complete knowledge of their own companies but with less-complete information about the market and competitors.

Gaming theory also owes a historical debt to mathematician John von Neumann, who worked out the quantitative theory of decision making under conditions of competition and uncertainty. His classic work, *The Theory of Games and Economic Behavior*, published in 1944, provided the vocabulary for describing the characteristics of competition and the quantitative methods needed for using computers in gaming.[13]

An important aspect of learning through virtual realities is the concept of *transfer*, also discussed in chapter 7, p. 155. Originating with Thorndike and other behavioral psychologists in reference to skills and practice, transfer refers to a student's ability to take learning in one context and apply it to a different context. Stated another way, transfer is taking previous learning and applying it to a new and novel situation. Learning through virtual realities is concerned primarily with taking learning in a carefully structured and supportive environment and transferring it to a complex, real-life environment. For example, students test methods, hypotheses, and strategies, seeing how other players respond to the situation, and then transfer this learning to the next level or the next puzzle.[14] This is why virtual realities should be lifelike and contain the critical attributes of the skill to be practiced.[15] Thus, role play, dramatic scenarios, and simulations and games by their very nature and design promote transfer.[16]

What We Know About Learning Through Virtual Realities

The roots of this way of learning are varied, but the common goal is to create a simulated reality that can be used to learn something about a role, a situation, or one's performance. Today these origins come to life in three types of virtual realities for education: role playing, dramatic scenarios, and simulations and games. These forms range from instructor-developed role-playing situations to semistructured minidramas to massive multiplayer online role-play games. Consider the following example of role play.

Kevin Brun teaches at the Law Enforcement Training Academy at Colorado Mountain College. One of the main methods used in teaching future police officers is to put them in actual situations to practice their skills. "Back when I was in the academy, we used to talk about these things. But it's more important to practice them," says Kevin. "Police officers need muscle memory to develop quick reaction times, and people need to realize what they are actually capable of doing under stress." While the academy uses many forms of high-tech simulations, some of the abilities being developed rely on being able to carry out basic roles successfully under various situations. In the Arrest Control class, role-playing methods are used to teach prospective officers how to arrest someone and, more importantly, what to do when someone resists arrest. After the instructors first demonstrate a typical arrest sequence, the students role-play the procedure in pairs. Kevin says, "Students have to use the right language to be successful. Turn around, put your hands behind your back, and so on." Then Kevin adds some complexity to the role play. What if someone pulls away? What if they don't take their hands out of their pockets? Students need to think through and practice what to do if any of these situations occur. Another common role play involves law enforcement students' walking into a situation where they don't know what to expect. In this role play, students have to stand still with their eyes closed, and they cannot move until they hear or feel something. They have no idea what will happen, but when they open their eyes, someone might be trying to take their gun or might be about to take a swing at them. They have to rely on their gut reactions and practice responding to uncertainty. "We actually have them wear heart rate monitors. Usually the heart rate goes way up before they open their eyes as they are anticipating something to come. But as they are responding, if they are doing what they've been taught, their heart rate usually goes down once the action starts. The heart rate drops as their confidence grows," he says. Students get to watch each other role-play these scenes so they can see how others react. "They can see someone else respond differently and think, there's something I should have done, or now I know not to do that!" he says. Using these methods helps Kevin's students make mistakes in a safe environment rather than in a real setting. "Some students may actually experience these things on the first week of the job, and they need to be prepared, not just physically but also mentally. I like to think of it as setting a mind-set for survival."[17]

Role Play

Role play is an activity where a limited number of students, usually two or three, take on specifically assigned and well-defined roles and act out an encounter that involves some goal or problem. In one of the classic business role plays, for example, one student takes on the role of a dissatisfied customer returning a defective shoe, while another plays the role of the clerk. The customer is told to obtain some satisfaction, and the clerk is instructed to bend as little as possible from the no returns policy. The players act out their differences as they assume their roles and try to negotiate.

The concept of role comes from the field of sociology and denotes a cluster of culturally prescribed behaviors associated with particular social positions.[18] For example, being a lawyer, social worker, doctor, diplomat, or police officer is a role, and each occupation carries with it certain role expectations, which can vary from organization to organization and even country to country. Some jobs involve role conflict in which one is expected to carry out some activities that interfere with others, such as the manager who needs to discipline an employee but wants to remain open and approachable when that employee has problems. Some sociologists (functionalists) maintain roles are set and prescribed by society, while others (interactionists) believe roles are modified and played differently by individuals with different personalities and varying interpretations of their roles. Sociology's best known role theorist, Irving Goffman, believed that all of life is, indeed, a stage and that much of human behavior can be understood in the way roles are played on that stage—sometimes in a sincere and realistic way, sometimes in an idealized manner, and sometimes cynically.[19]

Role play employs the concept of social role and is used for various purposes in education, such as diagnosing and analyzing a particular role, teaching students the content of the role, giving students an opportunity for practicing a role, or evaluating how well students can actually play the role.[20] Role play can be used for different purposes, and it is important to gain some clarity about what the precise purpose of the role-play activity is before using it. Students will be confused, for example, if they think the purpose is practice when in fact they are being evaluated.[21]

Arrangements for Role Play

Clarity of purpose, arrived at by establishing clear learning outcomes, helps guide a series of subsequent decisions about role-play arrangements that need to be made.

- *Single or multiple role plays.* Will one scenario be acted out in front of several observers, or will several role plays be enacted simultaneously? Several role plays get more people involved, but one carefully enacted role play provides an opportunity for more control, observation, and discussion.
- *High or low structure.* Will a general description of a situation be provided for participants to act out their roles spontaneously, or will the roles be carefully scripted? The scripted role play provides a highly focused demonstration, and the less-structured role play stimulates more involvement and allows for spontaneous variations that may better fit the real-world needs of students.
- *Number of roles.* How many roles will be presented at once? Will the players have alter egos or coaches they can consult about how to play their role and what to do next? Complications can arise when too many roles are being enacted at once, but there are advantages to getting more people involved as players or as alter egos.
- *Importance of nonverbal behavior.* Will emphasis be placed on the spoken lines or the nonverbal action? An emphasis on the content of the script provides more focus for ideas and language, but stressing nonverbal behavior may involve participants more in the emotional aspects of role playing. A role play could be acted entirely in pantomime.
- *Length of role play.* Will the role play last a few minutes or much longer? Perhaps there will be a need to pause or freeze the action at certain points for debriefing. Or a more involved role play might take place at short intervals over several months, allowing for greater complexity to be added over time.

Materials for Role Play

The materials used to initiate role play have some of the properties of instruments used for group activities; for example, materials set up a task and provide an excuse to act. Role-play materials must, however, emphasize roles—what people will do in a particular situation and how their efforts to play their roles will become complicated as the action progresses. Materials should be thought of less as instructions and more as efforts to create a setting or state of mind.[22]

The materials used to initiate role playing can include memos, e-mails, diagrams, capsule descriptions of characters, common situations, videos, websites, or actual scripts. In many cases instructors create their own materials for role play, but more and more materials are available through online sources. However the materials are developed, they should be brief enough to be understood quickly but should also be clear about what students are to do in a situation that can be acted out. The materials must also be related closely to purposes so that the situation developed provides a virtual reality of the expected real-world performance and has the potential to result in the intended learning outcomes.

The Teacher's Role

When using role play, the teacher often plays an important part in making decisions about arrangements and in developing materials, but the teacher is also the manager of the role play. The teacher chooses the appropriate students for each role, makes sure instructions are clear, assigns precise duties to observers, guides the role playing as it unfolds, and leads the subsequent discussion on the meaning of the role play.

The teacher often has (or seeks) inside knowledge about who would perform well or who could profit from a particular role. The teacher knows how to get the role playing started and when and how to stop it. The teacher is also sensitive to how the experience might affect the players, sometimes asking them to express how they were feeling during the role playing or being on the alert for strong emotional responses. Above all, the teacher needs to use the energy and motivation generated by the role play to explore the intended learning. Although the learning often comes in the process of the role play itself, it is valuable to debrief the role play so the participants and observers can identify and put into words what was learned. Sometimes the role play sparks a discussion that moves on to other matters and extends the learning well beyond the issues portrayed in the role play. The teacher carries the responsibility of creating the virtual reality and relating it to the intended learning, always keeping in mind the real-world context where the students will eventually use their learning.

A skillful teacher knows that the following different aspects of a role can be emphasized in role playing:

- Role conflict—when the student is asked to play two different roles that interfere with each other, such as a nurse who is supposed to get victims to safety but also empathize with their loss
- New role—when the role is full of puzzles and surprises, as with a new social worker facing a crisis on the first day at a community center
- Role relationships—when the people one interacts with are difficult, such as a residence hall assistant relating to an intoxicated student
- Role fatigue—when it becomes difficult to play the same role over and over again, always smiling, always pleasant, as with a hotel clerk at a front desk
- Role confusion—when one is unclear about his or her role, as with a law enforcement officer arriving on a domestic conflict scene after the couple has decided to make up
- Dual roles—when the player has two roles, as with a financial adviser who wants to sell an investment product, but who already has a long-standing friendship with the family[23]

Effective teachers also know that some role enactments involve *role reversal*, which is simply assuming the rigid parameters of a socially prescribed role; some involve role playing, where the student renders the role with some freedom to interpret; and some actually require role creating, when the student has to improvise the role using a high degree of spontaneity and inventiveness. The teacher also knows that most roles have a social aspect that emphasizes relationships and a psychodynamic aspect that emphasizes personality and the inner emotional life of the participant.

One of the favorite techniques used in this way of learning is role reversal, where two or more students play a role and then are asked to switch and play the other student's role. Role reversal enables students to walk in each other's shoes and develop empathy for what it is like to be in the other role. Although role playing relies on spontaneous synchronous interaction and may be difficult to accomplish in an asynchronous online course, many online role-play software programs allow students to run through a scenario independently, first taking on one role and then a different role the next time. The variety inherent in differing types of roles offers teachers many opportunities to guide the role play in a number of interesting directions. The skilled teacher is aware of this variety and uses it appropriately to tailor the activity to desired learning outcomes. Role play can be a fairly simple, easy-to-manage way of learning, but it has great potential because there are so many ways to craft and adapt the basic technique.

Dramatic Scenarios

Dramatic scenarios are similar to role play but are enactments of more complex situations, usually involving several characters and a problem that unfolds or evolves, much like a short scene from a play. Dramatic scenarios have their conceptual roots in *sociodrama* and *psychodrama*. Sociodrama tends to be concerned with social roles and relationships, while psychodrama focuses more on the inner life and private concerns of individuals. The techniques for both are quite similar, however, and both grew out of the work of their founder, J. L. Moreno.[24] Teachers can adapt the techniques used in sociodrama and psychodrama to enhance their work with dramatic scenarios in educational settings.

Most dramatic scenarios also involve roles, so the insights and suggestions about managing roles in role play also apply to dramatic scenarios. What distinguishes a dramatic scenario is the length of the action and the complexity of the situation. Like role play, the dramatic scenario relies on something to get it started. There is a scene to be enacted, a little drama to be carried out, hence the term *scenario*. In some cases the scenario will be carefully worked out ahead of time with scripts for each player, guidelines for those who will act as observers, a description of the scene, a summary of the action, and perhaps even props and costumes. In other cases the preparations will be less formal, the actors will be given only general instructions, and the action will need to be invented, as in improvisational theater. For dramatic scenarios, three stages borrowed from sociodrama apply:

1. Warming up is used to help the participants make the transition from the life they have been living, full of its immediate concerns, to the world of drama. Participants need to be clear about their instructions, the content of the scenario, and the general goals of the activity. They need to get ready to play.
2. Enactment is the actual portrayal of the situation. The portrayal needs to be taken with enough seriousness to create the virtual reality, but the emphasis should always be on the potential for learning, not the quality of the acting. Most of the learning should take place from the enactment itself.
3. Sharing is useful for exploring the feelings and ideas of the participants retrospectively, as well as the observations of those who may have been watching.

The dramatic scenario, like sociodrama, often produces some catharsis (satisfying expressions of emotion), some new insights (fresh ideas), or some role training (new ability) for carrying out a role effectively in a particular situation.[25]

Facilitating Dramatic Scenarios

Once the desired learning outcomes are well in mind, and the materials for the dramatic scenario are in hand, it is a good idea to give a brief overview of the roles and the action so students have some idea of what is coming. Before the day of the action, it is wise to ask if anyone is likely to find the topic upsetting, and if so, give them a chance to privately excuse themselves from active participation without penalty and with no questions asked.

Several valuable techniques drawn from sociodrama can be used to facilitate the action of dramatic scenarios.

- *Role reversal.* Players are shifted around to take other parts, either during the enactment or later in a rerun. Students can be moved to another role to develop empathy and gain a new perspective and then be returned to their original role to complete the scenario.
- *Double.* A student is assigned to one of the actors to serve as an inner voice or alter ego. The double may interrupt the dialogue to express the inner thoughts of his character or even use body language that portrays his character's unexpressed inner feelings.
- *Mirror.* A double actually takes the player's place for a while, so the player can step out and watch what has been happening. Sometimes the teacher becomes the double or mirror, to provide support, to challenge, to question, or to magnify feelings.
- *Empty chair.* A place is assigned to an imaginary additional character, someone the players can vent their feelings on, experiment with, or ask for advice as one might do with an imaginary mentor.
- *Soliloquy.* This technique, often used in plays—the most famous being Hamlet's "to be or not to be" soliloquy—provides a character the opportunity to emerge from the action and reflect on inner feelings. In dramatic scenarios the teacher may stand beside a student and call for a brief soliloquy on present thoughts or feelings.
- *Walk and talk.* The teacher may ask the student to pace back and forth in a walk-and-talk soliloquy to reduce tension and get out of a puzzling situation. Sometimes the teacher will actually walk the student out of the scene and talk it over to find a new approach to the

situation. A sensitive teacher knows when a student wants to say, "Give me a minute" and will arrange for a brief time-out as needed. After overcoming whatever it was the student was troubled about, the action can be resumed and perhaps played out more productively.

- *Freeze frame.* The teacher stops the action, as one might with a video. When the students hear the command to freeze, they are expected to stop where they are, so the teacher can comment on body language, expressions, tone of voice, communication, or arrangement in space. Sometimes observers will be asked to comment on the freeze frame.
- *Concretization.* Abstract expressions like "low man on the totem pole" or "bouncing off the walls" can be played out in concrete actions that represent feelings.
- *Sculpting.* A whole scene is arranged and dramatized through the arrangement of the players. For example, a dependent employee holding the supervisor around the knees is enacted to shed light on a situation everyone knows but does not want to talk about.
- *Future projection.* The teacher asks the students how they think a scene is going to play out sometime in the future.[26]

The skilled teacher not only sets the action in motion but knows how to use an array of techniques to structure the action as the drama unfolds so that learning is maximized.

Sharing the Learning

Students usually will recognize when the scene has been played out, and the teacher needs to end the enactment and begin the sharing.[27] Often the students will need an opportunity to express their feelings—frustration, embarrassment, confusion, satisfaction—and get out of their role. The observers, who have been patient in their observing, are eager to talk and want to comment. The teacher can help set ground rules for sharing, such as nonjudgmental observation, acceptance of divergent opinions, honest disclosure, and minimization of giving advice and drawing morals. Observers need to remember the day will come when they will be the players, so they should present their observations in the form they themselves would like to receive them. Sharing is very important to show how the dramatic scenario fosters learning that will result in improved performance. Students can also critique the experience, and if the scenario didn't go as well as planned, it can be strengthened before another run.

Although dramatic scenarios are more complex than role play and demand more knowledge and skill from the teacher, they offer great opportunities for creating a safe and inexpensive virtual reality for learning. Consider this example of a dramatic scenario.

> Jeff Borden has taught Communication in the Courtroom at Metro State College of Denver and at the University of Northern Colorado. This course brings together students from various majors to focus on some common and some independent course outcomes including nonverbal communication, oral communication, persuasion, argumentation, and reasoning skills. During the course, students participate in the "Trial of the Century." This large-scale dramatic scenario in which students play courtroom roles and attempt to determine the guilt or innocence of a defendant takes place over an entire weekend. At the beginning of the Friday class period, a guest lecturer begins a presentation, when Jeff, dressed in costume, bursts into the classroom yelling and making accusations about stolen keys. Shortly afterward the lights are turned out, and when they come back on, "Dr. Slain" is found lying on the floor, deceased and covered in blood. The students then jump into action, playing various roles. The attorneys for the defense and prosecution begin forming a case, witnesses are questioned, forensic scientists and criminologists help formulate theories based on planted clues, a jury is picked during voir dire, and the entire case culminates Sunday morning with a verdict from the jury. Jeff even recruits a sitting judge from the community to manage the proceedings. As the instructor, Jeff watches the action play out but takes on an observant and facilitative role. "After my 'death' scene at the start, I go back to my teacher role and facilitate," he says. "I am a reference for any team needing assistance or guidance and I also act as a director during the trial, occasionally stopping for poignant teaching moments." Students not only practice how to communicate effectively in the courtroom, but they enjoy the process so much they often invite family members to the closing arguments. "We often have a huge 'gallery' to present to, which adds even more realism for the students who are practicing these critical communication courtroom skills."[28]

Simulations and Games

Role play and dramatic scenarios have an element of virtual reality about them, but with simulations and games the virtual reality becomes more prominent and the complexity increases. The terms *simulation* and *game* are often used interchangeably in writing about them, and sometimes the terms *simulation game* or *simulation/game* are used, adding confusion. Simulations are representations of some aspect of the real world where abstract models are developed and then manipulated in dynamic ways to create learning.[29] Simulation involves abstracting elements of a social or physical reality so that a person can enter it and learn.[30] Simulations can lean in one of two directions: either they are set up to explore, understand, or practice social interactions among individuals or groups, or they are arranged to explore, understand, or practice aspects of the physical or mechanical world, such as an instrument, an apparatus, or a conveyance.[31]

A game is a type of simulation that often stresses competition or mastery; it is a contest with rules and a clear outcome.[32] Although in games, players or groups of players may compete against each other, often they work together against a common adversary or to control a natural event or destructive force. Games involve rules and goals, and they usually contain some element of enjoyment.[33] If we eliminate games that are played simply for entertainment, such as sports or board games, and if we also eliminate games that deal in abstractions and are designed primarily to stretch the mind or cultivate creativity, then we are left with serious games or educational games that are designed for educational purposes. In simulations, players often play a prescribed role, but in games the role of the player is manipulable, and the roles and goals are often defined and redefined by the players.[34] Not all simulations are games, some have no clear outcome or competitive element, and not all games are simulations because some games lack a component of virtual reality. Numerous games are fun and teach students about academic content, but we focus this way of learning on games and simulations that teach students to develop complex judgment. Simulations, and games that simulate, should be examined for their educational promise for bringing about desired outcomes. Consider the following example.

> In the teacher education program at the University of North Texas, Tandra Tyler-Wood uses a virtual simulation in her online and on-campus special education courses. "There is a real shortage of special education teachers today, and nearly all prospective teachers will work with students with diverse needs as more students are mainstreamed in our schools," says Tandra. "However, prospective teachers usually do not come into contact with a wide variety of students during their teaching internships in a real classroom. We need a manageable way to expose them to many different kinds of student needs." Tandra uses simSchool, a software program that simulates a classroom, to give them this experience.[35] While working in this program, her students take the role of a teacher as they view an image of a

classroom scene with different students sitting at desks. The teacher can run through the action of the classroom, choosing from a variety of lesson plans, sequencing activities, behavior management strategies, comments to make to students, and other classroom tasks while the action unfolds. "What is really powerful is that we can create custom students, with any number of exceptionalities," she says. Virtual students can be created by manipulating variables such as visual or physical abilities, personality dimensions such as agreeableness or emotional sensitivity, and academic achievement dimensions. By working through the simulation with these virtual students, prospective teachers become aware of students' unique learning needs and practice adjusting instruction accordingly. Tandra helps her students interpret the data gained from the simulation on aspects such as how well they allotted time for instruction, developed adaptations for students, or interpreted on-task behavior. "Students really like working with simSchool. They appreciate being able to experience a wide variety of potential students in a short time frame. And although a 'real' student may not react the same way as a 'virtual' student, through the simulation they gain confidence as they get the sense that they can anticipate and actually fix problems that might arise in their actual classrooms."[36]

Simulations are used more often than games in higher education because the teacher has more control over roles and rules, and can target specific learning aspects. Games can be powerful learning environments but are much more open-ended. James Paul Gee, a leader in educational gaming, says, "Digital games are, at their heart, problem solving spaces that use continual learning and provide pathways to mastery through entertainment and pleasure."[37] Games teach roles and judgment through cause and effect. Students take action, observe others' actions, and reflect on this action. Through this process, students begin to understand patterns of actions and how people relate, behave, react, and respond to each other.

Simulations and games are made up of certain components, and understanding the components is important for teachers who wish to use this way of learning effectively. Although scholars use a variety of terms to describe these components, we believe they can be reduced to a list of eight words that all begin with *R*:

- *Reasons*. There must be a clear purpose or set of reasons for the activity, something the simulation or game explores. The reasons will set the guidelines for other decisions about using the game and will give the activity a particular emphasis.[38] What learning is desirable? In what context will it be used? What is the fundamental purpose of the activity?

- *Reality.* Choices need to be made about what aspect of reality is to be portrayed. The simulation activity will incorporate some abstraction of reality as a model. What elements are highlighted, and which have been eliminated? How much and what kinds of reality are drawn into the model?[39]

- *Roles.* Roles need to be defined and allocated and a scenario needs to be provided. Who are the players, and what roles will they play? What will they do? How will the object of the activity get them into action? Where will the action carry them?

- *Rules.* The activity will have certain rules or procedures that set the parameters for the players. The rules actually drive the game and set up or limit possibilities. How will the rules be determined and communicated? Can the rules be broken or modified? How will the rules be enforced?[40]

- *Resources.* The activity will use certain resources. The game or simulation might occur entirely through computers or mobile devices or partly in the physical world. There might be a need for a simulated room or apparatus, graphic displays, problems, data banks, objects, videos, audiotapes, materials, supplies, implements for writing and recording, and so forth. What resources will this activity need, and at what times will they be needed?

- *Records.* The activity may generate information, data, scores, or possibly the need for calculations. What will be the accounting system for the activity? Who will keep track of the data that is generated and meet the needs for data analysis? What procedures or software will be used to establish the accounting system, and in what sequence will information be received and delivered?[41]

- *Running time.* The activity will have certain steps of play, phases, or sequences.[42] Sometimes these are incorporated into directions or intermittent commands. What is the simulated time frame (day, month, quarter) for the activity, and what amount of real time will be allocated for the simulated time? What cycles will the activity have, and how much time will be allocated for the various cycles? How much simulated time is represented in a cycle?

- *Results.* The activity will produce certain results, perhaps a successful or unsuccessful outcome, winners and losers, or a resolution of some type. To what extent is the resolution defined or open? How will the players know when the game is over? How will the activity be concluded?

As with the facilitator of the role play or the director of the dramatic scenario, the teacher has certain responsibilities in managing a simulation or game.[43] The first step is to select the game or simulation, and there are many off-the-shelf and downloadable games to choose from. Although there are many classic games—the Oregon Trail and SimCity have been available for decades[44]—new games with increasing levels of sophistication are being developed each year and are widely available commercially and sometimes for free. Kurt Squire identifies several aspects of what to look for in good educational game design: education games should pique players' interest, offer multiple ways of playing, encourage social interaction, and rely on academic knowledge and systemic understanding to achieve the goals.[45] Most educational games are labeled as such or are referred to as serious games. What the instructor does not want to do is mistake some of the many drill-and-practice exercises disguised as games for true educational games. Using drill-and-practice exercises that look like games is common enough to be given the popular moniker *chocolate-covered broccoli*. When teachers are bombarded with options for educational games, they need to remind themselves that the purpose of learning through virtual realities is the development of complex behaviors, judgment, and systemic thinking in lifelike environments.

If the games or simulations the teacher finds available do not adequately fit the desired learning goals, sometimes a game can be adapted (within the confines of copyright) to fit a particular purpose or time frame. Fantasy games have been used to explore teamwork and social behaviors. Even video games about football have used built-in sports franchise options to teach students about marketing.[46] However, it may be necessary to create a game or simulation from scratch. This will take more work—in the case of video games it could involve a team of outside experts and designers—but in the long run, that newly created product may leverage unique educational purposes well worth the time.

Once the simulation or game is chosen or created, planning for its use takes a high priority because once set in motion, the activity should run itself. Here is a planning checklist:

1. *Knowledge of the game.* The teacher should have a solid understanding of the game: what it does, what it doesn't do, the roles and rules, and what is needed to complete the game, or to win.

2. *Participation.* Prior to taking on the teacher's role, it is desirable to participate as a player to gain complete familiarity with how the simulation works.

3. *Materials.* If the game or simulation is not completely automated, materials need to be carefully developed and arranged for timely presentation.

4. *Role allocation.* With many games, students can choose their own roles. At other times, assignment to groups and to individual roles should be carried out through a deliberate process.

5. *Space arrangement.* The location should fit the activities planned and may include more than one space, arrangements for media, one or more home bases for the participants, the use of computers or mobile devices, laboratory space, or perhaps a specially designed simulated environment.

6. *Accounting.* Provisions should be made when data sets are used or when quantitative information is generated and has to be analyzed.

7. *Briefing.* Before the simulation begins, the teacher holds a briefing to make assignments, give an overview of the activity, provide materials, explain the roles and rules, and alert the students to the types of learning anticipated.

8. *Detached observation.* Once the simulation is under way, the teacher usually cultivates an air of studied detachment. Unlike the director of a dramatic scenario, the teacher of a simulation is more like a prop manager, trying to stay offstage, limiting visibility, and restraining the urge to intervene. If the simulation or game occurs virtually, the teacher can generally stay out of the way. If the simulation or game occurs in person, the teacher should generally maintain a poker face devoid of an expression of satisfaction or displeasure. There are several reasons for this: a well-planned simulation or game should be so well designed that it runs almost unassisted, the participants should own their activity, and the mood should not be interrupted, thus heightening the semblance of reality.

9. *Time management.* The teacher is primarily a time manager, initiating the action, helping participants make transitions through cycles, letting the students know how much time they have left or what deadlines they must meet, and making decisions about when to stop or whether to rerun. Thus, the teacher may circulate and observe but not direct or intrude, because the action, growing out of the roles and rules, will take care of itself.

10. *Just-in-time explanations.* The teacher should be prepared to stop the action and provide information, additional resources, or even short presentations when confusion or questions arise that limit the students' ability to complete the simulation or game.[47]

11. *Debriefing.* The teacher gets back into a more familiar role during the debriefing when the students are asked to describe their learning. The teacher should help students explore their actions and compare the actions and results of various students to discover the patterns and systems at work in the simulation. The key challenge here is to get the students to stop talking about the details of the activity and to extract from it the essence of the learning.

One advantage of simulations and games is that they can be run on any scale desired, ranging from a brief, focused game that lasts a portion of a class period to much more elaborate arrangements of roles and activities extending over a longer period of time. If the reality to be simulated is complex, then the virtual reality needed to simulate it may be difficult to create, consuming extensive time and resources. Consider the following example of a marketing simulation.

Carl Mela teaches Brand Management at Duke University. "Brand and product managers 'run' a small business and, as such, have profit and loss responsibility for brands. Yet few courses are intended to walk students through the steps necessary to achieve this objective," says Carl. "The goal of this course is to prepare such managers to build brand assets and create an enduring advantage for their brands in the marketplace." Carl uses a marketing simulation software program called PharmaSim where students take the role of a brand management team for a pharmaceutical company.[48] Students make decisions about factors such as pricing, advertising, promotion, and distribution and see how their marketing strategy performs by running the simulation. This program gives the students real-world experience in a way not usually possible within the confines of an academic term. Carl bases 30 percent of the students' grade on the quality of their marketing plan but only 5 percent on students' performance in the computer simulation. Although strong marketing plans usually lead to strong performance, this simulation is a place where they can see how their choices play out, learn from their mistakes, and get a sense of the complexities of managing brands and how many factors interact. "Importantly," he says, "I grade in phases to give students feedback as they proceed. In my experience, it is more common in organizations to have interactive feedback than all of the comments at the end of a task. In this regard, students have the chance to react to and learn from the feedback."[49]

Assessing Virtual Realities

Assessing learning through virtual realities can seem daunting. How can a teacher test a student's acting a role or playing a game? The goal, of course, is not to evaluate the acting or playing but the learning. The process may seem easier if the teacher goes back to the purposes for using virtual realities. When the goal is development of complex professional judgment and systemic thinking in a virtual setting, the teacher uses the desired outcomes for student learning to check on the learning gains and the goal attained. How much has the student improved professional performance, and how close is he or she to being an expert?

When using role play and dramatic scenarios, summative assessment is often based on how well a student's performance matches the expectations of the actual role the individual is portraying.[50] This is often a matter of observation and inference. The teacher can use rubrics to spell out what constitutes advanced performance in the area of a sales interaction, disaster management, or law enforcement and evaluate a student's performance accordingly. Such rubrics may be very specific, such as, "The sales associate politely acknowledges the customer's complaint while redirecting the conversation toward a solution" or, more general, "Students acting as station managers display leadership when developing an appropriate action plan." Rubrics help teachers get more specific about what they are looking for in students' actions.

By their very design, simulations and games are focused on formative assessment, self-assessment, and mastery. Rubrics such as those used for role playing and dramatic scenarios can be used, but in games, students work toward mastering each level or winning, both of which function as a kind of assessment. Some games automatically build in means for determining who has achieved mastery or a measured approximation of mastery. With other games students may need to create a presentation, present a proposal, write a reflection paper, or talk directly to the teacher to demonstrate what has been learned from the game. In any case, mastering games should be less about accumulating the most points and more about achieving measurable levels of professional expertise.

Games can also be designed to contain embedded assessments. Kurt Squire describes this process in a game about finding the source of contaminated water. The game contains "carefully placed red herrings" to determine which sources of evidence students use.[51] Such distractions highlight common misconceptions or faulty evidence students might use and can help determine how well students draw conclusions based on appropriate evidence.

Perhaps for this way of learning more than any other, the process of the activity is more important for learning than the final outcome. The feedback—from the teacher, other students or players, or the software or simulation itself—is what influences the development of judgment. What worked? What didn't? What happened to other factors or individuals when the student took certain actions? Self-reflection on this feedback is valuable for learning and should be encouraged. Although final summative assessment is often needed, when using virtual realities the teacher should ultimately reflect on the purposes of this way of learning to determine if, what, and how much to assess.

Technology That Supports Learning Through Virtual Realities

When students are learning with virtual realities, especially when they are using simulations and games, technology will often play an important role. Certainly role playing and other simulations can occur quite effectively without any use of technology. But many technologies developed to simulate a real experience can be quite valuable for this way of learning. Expensive and highly involved simulations, such as flight simulators to train airline pilots, have been around for decades and took years and considerable investments to create. Today computers, software applications, and mobile devices make simulated reality something anyone can experience.

Perhaps the simplest technology to use, but still highly valuable, is the video recorder, now widely available on many types of cameras, computers, and mobile devices. Role play and dramatic scenarios can be recorded and replayed, using the recording to focus on selected moments or key turning points in the action. Students can use instant replay to analyze their own behaviors and consider what they actually did or missed, what went well or poorly, and what they might have done differently. Sections of the role play or scenario can be replayed again after watching the recording in the sharing session. Because dramatic scenarios are more complex, the video may need to be more sophisticated, using more than one camera to capture nuances of the dialogue or zoom in on the action of a primary player. Students can independently view aspects of the video related to their role.

Standard commercial software can be used for creating virtual realities; for example, financial simulations using predesigned data sets in electronic spreadsheets are an easy way to create a simulation. The ideas behind capitalism portrayed in the classic board game Monopoly have been reinvented as multimedia video games such as Gazillionare! and Zapitalism![52] Many of the SimCity games and other multiplayer games are used to practice managing complex environments and analyze professional behavior.

Other technologies are more complex and involved. The application of virtual worlds to education has been evident for many years through Second Life, an online virtual world where people can create graphical representations of themselves, known as avatars, and exist in this space virtually.[53] Students and researchers have explored alternate identities, tested projects and proposals, developed archeological prototypes, and conducted experiments with nuclear materials in this virtual world without the extreme negative consequences possible in the physical world. Although Second Life has not yet gained the acceptance or momentum that was expected by this time, it remains a tremendous example of virtual simulation and the possibilities of learning through virtual realities.

The future of learning through virtual realities most likely lies with mobile devices most students now have with them at all times. For example, a number of leading educational gaming experts at Massachusetts Institute of Technology have collaborated on a game called Environmental Detectives.[54] This game simulates an environmental disaster in a local watershed, and teams of students walk around the actual locations with mobile devices that enable them to collect simulated field data, conduct mock interviews, and gather other information to try to pinpoint the source of the toxic spill and present their case. Mobile devices are now enhanced with augmented reality, the ability to add a computer-assisted contextual layer of information over what we see in the real world. It combines real and virtual elements on computer or mobile device screens. This form of enhanced reality has evolved from head-mounted goggle displays reminiscent of old sci-fi movies to a commonly used form of marketing and business relations images that are available today on anyone's smartphone or mobile device. According to the annual Horizon Report about the future of educational technology, through augmented reality, "Dynamic processes, extensive datasets, and objects too large or too small to be manipulated can be brought into a student's personal space at a scale and in a form easy to understand and work with."[55] Students explore museum pieces without actually touching them, and US Marine mechanics are trained to repair engines and other expensive machinery without harming any physical objects.[56]

Final Thoughts

Learning through virtual realities allows students to develop, practice, and test professional judgment before entering real-world settings. This way of learning can also be fun, so it's easy for teachers and students to get sidetracked from the learning objectives by the flair and appeal of many new products and the sheer fun of using them. Because of the fun factor, some students, teachers, and teachers' colleagues may not be convinced of the value of such activities in higher education—How can learning be fun?—and they may need to explore the origins and legitimize the purposes of this way of learning. Elementary and secondary school students are already creating their own games for learning, and they will soon be in college doing the same. Learning through virtual realities has an exciting future as advances in technologies open new possibilities for more lifelike and convincing simulations of reality in which learning can thrive.

Points to Remember

Teachers who want to facilitate learning through virtual realities effectively should do the following:

- ✓ Define a clear purpose for using virtual realities for learning.
- ✓ Design or select the activity to use.
- ✓ Define the type of professional behavior or judgment desired from students as an outcome.
- ✓ Find appropriate materials to support the activity.
- ✓ Arrange the logistical aspects, such as number of participants, type of roles needed, level of structure, and length.
- ✓ Identify the various roles that are needed and create the scripts or backgrounds to set them in motion.
- ✓ Decide what role or level of involvement, if any, the teacher will have.
- ✓ Define any rules necessary for the activity to proceed.
- ✓ Prepare students for the activity and any possible emotional reactions.
- ✓ Facilitate the action as necessary using techniques such as role reversal, student doubles, empty chair, soliloquy, and freeze frame.

✓ Stop, pause, or support the activity with additional resources, materials, technologies, or just-in-time explanations.

✓ Provide formative feedback and determine what aspects of the activity are appropriate for summative assessment.

✓ Debrief the experience with students to identify and discuss the essential learning.

Notes

1. Larry Johnson et al., *The 2011 Horizon Report* (Austin, TX: New Media Consortium, 2011), 21; John P. Hertel and Barbara J. Millis, *Using Simulations to Promote Learning in Higher Education* (Sterling, VA: Stylus, 2002), 12–13.

2. See, for example, http://www.anatomylab.com, developed by Mark Nielsen, biology professor at University of Utah.

3. "Peacemaker," 2010, Hybrid Learning Systems, http://www.peacemaker game.com/.

4. Omar Moore and Alan Anderson, "Some Principles for the Design of Clarifying Educational Environments," in *Gaming-Simulation: Rationale, Design, and Applications*, ed. Cathy Greenblatt and Richard Duke (New York: Wiley, 1975), 49–50.

5. Betsy Watson, "Games and Socialization," in *Gaming-Simulation: Rationale, Design, and Applications*, ed. Cathy Greenblatt and Richard Duke (New York: Wiley, 1975), 42–43.

6. René Marineau, *Jacob Levy Moreno, 1889–1974: Father of Psychodrama, Sociometry, and Group Psychotherapy* (London: Tavistock/Routledge, 1989), 25–49.

7. J. L. Moreno, *Psychodrama* (New York: Beacon House, 1946), 2.

8. Alice Gordon, *Games for Growth* (Palo Alto, CA: Science Research Associates, 1970), 4–6.

9. Kalman Cohen and Eric Rhenman, "The Role of Management Games in Research," in *Gaming-Simulation: Rationale, Design, and Applications*, ed. Cathy Greenblatt and Richard Duke (New York: Wiley, 1975), 233–35.

10. Ken Jones, *Simulations: A Handbook for Teachers and Trainers* (London: Kogan Page, 1987), 19–20.

11. Clark Abt, *Serious Games* (New York: Viking Press, 1970); "The Serious Games Initiative," accessed March 15, 2012, http://www.seriousgames.org/.

12. Thomas C. Keiser and John H. Seeler, "Games and Simulations," in *Training and Development Handbook: A Guide to Human Resource Development*, 3rd ed., ed. Robert L. Craig (New York: McGraw-Hill, 1987), 457–58.

13. John von Neumann and Oskar Morgenstern, *The Theory of Games and Economic Behavior* (Princeton, NJ: Princeton University Press, 1944).

14. Eric Klopfer, paraphrasing James Paul Gee, *Augmented Learning: Research and Design of Mobile Educational Games* (Cambridge, MA: MIT Press, 2008), 17.

15. David A. Sousa, *How the Brain Learns* (Thousand Oaks, CA: Corwin Press, 2001).

16. James Paul Gee, *What Video Games Have to Teach Us about Learning* (New York: Palgrave, 2003).

17. Thanks to Kevin Brun, Instructor at the Colorado Law Enforcement Training Academy, Colorado Mountain College, for granting permission to use his example. In discussion with the author, January 31, 2012.

18. Caroline Persell, *Understanding Society: An Introduction to Sociology* (New York: Harper & Row, 1989), 58–61.

19. R. P. Cuzzort and E. W. King, *Twentieth Century Social Thought*, 4th ed. (Fort Worth, TX: Holt, Rinehart and Winston, 1989), 272–84.

20. M. E. Shaw et al., "Role Playing," in *The 1979 Annual Handbook for Group Facilitators*, ed. J. E. Jones and S. W. Pfeiffer (San Diego, CA: University Associates, 1979), 182–93.

21. Phyllis Cooke, "Role Playing," in *The ASTD Training and Development Handbook*, ed. Robert L. Craig (San Francisco, CA: McGraw-Hill, 1996) 430–31. The following section on arrangements is adapted from Cooke.

22. Norman F. Maier, Allen Solem, and Ayesha Maier, *The Role-Play Technique* (La Jolla, CA: University Associates, 1975), 12.

23. Patricia Sternberg and Antonina Garcia, *Sociodrama: Who's in Your Shoes?* (New York: Praeger, 1989), 48, 50, 53, 104, 105.

24. Ibid., 4–7.

25. Ibid., 15–24.

26. Ibid., chap. 6, "Structuring the Action."

27. Ibid., chap. 9, "Mastering Directing Skills."

28. Thanks to Jeff Borden, PhD, Senior Director of Teaching and Learning at Pearson eCollege and Adjunct Faculty at Chaminade University and Southeast Community College, for granting permission to use his example. E-mail message to author, November 30, 2011.

29. Richard Barton, *A Primer on Simulation and Gaming* (Englewood Cliffs, NJ: Prentice Hall, 1970), 4–7.

30. Richard Dukes and Constance Seidner, *Learning with Simulations and Games* (Newbury Park, CA: Sage, 1978), 15.

31. Dennis Adams, *Simulation Games* (Worthington, OH: Charles A. Jones, 1973), 4–5.

32. Abt, *Serious Games*, 6–7.

33. Klopfer, *Augmented Learning*.

34. Kurt Squire, *Video Games and Learning: Teaching and Participatory Culture in the Digital Age* (New York: Teachers College Press, 2011).

35. "simSchool," 2012, http://simschool.org/.

36. Thanks to Tandra Tyler-Wood, PhD, Associate Professor of Learning Technologies at the University of North Texas, for granting permission to use her example. E-mail message to author, March 5, 2012.

37. James Paul Gee, "Deep Learning Properties of Good Digital Games: How Far Can They Go?" in *Serious Games: Mechanisms and Effects*, ed. Ute Ritterfeld, Michael Cody, and Peter Vorderer (New York: Routledge, 2009), 65–80.

38. Cathy Greenblatt, "Gaming-Simulation and Social Science: Rewards to the Designer," in *Gaming-Simulation: Rationale, Design, and Applications*, ed. Cathy Greenblatt and Richard Duke (New York: Wiley, 1975), 92–93.

39. Cathy Greenblatt, "Basic Concepts and Linkages," in *Gaming-Simulation: Rationale, Design, and Applications*, ed. Cathy Greenblatt and Richard Duke (New York: Wiley, 1975), 10–13.

40. Allan Feldt and Frederick Goodman, "Observations on the Design of Simulation Games," in *Gaming-Simulation: Rationale, Design, and Applications*, ed. Cathy Greenblatt and Richard Duke (New York: Wiley, 1975), 170–71.

41. R. H. R. Armstrong and Margaret Hobson, "Introduction to Gaming-Simulation Techniques," in *Gaming-Simulation: Rationale, Design, and Applications*, ed. Cathy Greenblatt and Richard Duke (New York: Wiley, 1975), 85–86.

42. Barton, *A Primer on Simulation and Gaming*, 29.

43. Ken Jones, *Simulations: A Handbook for Teachers and Trainers* (London: Kogan Page, 1987), 65–90.

44. "The Oregon Trail," 2011, The Learning Company, http://www.oregontrail.com/hmh/site/oregontrail/; "SimCity," 2012, MobyGames, http://www.mobygames.com/game/simcity.

45. Squire, *Video Games and Learning*, 36–37.

46. This example of Paul Swangard's class is described in Patrick Chinn, "Playing for a Good Grade," *IT Connections*, February 15, 2009, http://it.uoregon.edu/itconnections/playing-for-a-good-grade.

47. Squire, *Video Games and Learning*.

48. "PharmaSim: A Marketing Management Simulation," accessed March 15, 2012, http://www.interpretive.com/rd5/index.php?pg=ps4.

49. Thanks to Carl Mela, PhD, T. Austin Finch Foundation Professor at the Fuqua School of Business at Duke University, for granting permission to use his example. E-mail message to author, January 9, 2012.

50. Klopfer, *Augmented Learning*, 145.

51. Squire, *Video Games and Learning*, 198–200.

52. "Gazillionaire!" and "Zapitalism!" 2012, LavaMind, http://www.lavamind.com/.

53. "Second Life," 2002, Linden Research, http://www.secondlife.com.

54. "Environmental Detectives," accessed March 15, 2012, G2T, http://www.educationarcade.org/gtt/Handheld/Intro.htm.

55. Johnson et al., *The 2011 Horizon Report*, 17.

56. The Augsburg display cabinet from the J. Paul Getty Museum is described in Johnson et al., *2011 Horizon Report*, 17; Tim Folger, "The Big Idea," accessed March 15, 2012, *National Geographic*, http://ngm.nationalgeographic.com/big-idea/14/augmented-reality-pg2.

REFLECTING ON EXPERIENCE

Experiential Learning

Intended Learning Outcomes What students learn	Way of Learning Origins and theory	Common Methods What the teacher provides
Reflecting on experience Self-discovery and personal growth from real-world experience	**Experiential learning** Experiential learning, cognitive neuroscience, constructivism	Internships Service-learning Study abroad

Is this a kind of learning that bubbles up out of experience? Is this learning that occurs when students go out and get immersed in a real-life work, service, or travel experience? Could students learn more from the experience if they have a chance to reflect on it and make meaning of it? Is there a potential here for learning to see something in a new way? These are learning outcomes that are well served by experiential learning.

A law professor arranges for law students to engage in a monitored work experience known as an externship. Students craft a Learning Agenda Plan, write journal and blog entries, and share their observations with the teacher and other students. They meet once a week as a class, face-to-face or online, to make sense of their experience. Along the way they find out if they like the practice of law, and if so which kind of law practice best suits them.

Everyone learns from experience, we say, but alas, we all know people who never seem to do that. But what is experience and how do we learn from it? We say a new department chair is inexperienced, and we say the new dean is very experienced. We look back and say, "That was a painful experience, but actually it was a good learning experience." We often mention the words *learning* and *experience* in the same breath. What is the connection?

To the well-known educational theorist John Dewey, experience was interaction between the individual and the environment, and the experience itself contained a continuous flow of knowledge from previous experiences.[1] So experiences are more than just the present moment; they also draw together past and future. Parker Palmer says, "We are most powerfully affected by deep and sustained experiences, which leave enduring imprints on our very constitution and consciousness. We not only know more but see differently and become another human being through transformational experiences."[2]

Colleges and universities use various types of structured experiences to promote learning. They send students off campus for cooperative education work experience in business and industry. Some professional schools require students to complete an internship experience, often called an externship in law schools or a practicum in education or social work fields. Many universities today encourage students to have a study abroad experience, wilderness challenge experience, or service-learning experience. Unlike learning through virtual realities where learning experiences are simulated, these are real experiences that put students in a new or challenging situation that can result in various kinds of learning.

This way of learning is usually known as *experiential learning*. Although this term is sometimes misused to describe any type of active learning, it is the commonly accepted term for programs that draw upon experience for learning. The National Society for Experiential Education establishes best practices and provides training resources through its Experiential Education Academy.[3] Experiential learning refers to the use by colleges and universities of sponsored, structured, and guided experiences identified or established for the express purpose of contributing to the learning of their students. The main focus of this way of learning is making meaning from challenging real-life experiences. Research on the anatomy and physiology of the brain in the field known as *cognitive neuroscience* suggests that human beings are well wired for learning through experience.

Learning Through Experience

Not all experiences lead to learning. How is it that raw experience becomes educative? One of the pioneers in addressing this question was David Kolb.[4]

Drawing on the earlier work of Lewin, Dewey, and Piaget, Kolb sets forth a cyclical model of learning through experience.

According to Kolb, learning begins in concrete experience. A student is immersed in a potentially educative experience and begins to reflect on what that experience means. As the reflection deepens, the student formulates abstract conceptualizations about what has taken place. As the abstract conceptualizations are developed, they must be tested to see how they work. This testing is done through a process of active experimentation, which of necessity returns the student once again to concrete experience. For Kolb, "Ideas are not fixed and immutable elements of thought but are formed and reformed through experience."[5] Understanding is a process of continuous construction, built on the interaction of ideas and experience. "Failure to modify ideas and habits as a result of experience is maladaptive."[6] Therefore, one must engage in a continuous cycle of experience, reflection, abstraction, and testing, finally returning to experience once again. Kolb's work shows that experiential learning involves some steps, some phases, going into an experience and coming back, and above all a process of reflection, as illustrated in the following example.

> Ann Vessels directs the Legal Externship Program at the University of Denver Sturm College of Law. An externship consists of two parts: a monitored work experience in a private firm or company, government agency, nonprofit organization, or with a judge, and a weekly seminar in which students reflect upon and discuss issues related to their work experience. "The overarching goal of the Legal Externship Program is to provide opportunities for students to engage in critical reflection about the legal profession, their legal career, and their priorities and values as lawyers and individuals," says Ann. "Some of the specific goals of the program include increasing students' understanding of their own individual strengths and weaknesses as lawyers, exploring workplace issues and culture, and developing a sense of self-directed and lifelong learning." To ensure they get the most out of this experience, students complete a Learning Agenda Plan during the first week of their externship to articulate their personal and professional learning goals and areas in which they want to gain specific experience. This document is cosigned by the students and their supervising attorney. The weekly class sessions—or online sessions for those students completing externships in other states or countries—allow students to reflect and learn from their experience and from the experiences of fellow students. "Reflection is a key pedagogical tool in experiential learning," says Ann. "It both enhances and accelerates student learning. By

articulating their observations, students are better able to comprehend and integrate what they have learned so that it can become a basis for future action." To keep students reflecting on what they are learning, Ann has students write journals and blog entries throughout the experience. "Journaling allows students to make sense of what they are experiencing and link this experience to the bigger picture. For example, some students may think they want to practice a certain kind of law, but after externing in that area and reflecting on their experiences, they realize they should consider a different direction." Students write a blog post when they observe something interesting, and they comment on each other's posts. "They like the instant feedback they receive from each other and from me. And they appreciate knowing that others are experiencing similar issues," Ann says. These tools are a way for students to learn from each other's experiences as well as reflect on their own experience with the practice of law.[7]

One point is clear from this example of learning through experience: the learning doesn't happen automatically. As with other ways of learning, learning through experience needs to be facilitated. It has to be planned and arranged, settings need to be identified and selected, and participants need to be matched to the right setting and oriented to what learning from experience actually involves. Above all, someone must establish and facilitate the reflection process.

What We Know About Experiential Learning

What are the typical learning outcomes that experiential learning is particularly useful for developing? Through experiential learning students are able to

- develop awareness of the overall big picture structure of organizations, communities, and cultures;
- identify problems and opportunities in an unfamiliar setting;
- apply previous learning to new settings;
- improvise new on-the-spot solutions to problems and opportunities;
- test new ideas that emerge from practice;
- develop awareness of their own cultural identity and how it influences and interacts with the identities of others;
- use multisensory, interdisciplinary, and multicultural perspectives to understand unfamiliar situations;
- develop broader observational powers and reflective thought patterns;

- experiment with new patterns of verbal and nonverbal communication; and
- develop adaptability by reconsidering fixed responses and attitudes and then testing the alternatives.

Like other ways of learning, experiential learning has its distinct advantages for producing certain outcomes.

How much experience is needed for some or all of these learning outcomes to occur? Does a field trip count? How long and deep should this experience be to qualify as experiential learning? These are not easy questions, but three wonderful concepts come in handy to serve as criteria: *intensity, frequency*, and *duration*. How intense or deep is the experience? Are significant responsibilities involved as opposed to trivial routines? How frequently does the student engage in the experience, three half days a week or three hours one day a week? Has the student moved from being strictly an observer to an active participant? How long does the experience last, for a whole term or only for a few days? Note how the criteria interact. An interterm study abroad experience in which a student lives with a host family might involve significant intensity and frequency but may last only three weeks. A civic engagement experience in which a student volunteers every Friday over the course of a year involves a longer duration and frequency but perhaps less intensity. All three criteria should be present but not necessarily at the same level. Professional judgment should be used in applying the criteria, but at some point teacher and student need to be able to distinguish between a potentially educative experience and one that is merely fun or interesting.

Reflection-in-Action

What is the learning that takes place from the going out and coming back depicted in Kolb's experiential learning cycle? Is it a mere application of knowledge learned elsewhere to a practical setting, or is there a new, perhaps qualitatively different, kind of learning that grows from experience? Some would argue that knowledge constructed through experience is quite different from knowledge gained through formal classroom study. This case has been made by Donald Schön in a stimulating book titled *The Reflective Practitioner: How Professionals Think in Action.*[8] His argument is as follows:

- Professional education—the education of practitioners in law, medicine, theology, social work, engineering, and business—has been dominated by a model for training known as technical rationality.
- Technical rationality stresses the development of a standardized body of knowledge—information, principles, theories—that can then be applied consistently to recurring professional problems.
- Most professional training involves an early disciplinary or basic science phase, an applied science (skill) or applications phase, and a professional phase. In other words, first you have to learn the theory, and then you go out and apply it.
- The model of technical rationality has dominated professional education so completely that almost no one questions it.
- The world of professional practice today is not as neat and tidy as the model of technical rationality would suggest. The older model of more or less routine problems of practice standardized knowledge applies to is no longer functional. There are too many cases that are not in the books, too many unique and unpredictable elements, too many unstable contexts for the old formulas to work.
- What is needed today is a new way of preparing professionals that goes beyond the incomplete model of technical rationality, a new way of knowing called reflection-in-action.

Reflection-in-action, it turns out, is a way of knowing that grows out of experience and is applicable beyond professional education. It is a kind of knowing that is in our action. Professionals must think about what they are doing while they are doing it, and it is in this way they learn from experience. Schön's term *reflection-in-action* is a handy phrase for capturing the essence of what happens in experiential learning.

Origins of Experiential Learning

Because experiential learning takes many forms in colleges and universities, it is not possible to trace the origins of all of these movements here, but the roots are deep in history. For example, *cooperative education*, the alternation of work and study in various patterns, dates to the University of Cincinnati in 1903. Programs in more than 1,100 colleges and universities today are supported by three professional organizations that advocate work-integrated learning: the Cooperative Education and Internship Association, the

National Commission for Cooperative Education, and the World Association for Cooperative Education.[9]

Study abroad began with overseas study, popular in the late eighteenth and early nineteenth centuries, when more than ten thousand American students traveled abroad to study in Germany. American scholars studying abroad in German universities, one may recall, brought back the idea of graduate education and the lecture method that became the dominant paradigm of American higher education.[10] The earliest professional association was the Institute for International Education, founded in 1919 in the aftermath of World War I, to increase understanding among nations and bring about world peace.[11] The National Association of Foreign Student Advisors, with nearly ten thousand members, is the largest association dedicated to study abroad and other forms of international exchange.[12]

Civic engagement, formerly known as *service-learning,* dates to the founding of the Peace Corps and Volunteers in Service to America (VISTA) in the 1960s, but the movement took big steps forward in the 1980s and 1990s through federal government support and the professional leadership of Campus Compact, which now has a national office and thirty-five state offices.[13] Adventure-based education grew out of the Outward Bound movement in England, which had roots in the Gordonstoun School in the 1930s in Scotland, a training ground for survival and rescue techniques.[14] Mechanisms for using experience for learning were in place for most of the twentieth century, but they were often seen as soft alternatives—or even offbeat exceptions—to the dominant paradigm of classroom learning.

The idea of learning from experience also has its philosophical roots. Two famous philosophers who stressed the importance of experience in learning were John Dewey and Alfred North Whitehead. A constant theme in Dewey's writing was the reconstruction of experience, and he wanted to place more emphasis on natural, present-moment experience in learning.[15] Dewey was joined in this point of view by Whitehead, the great British mathematician and philosopher. Whitehead expressed a deep concern about inert ideas, which he described as "ideas that are merely received into the mind without being utilized, or tested, or thrown into fresh combinations." He also said, "There is only one subject-matter for education, and that is life in all of its manifestations."[16] Dewey and Whitehead, perhaps more than any others, are the philosophical ancestors of experiential learning, and some of their ideas became the foundation of the progressive education movement. David Kolb, Donald Schön, and other scholars continue to theorize about experiential learning and help add to its philosophical foundation.

Cognitive Neuroscience

The ideas these individuals explored as philosophers—that human beings are well suited to learning from experience—are now being supported by research on the anatomy and physiology of the brain in an interdisciplinary field known as cognitive neuroscience. As far back as Roman times, people began to make observations about the brain. Galen, who administered to wounded gladiators, noticed that "contestants sustaining injury to the arm, leg, or torso retained their powers of thought, whereas those who sustained injury to the head or the brain did not." From these observations he inferred that the brain was linked to thought.[17] It was not until the twentieth century, indeed the last part of that century, that this kind of empirical observation enabled cognitive neuroscience to emerge and accelerate as a discipline.

The great-grandfather of brain research was Santiago Ramón y Cájal, who first formulated the idea that individual brain cells (neurons) signal each other at synapses, the little gaps between cells. By the late 1940s Hodgkin and Huxley discovered how the electrochemical conduction of an impulse along an axon (stretched-out thread of a brain cell) works, something like a burning fuse, and they won a Nobel Prize for their work in 1963.[18] The first department of neurobiology was established at Harvard in 1966.[19] Some of the earliest brain research focused on localization of function, that is, determining what takes place in different parts of the brain. This research was done with patients who had natural or induced (surgical) brain dysfunction and is referred to as the *lesion method*. According to Banich and Compton, "If damage to a particular brain region results in an inability to perform a specific mental function, scientists usually assume that the function must have depended on that brain region."[20] The focus on brain mapping stressed differences in function rather than coordination and integration of these functions.

After the mid-1970s, brain research was accelerated by the emergence different brain imaging techniques.[21] Computerized axial tomography (CAT or CT scan) provides "slices" of brain tissue that can be analyzed for tissue density.[22] Magnetic resonance imaging (MRI) provides even sharper and clearer images, and diffusion tensor imaging (DTI) has the potential to "provide information about the anatomical connectivity between different brain regions."[23]

Newer technologies that support brain research add not only to the understanding of brain anatomy but to brain function. Functional magnetic resonance imaging (fMRI) and positron emission tomography (PET) "allow researchers to observe the entire network of brain structures that participate in performing particular cognitive functions, by revealing all brain regions that are active in that function."[24] In particular, fMRI techniques allow researchers to track levels of oxygen-rich blood in activated areas of the brain, offering proof of which areas of the brain are working simultaneously on which tasks.[25] For most activities, one might say the brain lights up like a blinking Christmas tree, because so many parts of the brain are involved in what we once thought were relatively simple unitary functions.

What behaviorists believed could never be done—get inside the black box of the mind—and what the cognitive psychologists were so clever at doing by inference—understanding cognitive processes—is now being done through the work of cognitive neuroscientists, who are describing in detail how the brain works through technologies that help get them inside the brain. The following discussion may seem a bit technical, but we believe it is important to explore what is known about how our bodies and brains take in information from experience before we make inferences about learning through experience.

How the Brain Works

To understand how the brain works, the place to begin is not with the brain but with the components of the nervous system that feed information to the brain. Think of the brain as receiving sensory information, figuring out how to evaluate that information, and then acting on it. Just as the circulatory system has veins, arteries, the heart, and blood, the nervous system has various components connected in special pathways to and in the brain.

Sense Organs and Receptors

Sensory information comes to the brain through various receptor mechanisms designed for picking up raw data from experience.

Eyes

The two eyes are the site of 70 percent of the body's sensory receptors. Light rays (photons) come through the regulatory system of the cornea, iris, and lens and land on the 120 million rods and 7 million cones on the retina. Rods process dimly lit black-and-white moving elements of an image, and cones process clearly detailed color elements.[26] One million optic fibers from each eye cross over to the opposite side of the brain, joining the remaining fibers from the other eye. The sensory data are headed for the thalamus, the brain's initial processing and relay area. Information goes quickly to the amygdala to sort out anything alarming and lands in the occipital lobes at the back of the brain "where columns of neurons are arranged to respond to specific patterns of lines, angles, segments and movements in the visual field."[27] This visual information is then sent forward to an area of the cortex that "combines line segments into shapes, colors them, combines them, and contemplates their meanings."[28]

Ears

Ears provide a twenty-four-hour monitoring service for sound waves coming through the air laden with information that can be identified by pitch, volume, and timbre (tone quality). Sylwester said, "The process begins in the outer ear where sound waves strike our ear drum and cause it to vibrate. Our middle ear increases the strength of these vibrations about 22 times through the mechanical actions of the body's three smallest bones. They relay the increased vibrations to the cochlea, a fluid-filled tube in the inner ear shaped like a snail shell. Each of 25,000 hairlike receptors in the cochlea is tuned to a specific sound frequency."[29] The auditory nerve, which contains nerve fiber for each of the cochlear receptors, takes the information to the thalamus and back up to auditory processing centers in the brain located just above the ears. The brain can recognize half a million different sounds across ten octaves of pitch.[30]

Skin

The body's six-pound, twenty-square-foot double-layered surface with its half million nerve endings keeps the brain well informed about anything that touches the body as well as overall external conditions such as temperature. A patch of skin about the size of a quarter "averages more than 3 million cells, 250 sensory receptors, 100 sweat glands, 50 nerve endings, and three feet of blood vessels."[31] Touch information is "initially processed in the cortex in two narrow bands of neural tissue that spread from ear to ear across the top of our cortex."[32] Hands, face, thumb, and tongue get the most space in the brain.[33]

Nose

Millions of bare neural endings project through two postage-stamp-size mucous membranes to collect data from no more than thirty different odor-bearing molecules floating through the air. Smell is the only sense that doesn't go through the thalamus on its way to other parts of the brain, in this case the olfactory bulbs.

Tongue

More important to educators as a motor organ for speaking, the tongue is "a four-inch slab of muscle with 9,000 taste buds arranged in groups of about 100."[34] The mouth also registers temperature, touch, and pain, and the brain integrates sensory messages into "smooth hot chocolate or crunchy peanut brittle."[35]

Lumbar and Cranial Nerves

In addition to these very specialized receptors, the body in general is sending information to the brain all the time through the cervical, thoracic, and lumbar nerves that enter the spinal cord at assigned points along the spinal column. These, plus the twelve cranial nerves, deal with sensory (reception) and motor (action) functions regardless of whether we are conscious of their activity as they go about dealing automatically with such things as breathing and heart rate.[36]

The important thing to note about sensory systems is that they are the interface with experience. From a student's point of view, they let you know what's happening.

Integrative Mechanisms

Picture all this information coming in simultaneously to the brain from the eyes, ears, nose, skin, tongue, and spinal cord. What does the brain do with it? Although the earliest years of brain research stressed localization of function, resulting in a Nobel Prize in 1981 for Roger Sperry at the California Institute of Technology for his work on hemispheric specialization, the main theme of the latest brain research has been on interconnectivity, the ability of one part of the brain to connect to and communicate with other parts. Ironically, a spate of theories on left-brain/right-brain learning resulted, but Sperry's work was actually more focused on the corpus collosum, "a massive tract of more than 250 million nerve fibers that connects the hemispheres."[37] Consider the following selected examples of how the brain is wired to carry out its essential integrative functions.

- Auditory information from both ears converges, and this convergence is thought to be "important for localization of sounds in the horizontal dimension."[38]

- The eyes capture the main object in central vision, while the mid-brain visual system makes fine discriminations necessary for object recognition.[39]
- Almost all sensory information coming into the cortex and almost all motor information leaving it goes through the thalamus, a relay center in which "the neurons from one area of the brain synapse onto neurons that then go on to synapse somewhere else in the brain."[40]
- Tactile information from the skin along with information about pain and temperature is sent by neurons that connect in the dorsal (back) regions of the spinal cord before going to the thalamus and then to the cortex.[41]
- The frontal lobes coordinate information "associated with planning, guidance, and evaluation of behavior," executive functions that also allow us to "predict and consider future consequences of our behavior."[42]

These examples can be multiplied endlessly to illustrate the point that various regions of the nervous system and brain with their unique specializations are connected, integrated, and interrelated in complex ways for efficient processing of experience.

As more knowledge has been gained about the larger structures (gross anatomy) of the brain, a better understanding of what takes place to facilitate interconnectivity at the cellular level has also been developed. Without going into detail about the structure and physiology of brain cells, let it be said that brain cells are like little trees with lots of branches (dendrites) reaching out in many directions to connect with (or synapse to) dendrites of other nerve cells. Transmission of messages is both electrical and chemical, and cell branches can connect to as many as one thousand other neurons (nerve cells).[43]

As discoveries about hemispheric specialization, also referred to as lateralization, were announced, educators latched on to these left- and right-brain differences making what have proven to be unwarranted leaps and false generalizations. Although differences in hemispheric activity exist, mainly in the way the work of the brain gets done, these differences in processing are seen now as connected and complementary, not opposing and unitary. These lateralizations have been discovered in other primates and more distant species. It appears, for example, that in chickens "searching for food is lateralized to the left hemisphere and maintaining vigilance for a predator is lateralized to the right hemisphere." This results in a useful division of labor, but pity the poor chick that sees itself as either left brained or right brained, for it will surely die either of starvation or in the clutches of a predator.[44] The preponderance of evidence from neuroscience suggests that lateralization of brain activity is highly coordinated. Each hemisphere contributes in some way to nearly all complex mental functions.[45]

Motor Control

The brain also organizes and initiates movement of various kinds, and although widely differing parts of the brain are involved in motor activity, the story is essentially the same: the brain is well integrated for movement. Movement can include locomotion, such as getting from place to place; athletic movements, such as serving a tennis ball; and fine motor activity, such as writing and speaking.

Movement, such as serving a tennis balls, is often taken for granted as the brain simply telling the arms and legs what to do. In fact, the brain takes this complicated challenge and breaks it into component tasks that are handled by widely dispersed but connected areas. Movement actually involves developing a model of the anticipated movement, selecting the types of movement and their order, timing the patterns of muscle activation, controlling the force and direction of the movement, stopping the movement, and switching to another movement. The major players in this activity are the cerebellum, the basal ganglia, and the primary areas of the cerebral cortex.[46] Each location is playing its part simultaneously in a complex action that comes out as the smooth result of coordinated efforts.

From Brain Research to Experiential Learning

The story of how the human brain works is compelling and awe inspiring in itself, but humans also have more brain to work with than other species. Human brains are on average six times larger relative to body weight than the brains of other living mammals. (Dolphins are notable big-brain exceptions.) If a giraffe might be thought of as a "neck freak," and an elephant might be thought of as a "nose freak," then human beings are "brain freaks."[47] What is to be made of this intricately complex and oversized brain? Based on what is now known from the field of cognitive neuroscience, what implications can be drawn for learning?

This is dangerous territory, because the tendency is to overreach the evidence with elaborate theories and unwarranted conclusions. Educators have done this before, many times. Fools rush in where angels fear to tread, so to avoid foolishness we will try to limit our observations to ten principles from neuroscientists' convincing description of how the brain receives, copes with, and acts on experience. Note that these principles are not offered as a generalized theory of learning, but simply as theoretical support for learning from experience as one way of learning among others.

1. *Learning is not isolated from experience but grows out of experience.* The brain is not just a brain; it is part of a larger neurological system whose purpose is to connect human beings to the world of experience. As Robert Sylwester observes about the brain in *A Celebration of Neurons: An Educator's Guide to the Brain*, "Imprisoned and protected within the darkness and silence of our skull, it depends on its sensory and motor systems for external access. Our sensory and motor systems developed to enhance survival, but our conscious brain also uses them to reach out and explore cultural interests and abstract diversions—to smell flowers, observe sunsets, thrill to thunder, run races, throw Frisbees."[48] One might say the main purpose of the extended nervous system is to connect the self to experience.

2. *Learning is not passive but active.* Studies in brain development suggest that survival was an important driver in brain evolution, and as we know, survival is active, not passive. In *Human Brain and Human Learning*, Leslie Hart notes that *Homo sapiens* learned how to breed, live, survive, and dominate where less-developed animals could not. Present brain structures and processes were developed for survival long before the relatively recent development of civilization.[49] The brain is best adapted for active engagement for survival.

3. *Learning is not primarily auditory but multisensory.* Although the neural mechanisms for hearing are very sophisticated, this is but one channel from experience along with sight, touch, smell, and taste. As Leslie Hart wrote, "We identify an object, for example, by gathering information—often in less than a second—on size, color, shape, surface texture, weight, smell, movement, any sound it may make, where it is found, what else is with it . . . how other people are responding to it, and so on. All of these investigations by the brain to answer the question 'What is this?' go forward along many different paths, and branching paths, among the brain's trillion of connections, at the same time."[50]

4. *Learning is not linear but iterative.* Although something is to be said for the linear step-by-step approach to learning employed in formal education, it did not occur until well after the nonlinear informal methods of learning humans used to develop clothing, tools, weapons, utensils, housing,

dance, music, language, and religion.[51] Logic is a latecomer to this process. Rather, much like Kolb's experiential learning model, human learning goes in productive circles as people learn to recognize, remember, and use patterns, calling forth these patterns, improving upon them, and revisiting them through recurrent iterations.

5. *Learning is not sequential but spontaneous and simultaneous.* Formal learning usually involves arranging fragments of things to be learned in sequential order and sticking to that order. Hart offers this persuasive illustration of how young children learn baseball:

> Watch Little Leaguers play baseball, and you can marvel at their skill and grasp of an intricate game, and related knowledge, picked up over years in random fashion, mostly by participation as opportunity offered. If the game were to be taught logically, there would be a unit on its origins and history, on terminology, on the playing field geometry, on hitting, on fielding, base-running and so on down the list. Obviously, none of the players learned this way. They "picked up" the game by exposure over many years, in an utterly random, unplanned way—perhaps with no formal teaching at all.[52]

As with baseball, much learning comes from being given a glove and being told where to stand, that is, by being placed in an experience and told to learn from it.

6. *Learning is not so much about accumulating information as making meaning of information.* The brain does accumulate information, vast amounts of it, and calls it up as needed. The executive function of the brain draws on memories and previous experience to make meaning of current experience. A group of philosophers and psychologists known as *constructivists* stress that knowledge is no mere copy of reality but a construction of the meaning of selected phenomena. Stated in its more radical form, "Knowledge does not exist outside of a person's mind."[53] Jacqueline and Martin Brooks explain constructivist principles in *In Search of Understanding: The Case for Constructivist Classrooms* as follows: "Each of us makes sense of our world by synthesizing new experiences into what we have previously come to understand. . . . We either interpret what we see to conform to our present set of rules for explaining and ordering our world, or we generate a new set of rules that better account for what we perceive to be occurring. Either way, our perceptions and rules are constantly engaged in a grand dance that shapes our understanding."[54]

Brooks and Brooks provide a provocative illustration of this idea in the example of a young girl whose concept of water has been shaped only by her experience of water in a bathtub and swimming pool. Water is calm and moves when she moves. But when she goes to the shore, she has to construct a new meaning for water as salty and coming at her in strong waves. "In this instance," the authors note, "the interactions of the child with water, and the child's reflections on those interactions, will in all likelihood lead to structural changes in the way she thinks about water."[55]

7. *Learning is not fragmented but holistic.* The human brain appears to be well designed for taking in several sources of sensory information at once, comparing these with previously stored information, and constructing new meanings almost simultaneously. This activity is akin to what is often referred to as *holistic learning,* a type of learning that stresses the importance of spontaneity and integration in learning, not only in subjects studied but in methods of study.[56] The word *holistic* at least seems to provide an apt image for widely dispersed but interrelated brain functions that occur almost instantaneously.

8. *Learning is not confined by perceptual limitations but can be augmented by sensory and computational extensions.* As cognitive neuroscientists have detailed human capacities for receiving information, such as the range of the spectrum for the eyes or the range of sound frequencies for the ears, they have also become acutely aware that there is a wider range of phenomena available in experience than the raw human senses can pick up. One might say there is more out there than meets the eye. The unending human quest to know more than what the senses provide has resulted in an amazing array of technologies that extend the capabilities of perception, the most obvious of which are the microscope and telescope. These are of course only the beginning of a deluge of new inventions that help humans see, hear, and even walk when impaired. Interestingly, the field of neuroscience itself exists largely as a result of technological extensions of the senses developed in the last twenty years.

9. *Learning is not meant to be arduous but natural.* The old idea that the brain is a muscle to be exercised coincided nicely with the old fitness motto "No pain, no gain." Formal learning in classrooms has been set up in a variety of unnatural ways over the years with inventive forms of psychological and physical coercion (sometimes painful) used to obtain compliance to behavior that no one enjoys. The findings of cognitive neuroscience suggest a nervous system that is surprisingly well equipped and eager to go. Frank Smith, a linguist and author of many books on literacy and reading,

describes in his book *To Think* how learning should be a natural common-place process, the normal business of the brain:

> The brain picks up huge amounts of "information" on our journey through life, but only incidentally, the way our shoes pick up mud when we walk through the woods. . . . If learning is normally so easy, why should it sometimes be so difficult? Learning is easy when it is part of the flow of events in which we are involved, when we can make sense of what we are doing, when the brain is in charge of its own affairs. Just like remembering and understanding, learning is easy when it is not a particular focus of attention, when it happens to us in the course of doing something else. We learn best when we are engaged in an activity that is interesting and meaningful to us, when our past experience is relevant. On the other hand, learning is difficult when it is a deliberate attention. . . . Learning is difficult when it is contrived.[57]

10. *Learning is not conclusive and terminal but continuous.* The brain is full of self-corrective mechanisms, such as the ability to determine danger, provide multiple perspectives, use several senses at once, and check on the effects of action. The brain checks and double-checks itself. Constructivist psychologists suggest that as we encounter new experiences, we *assimilate* them if the new experiences more or less fit our previous meanings, we *accommodate* them if we need to change our interpretation, or we differentiate and *integrate* them when two sets of new interpretations don't fit.[58] Piaget called the process of adjusting meanings to experience *equilibration*.[59] Consider this example of learning through a service-learning work experience.

> Lydia Bell directs Project SOAR (Student Outreach for Access and Resiliency) at the University of Arizona. Under this project, which is associated with for-credit classes in the College of Education, students engage in twenty-five hours of service work in underresourced middle schools throughout the Tucson public school district. The students serve as mentors to middle school students, meeting with them weekly to help them set goals, explore their academic strengths, address self-esteem and peer conflict issues, and focus on career and college exploration. One of the main goals of the affiliated college courses is to examine issues of college access, those individual, cultural, social, and environmental factors that affect an individual's academic achievement and path to higher education. "It's one thing to explore these issues theoretically," says Lydia, "but by examining them personally, acting as a mentor to a student who is directly impacted by these forces of limited college access, the undergraduates really discover

a lot about themselves and the society in which we live." Lydia feels that reflection is a critical part of this service-learning experience. As they learn about college access issues, mentors not only reflect on their own experience as precollege students but compare these reflections with the experiences of their mentees. "Reflection is so imperative. Without it, it would be service; the reflection is what makes it a service *learning* experience," Lydia says.[60]

How Teachers Facilitate Experiential Learning

College teachers and related staff members play an important part in ensuring that learning results from the experiences provided by such programs as cooperative education, internships, civic engagement, wilderness challenge, or study abroad. All these programs provide experiences for learning that are most likely to be engaging, active, multisensory, nonlinear, spontaneous, holistic, natural, and productive of meaning. Most students find them challenging but fun. But these potentially educative experiences can become even more valuable and enjoyable with a bit of structure and a touch of facilitation. The following are some important ways facilitators get involved:

- *Selection and approval.* Not all experiences have the same educational potential. Some are more stimulating, more challenging, and more broadening than others. Knowing the setting well enough to approve of its educative prospects is important.
- *Matching.* A setting that works for one student may be either too challenging or too boring for another. To be effective for a student, the setting should include real and meaningful experiences or responsibilities, not just surface-level exposure. The student and facilitator work together to identify which experience is the best match for that student at that time.
- *Setting of goals and responsibilities.* The student and facilitator collaborate to elaborate broad learning outcomes that should result from the experience while leaving room for spontaneous learning from the unexpected. Having goals helps focus attention and energy. In many situations, especially those that involve working closely with community partners, students benefit from setting up and agreeing to a list of student responsibilities.[61]
- *Orientation.* Knowing what to look for and expect helps the student anticipate dimensions of the experience that might otherwise be overlooked. Sometimes it is necessary to provide background knowledge,

to develop and practice certain skills, or to anticipate how to manage certain types of situations. An orientation includes learning about what a specific experience has to offer and how to gain the most from it.

- *Ongoing reflection.* From the first day onward, the student commits to writing impressions, puzzlements, and reflections about the experience through logs and journals. These are not just accounts of what takes place but deeper reflections on personal changes, changes within the setting, and the meaning of various aspects of the experience.

- *Periodic review.* At certain key points during the experience, the facilitator interacts in person, on the phone, or online to discuss what has taken place, what learning is occurring, and what next steps should be considered. The facilitator provides support and feedback as needed to support the student during the experience.

- *Final review.* At the end of the experience, a final reflection paper, video essay, or other follow-up project enables the student to pull together interpretations, extract meanings, and relate the experience to previous or additional learning.

Facilitating Reflection

Consider the following example of a teacher using reflection to support experiential learning.

Ruth Benander teaches English at the University of Cincinnati and is responsible for many study abroad programs. Although most study abroad programs have course-specific learning outcomes in terms of literature or language study, Ruth's programs also contain culture study goals. "We want students to be able to notice and analyze details and events, and view these with personal insight to create new points of view that go beyond just personal feelings," says Ruth. She and others in the field have realized over the years that study abroad by itself does not automatically result in cultural awareness and sensitivity, and even student reflection by itself can be superficial. "When students are asked to reflect, they often get stuck at *describe.* This is typical for an unstructured prompt that simply says, 'Reflect on your experience.'" To specifically address the experiential learning component, students are asked to write reflections in the form of public blogs. The prompts for these reflections are carefully structured to lead students through describing key elements of the historical and cultural context, comparing observations and perspectives of the host culture to observations and perspectives of their own culture, and synthesizing competing interpretations to create new insights. For example, a prompt about behavioral norms reads:

> Notice people's attitudes such as how people think about time, personal space, how to treat foreigners, or just general notions of what is right and what is wrong. Pay attention to how people respond to inappropriate behavior. Note what clues you use to figure out the attitudes of the people in the new place.
>
> a. Describe the attitudes you have noticed.
> b. Compare what you have learned with your assumptions before you came.
> c. Explain what insights this critique has given you about the new culture or how you need to behave.

The role of the instructor is to help students frame the experience and relate it to academic content and their personal lives. "The cross-cultural aspects of the experience at first unsettle a student, and the first response can be resistance to what is unfamiliar," Ruth says. "This can cause anxiety which might manifest as anger or fear. The job of the instructor is to help students understand where the anxiety is coming from, process the anxiety, and learn to use it as a way to form new ways of understanding unfamiliar situations." Critical analysis takes effort, and students need careful scaffolding to be able to do this complicated task. "We found that if we did not structure our reflective blog prompts appropriately, all we got was egotistical description. Once we changed the prompts to lead students from description to creation of a new perspective, we consistently got excellent reflections, student anxiety went down, and students began to see the confusion of novelty not as a threat but as a great opportunity for another cool reflection."[62]

Reflection is an intentional process of learning something from what we see and what we do. We often reflect because we experience discomfort, and our minds want to return to a balanced state. According to Dewey, "The function of reflective thought is, therefore, to transform a situation in which there is experienced obscurity, doubt, conflict, disturbance of some sort into a situation that is clear, coherent, settled, harmonious."[63] Journal writing is especially well suited to reflection because it involves deliberate thinking and putting thoughts into words, simulating a dialogue with one's self.[64] Journal writing is attractive because it can be open-ended and allow a lot of freedom for individual student reflection. However, for journal writing to be successful, it should be fully integrated into the learning experience. Students need some direction and purpose so their reflection time can be the most productive. Techniques such as using guiding questions or asking students to list words that describe feelings or writing a dialogue with a community partner can help students reflect from different angles.[65] Some helpful guiding questions include

- What did you do today?
- What did you see or observe at this site?
- How did you feel about the experience?
- What connections did you find between the experience and course readings?
- What new ideas or insights did you gain?
- What skills can you use and strengthen?
- What could you apply from this experience in the future?[66]

The key to learning from experience, as opposed to just having an experience, is reflection. Helping students reflect on the experience is clearly the most important thing the teacher or facilitator does. Although the brain is well equipped to absorb wave after wave of new sensory information, it also needs time and encouragement to use its executive powers to connect that information, construct new interpretations, and take action. This is best done through a structured conversation with a skilled helper outside the experience.

What is this structured conversation about, and how does the teacher help the student reflect on experience? Facilitating reflection is a form of helping. A valuable resource for reflecting on reflection is a popular text often used in basic counseling courses by Gerard Egan, *The Skilled Helper: A Problem-Management and Opportunity Development Approach to Helping.*[67] Egan notes that helping (his more general and preferred term for counseling) provides a context not only for solving problems but also for engaging missed opportunities and unused potential, occasions to deal more creatively with our work, ourselves, and others.[68] This is an especially useful resource for teachers who hope to facilitate reflection on experience. Students in the midst of an experience often find themselves in a predicament, and they need to reflect on the problem-causing aspects of their experience, but just as often, perhaps more often, they find themselves in a situation in which they are at a loss to know what they can learn from it. The teacher, as skilled helper, helps the student reflect on the experience not only to address problems but to capitalize on opportunities for learning. To make this happen, Egan suggests dividing the helping process into three stages: the current picture, the preferred picture, and the way forward.[69]

The Current Picture

The place to begin is with helping students focus on telling their stories, that is, to describe their experience and begin making initial assessments of it.[70] The teacher provides a safe setting for a student to tell his or her story and uses active listening skills to draw out perceptions and feelings. The first step in facilitating reflection is to understand the story. Sometimes at this stage, however, the student may be so immersed in the experience that he or she does not have much insight about it or may be reluctant and resistant to talk openly about it.[71] Reluctance may develop when a student lacks trust, is uncomfortable with the potential intensity of the helping exchange, worries about what might be uncovered, or is anxious about change in general. Resistance can surface when a student feels too forcefully challenged. Helpers regard reluctance and resistance as normal, recognizing it in themselves from time to time, and are skillful at challenging the student (within a climate of support) to reflect more deeply on the experience through skillful probes, prompts, and questions.[72] If the teacher sees the world only as the student sees it, the teacher has little to offer.

What needs to be challenged? Egan lists such things as "self-defeating mindsets, dysfunctional behavior, and discrepancies between thinking and acting."[73] Also to be challenged are "distortions, evasions, games, tricks, excuse making, and smokescreens."[74] Challenging, of course, needs to be done in an overall context of support and acceptance and is usually better received when there is empathy, appropriate self-disclosure from the facilitator, and occasional humor. A key goal is to uncover blind spots, "the things we fail to see or choose to ignore that keep us from identifying and managing problem situations or identifying and developing opportunities."[75]

Once the experience has been set forth, understood, and challenged, the teacher tries to help the student define what is most important, begin to work on a subproblem, and pick an aspect of the problem where there is likelihood for general improvement.[76]

The Preferred Picture

The teacher and student try to arrive at a description of what the situation will look like if the problems and lost opportunities in the experience are to be managed successfully. What are the possible scenarios for this situation? This phase of the reflection is solution focused and incorporates goal setting, the discovery of possibilities for a better future, and the crafting of change agendas and commitments as the triggers for action.[77]

The Way Forward

The focus now is on implementation. If we know now where we are in this experience, and we are clear about where we would like to be, how do we get there? The teacher becomes a partner in generating action strategies by asking questions that begin with phrases such as: Have you considered . . . ? What if . . . ? What do you need to do to . . . ? Who could help you to . . . ? This discussion is aimed at developing specific strategies for implementing goals, choosing strategies that fit the individual's situation, resources, personality, and preferences, and become viable plans capable of implementation.[78]

A structured reflection process turns mere experience into learning. For the most part, the brain will do what it is best designed to do with experience, but it sometimes needs a little counsel from a skilled helper. Through the reflection process the student is challenged to think about the experience realistically, put feelings and ideas into words, formulate preferred scenarios, and put plans into action. Far from being soft or fuzzy, learning from experience is challenging and demanding. A skilled teacher/facilitator will quickly end the games of a chronic complainer but will also provide an opportunity for a timid person to discover and develop his or her unrealized potential.

Egan's scenarios are similar to a simple model for facilitating experiential education developed by the Campus Outreach Opportunity League, an organization that supported student participation in service-learning and experiential education in the 1980s and 1990s. Its model, based on Kolb's experiential learning model, is perhaps an easy way of remembering these three scenarios in the form of three questions: What? So what? and Now what?[79]

Developing Awareness of Personal Identity and Cultural Differences

One of the noted outcomes of engaging in experiential education is a heightened awareness of one's personal identity and the development of intercultural competence.[80] As the world becomes increasingly diverse and multicultural, experiential learning is poised to offer students valuable insights into their own identities as well as the sensitivity to work in multicultural settings. Becoming interculturally competent begins with awareness of one's own culture, minority or majority characteristics, and associated complications or privileges. White students of European backgrounds may at first resist the notion that they even have a racial or cultural identity. Drop them off in Taipei, Taiwan, or Mumbai, India, and they may be forced to define themselves more clearly. Immersing students in the actual experience of diversity creates awareness of personal identity just by being in settings, situations, and groups where contrasts are obvious. It is important to be aware of one's identity before being able to eventually accept one's place and value the place of other people in a multicultural world.

Study abroad programs seem especially well suited to fostering intercultural competence, but considerable work must be done by facilitators to provide the guidance necessary for students to go beyond surface-level learning of the differences of other cultures, such as food, dress, and customs. Students need in-depth exposure and constant reflection on what diversity means to truly change perspectives and gain intercultural skills. Unfortunately, without such guidance, previously held cultural stereotypes can simply be reinforced.

Similarly, domestic multicultural learning experiences are well suited for developing awareness of oneself, empathy for others, and challenging an individual's worldview.[81] Self-identity and personal biases emerge in such situations, allowing for the growth in awareness that is necessary before students can be expected to understand the culture and identity of others. Yet awareness is only one part of intercultural competence. According to Prieto, "It is quite possible for students to have gained an awareness and fact-based understanding of other cultures but still hold sexist, racist, and homophobic attitudes (and cultural privileges) as yet unexamined and unchallenged."[82] Once again, students need guidance and reflection in their development of a true appreciation of identity and diversity. Intercultural service-learning in particular has been shown to reduce negative stereotypes among students because of its in-depth work arrangements and constant reflection. Such experiences have the "power to break down stereotypes and build appreciation for the many insights to be gained as a result of cultural diversity."[83] Consider again the service-learning example introduced on p. 259.

> Returning to Lydia Bell and the Project SOAR service-learning program, we see that issues of identity and intercultural awareness are a vital part of this experience. These students, who mentor in middle schools, also meet

weekly in smaller groups with teaching assistants to process and reflect on the experience. "They need smaller groups to establish trust and be able to discuss their successes and challenges with each other," Lydia says. "We discuss issues of social capital, cultural capital, and the American Dream. It is hard for many of our students to grapple with these issues, for some, taking a critical perspective is very new." Students are also asked to write periodic reflections on specific questions and often have very insightful comments about the idea of equal opportunity for college in America. But the directors of Project SOAR have not always seen such introspective reflections. "About five years ago we were examining student reflection papers and realized that although some mentors developed very close relationships with their mentees and others did not, some student reflections in both situations remained at a surface level of intercultural understanding," she says. "These comments seemed to fall into either a 'fatalist' group, a feeling that 'these kids are doomed,' or a 'savior' group, a feeling that the college student had come in to save the day. Neither opinion really showed a depth of intercultural sensitivity and awareness." These comments were from students of all ethnicities and economic statuses. So Lydia and her colleagues reworked the course and the focus of the reflection papers. "Now we start early on with the concept of 'funds of knowledge,' an idea that no one comes to school as an empty vessel but rather all kids bring something with them," she says. "Some kids might not have learned about math and chemistry in the classroom yet, but they have learned similar principles in the kitchen. We ask the mentors to search for and reflect on the funds of knowledge of their mentee, to be thoughtful about their strengths, rather than focus only on the gaps and differences." The students also read studies about stereotype threat and the power of expectations, and are asked to reflect about the expectations they should have of their mentees. "The mentor has no background information about their mentee, they don't know their family or what their siblings were like in school, they see them with fresh eyes and are in a unique position to expect the best from them and challenge them to live up to positive expectations," Lydia says. These course changes have shown positive outcomes. "Of course it's never perfect, but we now see stronger reflection papers after we've intentionally focused student reflections toward digging deeper and going beyond stereotypes."[84]

Assessing Experiential Learning

As with every way of learning, assessment needs to support the intended goals. As a starting point, revisit the typical learning outcomes of experiential learning listed on pp. 246–47. Because experiential learning is based on making meaning from experience through reflection and awareness, assessment methods that show evidence of personal growth fit nicely with this method. Journals, blogs, written or video essays, photo exhibits, digital storytelling projects, and presentations are all methods that help students pull out and make visible the learning they have gained from their experiences.

When using this way of learning, teachers should examine closely their formative, or process goals, and their summative, or product goals to ensure their assessment measures match the goals. Most experiential learning outcomes are process focused, making summative assessment difficult or even irrelevant. Mixing formative and summative purposes can be confusing to students. If methods such as journals or discussions are used for grading purposes, students are less likely to freely share their thoughts, opinions, and observations. To address this problem, many teachers grade only for completion of such assignments and provide ample feedback along the way to ensure that learning is occurring.

Journals and blogs are a popular and complementary activity to experiential learning and can provide evidence of learning and growth from structured experiences. Some students do well with open-ended journal assignments, but many students, especially undergraduates, need some direction on the purpose and goals of the journal to take it seriously. Beyond the development of focused questions described in this chapter, rubrics can be used to help students direct their reflections. Rubrics can focus on logistical aspects such as length and quantity but may also give guidance on aspects of critical reflection such as testing new ideas, linking observations to readings or theories, or developing new patterns of communication. Students can use these rubrics to critique their own journal entries and discover what they may have left out. Journals are primarily used for formative purposes for the reasons previously mentioned, but there are ways to use them for summative assessment. Sometimes students are asked to write in a journal or blog for the duration of an experience and then choose their two to three best entries for grading. They might be given the chance to revise these entries based on a new perspective, outlook, or sense of meaning; or they may be encouraged to create a summary entry as a metareflection. However, other teachers argue that journals should be left as an artifact of that point in time and even suggest that teachers not mark on the entries themselves in order to preserve them as the student's work, instead using sticky notes or a separate document to record their marks or observations.[85]

When the experience is more structured, such as an internship, service-learning, or a work project, it can be helpful to identify what constitutes success.[86] This might be the completion of some tangible project, or it might be making a certain contribution to a setting within a number of hours served. Once the goals have been defined in these terms, it is possible to gather evidence of success from the student, facilitator, and community partners. Keep in mind the student is also in a valuable position to give feedback to community partners about the experience and success of the project.

Technologies to Support Experience-Based Learning

Although the human brain is well suited to absorbing learning in a natural environment, its marvelous capabilities can be further supported and extended by various media. Multimedia tools such as cameras and voice and video recorders can capture various aspects of an experience, including close-ups that provide detail that might be lost. Students may videotape themselves during an experience to gain additional insight into their actions, mannerisms, and performance. Voice recorders are good for interviews or live conversations with people otherwise involved in the experience and may also be used for making on-the-spot observation notes to save what could be forgotten. Such tools can aid reflection and in making honest assessments of an experience.

Media are also used to allow students to keep in touch with the facilitator during an experience, especially for study abroad or internship experiences. Telephone, e-mail, text messaging, and online voice or video conferencing are some of the options available to students to check in with their facilitators and provide periodic updates. Such tools can also allow students to interact with each other during their experiences, comparing and contrasting examples and gaining insights into other types of situations.

Blogging is a popular means of electronic journal keeping because it allows entries to be posted on the Internet to share with other students, the facilitator, and a wider audience. Blogging can be fun, and students often find it easier to post short entries more often using this medium. With blogs, students can more easily share video and images and tag and search for related entries. Students can also create video essays as an even more personal means of journaling. However, the public nature of blogs can mean that students do not share their thoughts and opinions deeply or freely. Blogging for experiential learning may best be done in a small community, using privacy settings to allow some entries to be private. In addition, students should be made aware of any privacy concerns for themselves and their community partners when posting reflections publicly online.

Additionally, the media used to record and keep track of a student's experience may produce material that can be used later in final reflections or presentations. A difficult task in any presentation about an experience is helping others understand the experience at a deep enough level to perceive why the experience was educational and why it is being interpreted as it is. The presentation can be enhanced by media that animate the experience, ranging from the simple use of still images or video to a full-fledged multimedia presentation. *Digital storytelling*, using images, words, and music to create a short video, is an increasingly popular and powerful method of sharing the key learning aspects of an experience.[87]

Final Thoughts

Experiential education is powerful learning, and students often describe such experiences as life-changing. Jack Mezirow coined the term *transformative education* to describe learning that changes us in psychological, convictional, and behavioral dimensions. Sometimes true transformative education can happen with one isolated experience, but that is rare. It is more likely to occur through such experiences built over time, often in alternation with other ways of learning. Parker Palmer reminds us that experiential learning is not frivolous or superfluous but is rather an essential aspect of academia: "Great science, original science, the science on which so much of modern culture is built—depends on our subtle faculties as much as it does on objective data and logical analysis. It depends on bodily knowledge, intuition, imagination, and aesthetic sensibility, as you can learn from any mathematician who has been led to a proof by its elegance. The hard sciences are full-body sports, enterprises that depend on experiential immersion in the phenomena and the process."[88] One might ask: Is a college education truly complete without experiential education?

Service-learning, study abroad, internships, and other types of learning experiences are becoming more common in higher education. However, before letting students loose, teachers should familiarize themselves with the principles of experiential learning to ensure that the experiences they provide are potentially meaningful and that students have a chance to reflect and make meaning from them.

Points to Remember

Teachers who want to use experiential learning effectively should do the following:

- ✓ Use this way of learning for the purpose of involving students in experiences that are engaging, active, multisensory, nonlinear, spontaneous, holistic, natural, and productive of meaning.
- ✓ Select and approve potentially educative experiences that have appropriate levels of intensity, frequency, and duration.
- ✓ Carefully match the experience with the student's needs.
- ✓ Work with the student to establish personal learning goals and define responsibilities.
- ✓ Orient the student to the experience by providing necessary information or skill development.
- ✓ Provide means, technological or otherwise, to keep in touch with the student during the experience.
- ✓ Guide the student's ongoing reflection with probing questions about the current picture that go beyond personal or superficial reactions, and then help the student design a preferred picture and a way forward to take action.
- ✓ Check in with students for periodic updates.
- ✓ Provide an opportunity for students to create a final presentation, project, or story to demonstrate the meaning they have drawn from the experience.

Notes

1. Dannelle Stevens and Joanne Cooper, *Journal Keeping: How to Use Reflective Writing for Effective Learning, Teaching, Professional Insight, and Positive Change* (Sterling, VA: Stylus, 2009), 20.

2. Parker Palmer and Arthur Zajonc, *The Heart of Higher Education* (San Francisco: Jossey-Bass, 2010), 108.

3. "Experiential Education Academy (EEA)," accessed March 15, 2012, National Society for Experiential Education, http://www.nsee.org/experiential-education-academy.

4. David Kolb, *Experiential Learning: Experience as the Source of Learning and Development* (Englewood Cliffs, NJ: Prentice Hall, 1984), 22–23.

5. Ibid., 26.

6. Ibid.

7. Thanks to Ann Vessels, JD, Lecturer and Director of the Legal Externship Program, Sturm College of Law, University of Denver, for granting permission to use her example. E-mail message to author, December 15, 2012.

8. Donald Schön, *The Reflective Practitioner: How Professionals Think in Action* (New York: Basic Books, 1983), 3–69; see also Schön, *Educating the Reflective Practitioner* (San Francisco: Jossey–Bass, 1987), 3–22.

9. Cooperative Education and Internship Association, accessed March 15, 2012, http://www.ceiainc.org/; National Commission for Cooperative Education, accessed March 15, 2012, http://www.co-op.edu/; World Association for Cooperative Education, accessed March 15, 2012, http://www.waceinc.org/.

10. John S. Brubacher and Willis Rudy, *Higher Education in Transition: An American History: 1636–1956* (New York: Harper, 1958), 172–73, 86.

11. "Higher Education Institutional Development," accessed March 15, 2012, Institute of International Education, http://www.iie.org/What-We-Do/Higher-Education-Institutional-Development.

12. "About NAFSA: Mission, Vision, Values," accessed March 15, 2012, Association of International Educators, http://www.nafsa.org/about.sec/organization_leadership/.

13. Campus Compact, *2010 Annual Membership Survey Results: Executive Summary* (Boston: Campus Compact, 2011).

14. James Kielsmeier, "Growing with the Times: A Challenge for Experiential Education," in *Experiential Learning*, ed. Richard Kraft and James Kielsmeier (Dubuque, IA: Kendall Hunt, 1995), 3.

15. John Dewey, *Experience in Education* (New York: Touchstone, 1997).

16. Brian Hedley and Russell Dewey, *Whitehead: Philosophers as Educators* (Carbondale, IL: Southern Illinois University Press, 1986), 85.

17. Marie T. Banich and Rebecca J. Compton, *Cognitive Neuroscience*, 3rd ed. (Belmont, CA: Wadsworth, Cengage Learning, 2011), 53.

18. Ibid.

19. Dale Purves, *Brains: How They Seem to Work* (Upper Saddle River, NJ: Pearson Education, 2010).

20. Banich and Compton, *Cognitive Neuroscience*, 53.

21. Ibid., 59.

22. Ibid., 60.

23. Ibid., 61.

24. Ibid., 63.

25. Ibid., 65.

26. Robert Sylwester, *A Celebration of Neurons: An Educator's Guide to the Human Brain* (Alexandria, VA: Association for Supervision and Curriculum Development, 1995), 61.

27. Ibid., 62.

28. Ibid., 62.

29. Ibid., 63.

30. Ibid.

31. Ibid.

32. Ibid., 64.

33. Ibid.

34. Ibid., 66.

35. Ibid.

36. Banich and Compton, *Cognitive Neuroscience*, 9.

37. Ibid., 92.

38. Ibid., 23.

39. Ibid., 20–22

40. Ibid., 13.

41. Ibid., 19.

42. Ibid., 25.

43. Ibid., 35.

44. Ibid., 100.

45. Ibid., 98.

46. Ibid., 131–32, 143.

47. Carl Sagan, *The Dragons of Eden: Speculations on the Evolution of Human Intelligence* (New York: Ballantine, 1997), 35.

48. Sylwester, *Celebration of Neurons*, 55.

49. Leslie Hart, *Human Brain and Human Learning* (New York: Longman, 1983), 46.

50. Ibid., 5.

51. Ibid., 60.

52. Ibid., 109.

53. Catherine Toomey Fosnot, *Constructivism: Theory, Perspectives, and Practice* (New York: Teachers College Press, 1996), 3.

54. Jacqueline Grenno Brooks and Martin G. Brooks, *In Search of Understanding: The Case for Constructivist Classrooms* (Alexandria, VA: Association for Supervision and Curriculum Development, 1993), 4.

55. Ibid., 5.

56. See Carl Flake, *Holistic Education: Principles, Perspectives and Practices* (Brandon, VT: Holistic Education Press, 1993).

57. Frank Smith, *To Think* (New York: Teachers College Press, 1990), 12, 40.

58. Fosnot, *Constructivism*, 13–14.

59. Jean Piaget, *The Equilibration of Cognitive Structures: The Central Problem of Intellectual Development* (Chicago: University of Chicago Press, 1985).

60. Thanks to Lydia Bell, PhD, Assistant Professor of Practice and Director of Project SOAR, University of Arizona College of Education, for granting permission to use her example. In discussion with the author, February 28, 2012.

61. For a sample checklist of student responsibilities, see Christine Cress et al., *Learning through Serving: A Student Guidebook for Service-Learning across the Disciplines* (Sterling, VA: Stylus, 2009), 30.

62. Thanks to Ruth Benander, PhD, Professor of English and Communication, University of Cincinnati, Raymond Walters College, for granting permission to use her example. E-mail message to author, February 1, 2012.

63. John Dewey, *How We Think: A Restatement of the Relation of Reflective Thinking to the Educative Process* (Boston: D.C. Heath, 1933), 100–101.

64. Stevens and Cooper, *Journal Keeping*.

65. These and other journal-writing techniques can be found in Stevens and Cooper, *Journal Keeping*, 107.

66. Adapted from Cress et al., *Learning through Serving*, 9.

67. Gerard Egan, *The Skilled Helper: A Problem-Management and Opportunity Development Approach to Helping*, 9th ed. (Belmont, CA: Brooks/Cole Cengage Learning, 2010).

68. Ibid., 6–7.

69. Ibid., 72–80.

70. Ibid., 97–101.

71. Ibid., 116–24.

72. Ibid., 189–99.

73. Ibid., 212.

74. Ibid., 219.

75. Ibid., 223.

76. Ibid., 266–68.

77. Ibid., 290–349.

78. Ibid., 354–77.

79. As described in Janet Eyler and Dwight E. Giles, *Where's the Learning in Service Learning?* (San Francisco: Jossey-Bass, 1999).

80. Cress et al., *Learning through Serving*.

81. Carlos M. Diaz-Lazaro, Sandra Cordova, and Rosslyn Franklyn, "Experiential Activities for Teaching about Diversity," in *Getting Culture: Incorporating Diversity across the Curriculum*, ed. Regan A. R. Gurung and Loreto R. Prieto (Sterling, VA: Stylus, 2009), 191–99.

82. Loreto R. Prieto, "Teaching about Diversity: Reflections and Future Directions," in *Getting Culture: Incorporating Diversity across the Curriculum*, ed. Regan A. R. Gurung and Loreto R. Prieto (Sterling, VA: Stylus, 2009), 27.

83. Eyler and Giles, *Where's the Learning in Service Learning?* 29.

84. Lydia Bell, in discussion with the author, February 28, 2012.

85. Stevens and Cooper, *Journal Keeping*.

86. Cress et al., *Learning through Serving*.

87. See the Center for Digital Storytelling website for more on this method, accessed March 15, 2012, http://www.storycenter.org/.

88. Palmer and Zajonc, *Heart of Higher Education*, 21.

PART THREE

TRANSFORMING COLLEGE TEACHING

II

MORE PURPOSEFUL, EFFECTIVE, AND ENJOYABLE TEACHING

In this book we have presented seven ways of learning, each of which appears to be right or true when used to bring about a particular set of learning outcomes. There are vast theoretical differences between learning from experience with all the senses simultaneously and spontaneously involved (experiential learning), and building skills systematically and efficiently by breaking a task into predetermined and carefully reinforced steps (behavioral learning). The teacher's job is not to resolve these scholarly differences—leave that to those who study learning—but rather to raise the pragmatic question: Which way of learning works best to get the desired results?

More Purposeful Teaching

The subtitle of this book describes it as a resource for more purposeful, effective, and enjoyable college teaching. The first step toward becoming more purposeful is to recognize and understand traditional teaching as a paradigm. As long as we teachers always do what we have always done, we will not need to think very deeply about purposes—what to do is embedded in the lecture paradigm. That's the purpose of a paradigm. Once it is recognized as a paradigm, other options can be considered.

The next step is to think seriously about the learning outcomes for a program, course, or lesson. This is crucial to making good use of this book. Having solid learning outcomes in place makes it easier to choose the ways of learning that best match those goals. Don't skip this step; it is crucial for becoming more purposeful in one's teaching.

More Effective Teaching

The next challenge is implementation, which takes preparation and practice and a willingness to attempt the unfamiliar. Each chapter in this book provides specific advice on how to facilitate a particular way of learning and includes appropriate technologies and assessment methods. Study the specific advice in each chapter, think about your role, plan what you intend to do, and observe carefully how it is working. Be willing to make adjustments on the spot or modify the lesson the next time you use that way of learning.

Each way of learning requires some adaptation in the subject matter content and the audience of students. Using inquiry in the chemistry lab is not the same as asking searching questions about a poem in an online literature class. There is something quite valuable in Lee Shulman's idea of *pedagogical content knowledge,* that there are unique elements in the way teaching methods are used in each specific discipline.[1] Clearly, teachers must rely on their best professional judgment in making these adaptations as subject matter experts. Similarly, professional judgment is needed in making adaptations for the particular audience of students. Older students will respond differently than recent high school graduates. Motivation will surely make a difference. Differences in race, ethnicity, or gender may need to be taken into account. Teachers should be attuned to many levels of student diversity to make adaptations appropriately and with sensitivity. Although adaptation is important, knowledgeable and purposeful facilitation of a clearly delineated way of learning will almost always carry the day.

More Enjoyable Teaching

Isn't it odd how we in academia have come to refer to research opportunities and teaching loads? What takes the joy out of teaching? Surely the greatest impediment to enjoyable teaching is students who don't learn. Teachers often have unexpressed ideas about what they hope students will learn, but they sometimes have well-meaning but erroneous ideas about spoon-feeding and making the learning process rigorous by keeping their hopes covert and mysterious. In fact, teachers who make their hopes for students explicit are less likely to be disappointed with the results.

When all aspects of a course are aligned and working well—the goals, ways of learning being implemented, assessment and feedback techniques—students learn more and are more satisfied. Contrary to popular belief, students are not satisfied when a course is easy but when it is challenging and they have become proficient in the subject matter or have accomplished something. Satisfied students learning—this is what brings joy to a teacher.

Although the greatest satisfaction is seeing students learn, other enjoyment results from the process. In general, faculty members like to learn, and becoming expert at using one or more new ways of learning has its own satisfactions. Teachers not only have the opportunity to learn new things, they may discover that facilitating different ways of learning is actually fun. Essentially, teachers are laying plans, trying new things, and seeing what happens—all of which draw on their creative energies. It is quite rewarding to watch students think critically or creatively, solve problems, explore attitudes, or learn from a new experience. Over our years of watching faculty colleagues as teachers, we have observed that those who appear to enjoy their teaching most are those who are in a perpetual state of experimentation and exploration.

The Larger Task of Improving College Teaching

Teachers can do many things on their own to make their teaching more purposeful, effective, and enjoyable, but a larger problem exists: the overall postsecondary environment where individual teachers work is not well designed to help this kind of teaching thrive. This is the point where college teachers who have become successful are called on to become advocates for teaching, to contribute to and become leaders in the field. Here are some big-picture observations to ponder.

We described the traditional lecture paradigm for college teaching in chapter 1 as an accepted model of what college teachers generally do without having to think much about their teaching. In spite of many challenges and changes, the dominant paradigm still holds sway. Why? It is surrounded by and supported by three other strong paradigms: the student paradigm, the promotion and tenure paradigm, and the graduate education paradigm.

The Student Paradigm

The student paradigm is characterized by alternating passive and adversarial behavior. Many students come to college "academically adrift," not sure what career they want to pursue and "at odds with academic commitment."[2] They quickly learn to play a passive role. Their job is to take notes, earn points for participation, and perform well on tests. They are exposed to a limited range of teaching methods, and the traditional arrangement for learning—wise professor dispensing information to uninformed students— sets up an invidious hierarchy of authority and ill will. Certain students have learned from previous experience that to survive one does whatever one can to outsmart the teacher short of getting caught cheating. Not every student plays this game; some own and manage their learning, some drop out.

Into this strong student paradigm comes a change-oriented teacher— perhaps with our book in hand—a ready advocate of different ways of learning. Instead of the traditional lecture, students are asked to participate in an inquiry, a group activity, or a problem-solving activity. The accepted arrangements in the classroom are upended, role expectations are altered, and the invidious hierarchy begins to crumble. Some students will feel cheated, others confused. Complaints of "I paid good money to learn from the teacher, not teach myself" may arise because the traditional lecture paradigm is supported by the traditional student paradigm. Over the years, there has been a collusion between teachers and students in support of their respective paradigms. Noted student development researcher George Kuh calls it "the disengagement compact," an unspoken treaty that promises, "I'll leave you alone if you leave me alone."[3]

What has to happen, of course, is that the student paradigm also has to change. Students need to accumulate experiences with purposeful and effective teaching. Students must gradually learn to manage their own learning and set goals and expectations with their teachers about what they want to learn so they can come to regard the teacher as an ally in learning. The seven ways of learning described in this book have the side effect of breaking down the student paradigm. When that relationship changes, many positive results can occur, not the least of which is increased enjoyment of the learning process in students and faculty alike.

The Promotion and Tenure Paradigm

Although the processes for appointment, promotion, and tenure vary considerably by institutional type, a high degree of similarity also exists through what might be called the universal P&T paradigm. Although nearly half of all courses are being taught by adjunct and non-tenure-track faculty, the tenure-track model is what shapes and drives the paradigm. What most faculty members aspire to is a tenure-track appointment, and even though there is great variation in institutional expectations most tenure-track appointments are shaped by the practices and expectations at more prestigious research universities, which place far more emphasis on research and scholarship than teaching. Faculty members have limited time, energy, and focus, and the balance usually gets tipped toward research and away from teaching, because the paradigm dictates scholarly productivity as the means for getting ahead in academia, not just at one's own institution but everywhere.

Into this strong research paradigm comes the change-oriented teacher—perhaps with our book in hand—a ready candidate for exploring different ways of learning. The will is there along with the knowledge and enthusiasm for trying something new. However, teaching this way, even when it is more purposeful, effective, and enjoyable, takes time away from research. The least time-consuming method of teaching is found in the dominant lecture paradigm, not because effective lecturing is easy, but because it is familiar, replicable, and requires little learning or reflection.

What should happen, of course, is that greater weight should be given to effective, creative, and brilliant teaching in the promotion and tenure process. This is desirable in any college or university, because teaching students is a central mission of all types of postsecondary institutions. Clearer distinctions could be made, however, about the importance of research and scholarship in different types of institutions. Likewise, clearer differentiation could be made by institutions in faculty roles by assigning greater weight and time for research to certain faculty who have proven themselves capable of genuine scholarship, and a similar weighting process for those who have proven to be (and want to be) effective teachers. In other words, the dominant paradigm can be challenged and replaced with a more differentiated, pragmatic, and satisfying—not to mention fair—set of arrangements for the promotion and tenure process, beginning with a better balance between teaching and research. This includes recognition for work done each year just to stay current in the subjects taught, teaching methods used, and scholarly inquiry about learning. The valiant efforts started by Ernest Boyer in the 1990s to validate the scholarship of teaching and learning have met with many successes, albeit slow and scattered.[4] The seven ways of learning described in this book have the side effect of challenging the dominant universal P&T paradigm, posing serious questions about the lopsided emphasis on research and the lack of recognition for the scholarship of teaching and learning.

The Graduate Education Paradigm

The preparation of new college teachers takes place in graduate schools where the emphasis is almost exclusively on building subject matter specialization and development of research skills. Although some bold attempts have been made to teach potential college faculty about teaching, such as the doctor of arts degree and the Preparing Future Faculty program, most have not changed graduate education substantially. Graduate education is governed by another strong paradigm, a set of presuppositions and norms about what is supposed to happen when students earn advanced degrees. Learning how to teach or to think systematically about learning is not part of the paradigm, and therefore is not something a graduate student typically experiences.

Into this strong paradigm comes a change-oriented teacher—perhaps with our book in hand—to suggest to colleagues that there really is substance to the study of learning and that serious thought should be given to altering the curriculum to prepare graduate students for their teaching role. What should happen is that program advisers should identify graduate students who aspire to college teaching and provide them with opportunities to learn about teaching and learning through challenging courses and intelligently supervised internships for teaching that go beyond the typical teaching assistant role. In addition, all who will teach as part of their future roles should be given at least some background in ways of learning and teaching methods. What would happen if colleges and universities gave more consideration in the hiring process to such candidates? The credential review process would focus on teaching capabilities as well as research potential, and the interview process would include carefully evaluated demonstrations of ability to teach using methods other than the dominant lecture paradigm.

Leaders for Learning

All four paradigms conspire to maintain a status quo in college teaching that makes it difficult for alternate ways of learning to thrive. Exceptions exist, and many people have worked hard to bring about creative alternatives, but the hope is not just to continue to generate exceptions but to change the paradigms fundamentally. The old way of teaching is no longer sustainable in light of what is now known about learning, technology, and assessment.

Advocates for better-informed and more effective methods of teaching, what we are calling leaders for learning, can contribute at many levels and in different roles. The first step, of course, is to develop one's own teaching by experimenting with the different ways of learning and becoming expert in at least some of them. Some teachers might develop skills in particular areas whereas others might get involved at the institutional level in centers or initiatives for faculty development, or nationally through professional organizations and conferences, such as the Lilly Conferences on the Scholarship of Teaching and Learning, the Teaching Professor conferences, or the International Conference on College Teaching and Learning.[5] Many might become engaged in organizations and conferences dedicated to teaching in their particular discipline or become involved in national groups related to specific ways of learning. For those teachers who become engaged as leaders for learning, the essential organization for support of faculty development is currently the Professional Organizational Development Network.[6] All of this is important support for helping teachers incorporate what is known about learning into their teaching one teacher at a time.

Leading the transformation of the dominant paradigms is another matter, not so easy yet also very important. Helping others see the paradigms for what they are is an important first step. Demonstrating other ways of learning as options, and using evidence to support their effectiveness, might be easier than attacking the lecture paradigm head-on. But ultimately someone is just going to have to do some things differently if the four dominating paradigms are to be altered or transformed. This is where department chairs, faculty senate members, deans, provosts, presidents, and, yes, students must get involved. Individual change is important, but accumulated individual changes do not necessarily produce structural changes. The interlocking dominant paradigms require leaders for learning who will work with other leaders to do things differently.

The Future of Teaching

Making predictions about what will happen to college teaching in the next ten to twenty years is difficult and perilous, but the handwriting is on the wall, so to speak, for those who can read it. Instead of predictions, we offer a list of trends to watch for as well as forces and activities to take into account that may add up to big changes for college teaching.

- Well-grounded knowledge about learning will continue to emerge and become more widely known and understood.

- Students, their parents, and employers will continue to raise questions and want explanations about the value of a college education.
- Technologies with implications for education will continue to emerge at a rapid rate and will produce high-impact changes in the way students interact with information.
- Technologies that make it easier to diagnose and individualize student learning will, in many instances, change the instructor's fundamental role.
- The uses of class time will continue to be debated as teachers explore what kind of learning happens best in the classroom, online, or independently.
- Online and hybrid learning, already a viable option for adult learners, will become a part of the regular mix of classes.
- Business enterprises and publishers will provide subject matter content for a price, as simultaneously more free online educational materials also become available.
- Libraries will become even more fully digitized while providing increased and flexible study space for new ways of learning.
- College teachers will talk to each other more about teaching and will play more diverse roles in course design and on instructional teams.
- Seat time, credit hours, and grades will become harder and harder to define and justify.
- Dominant paradigms will continue to be called into question, and clarity will be a premium asset in a world of college teaching that could get even more confused with fads and cure-alls.

As we mentioned in chapter 1, every paradigm is replaced eventually by a newer and better idea. We hope this book is a valuable resource for those who are creating the new paradigm for college teaching and learning. Our hope is that more and more college teachers working as partners with students will introduce students to a greater number of ways of learning, that these teachers will be more purposeful and effective as facilitators of learning, and that they will find in the end that they truly enjoy teaching more than ever.

Notes

1. Lee Shulman, "Those Who Understand: Knowledge Growth in Teaching," *Educational Researcher* 15 no. 4 (1986): 4–14.

2. Richard Arum and Josipa Roksa, *Academically Adrift: Limited Learning on College Campuses* (Chicago: University of Chicago Press, 2011), 3.

3. George D. Kuh, "What We're Learning about Student Engagement from NSSE," *Change* 35, no. 2 (2003): 28.

4. See Ernest L. Boyer, *Scholarship Reconsidered: Priorities of the Professoriate* (Princeton, NJ: Carnegie Foundation for the Advancement of Teaching, 1990); and Pat Hutchings, Mary Taylor Huber, and Anthony Ciccone, *The Scholarship of Teaching and Learning Reconsidered: Institutional Integration and Impact* (San Francisco: Jossey-Bass/Carnegie Foundation for the Advancement of Teaching, 2011).

5. Lilly Conferences on College and University Teaching, accessed January 30, 2012, http://lillyconferences.com/; The Teaching Professor, accessed January 30, 2012, http://www.teachingprofessor.com/; Center for the Advancement of Teaching and Learning, accessed January 30, 2012, http://www.teachlearn.org/.

6. Professional and Organizational Development Network in Higher Education, accessed January 30, 2012, http://www.podnetwork.org/.

James R. Davis is the author of a previous book about teaching, *Better Teaching, More Learning: Strategies for Success in Postsecondary Settings*, (Phoenix, AZ: Oryx Press and the American Council on Education, 1993). As a professor, Davis used it in his graduate courses on college teaching, and the book provided a certain visibility that led to invitations to lead workshops on teaching across the United States and in foreign countries (Brazil, Saudi Arabia, and Republic of China). Davis then wrote a second book with his wife, Adelaide, repurposing and restructuring previous research material from *Better Teaching, More Learning* as a guide for trainers in business, government, and nonprofit settings: *Effective Training Strategies: A Comprehensive Guide to Maximizing Learning in Organizations* (San Francisco: Berrett-Koehler, 1998). Over several years Davis has filled various administrative positions at the University of Denver, including Director of the Center for Academic Quality (faculty development and assessment), Director of the School of Education, and Associate Vice-Chancellor for Academic Affairs. During that time, as Professor of Higher Education and Adult Studies, Davis maintained his role as teacher, author of scholarly books, and adviser of doctoral candidates' dissertations. For ten years Davis served as Dean of University College, the college for professional and continuing education at the University of Denver. He is recently retired and has professor emeritus status. He holds degrees from Oberlin College and Yale University, and his PhD from Michigan State University in Higher Education Administration.

Bridget D. Arend is Director of University Teaching at the University of Denver's Office of Teaching and Learning. Her work puts her in direct daily contact with faculty who want to reflect on their teaching, which gives her firsthand knowledge of what college teachers think about and struggle with today. Arend brings a background and focus on the current literature on teaching, emerging technologies, online learning, and assessment. She has also identified and gathered all the teaching examples for this book through her networks of colleagues across the country. She teaches adult learning and educational technology courses for the Morgridge College of Education and

University College at the University of Denver and uses the seven ways of learning in her own teaching, in her faculty development work, and in one-on-one consultations and workshops. She holds degrees from the University of Colorado Boulder, and her PhD in Higher Education and Adult Studies is from the University of Denver.